Veiled Superheroes

Veiled Superheroes

Islam, Feminism, and Popular Culture

Sophia Rose Arjana
with Kim Fox

Foreword by
Wajahat Ali

LEXINGTON BOOKS
Lanham • Boulder • New York • London

Published by Lexington Books
An imprint of The Rowman & Littlefield Publishing Group, Inc.
4501 Forbes Boulevard, Suite 200, Lanham, Maryland 20706
www.rowman.com

Unit A, Whitacre Mews, 26-34 Stannary Street, London SE11 4AB

British Library Cataloguing in Publication Information Available

The hardback edition of this book was previously catalogued by the Library of Congress as follows:

Library of Congress Cataloging-in-Publication Data Available

ISBN 978-1-4985-3652-3 (cloth : alk. paper)
ISBN 978-1-4985-3654-7 (pbk : alk. paper)
ISBN 978-1-4985-3653-0 (electronic)

∞™ The paper used in this publication meets the minimum requirements of American National Standard for Information Sciences—Permanence of Paper for Printed Library Materials, ANSI/NISO Z39.48-1992.

Printed in the United States of America

For Nabra Hassanen and all the other amazing
Muslim girls and women in the universe.

Contents

Foreword   ix
Wajahat Ali

Introduction   xv

1   Muslim Women in Western Popular Culture   1

2   The Muslim Body, Veiling, and Contestations of Islam   23

3   *Ms. Marvel*, Islam, and America   47

4   *Burka Avenger* and the Subversive Veil   71

5   *Qahera*, *Raat*, *Bloody Nasreen*, and the Vigilante Superhero   91

Conclusion: Islamic Feminism and Muslim Chivalry   115

Bibliography   129

Index   145

About the Author   149

Foreword

Wajahat Ali

Iboo is flying in the dark purple sky, wearing his Superman costume and cape, heroic and majestic with his toddler right fist raised toward the heavens. Beside her three-year-old brother, baby Nusayba floats with regal grace, her eyes reflecting a glint of sweet fierceness. She's holding a golden lasso and rocking Wonder Woman gear.

This painting proudly hangs in our family room. I commissioned the talented artist Rusty Zimmerman, my old high school friend, to do a unique superhero portrait of my two kids. If so, I've left space on the painting for Lil' Batman or Batwoman in case the wife wants a third baby. The Trinity will be complete featuring the most iconic heroes of the DC comic book universe.

Now, you'd think everyone would find this painting to be absolutely awesome. Surprisingly, it's divisive. Many peers believe it's childish, unworthy of prime family room real estate, and should be relegated to Ibrahim's bedroom, Others are less blunt, more passive aggressive, and some just nod and smile but quietly judge with their eyes.

Comics books are allegedly for kids. According to a college friend, they're cheap rags that little boys read. "What? You? You're reading these? I was wondering what kid would be on this flight with these?" asked an astonished fellow passenger and Aspen Ideas Festival participant when she saw me sit down and read the comic books I had left on my seat. I did so unapologetically. She remained confused.

In the 1950s, comic books were seen as the "10-cent plague." They were cheap, filthy, licentious smut that was degrading and corrupting the minds of our impressionable young men. (Check out David Hajdu's excellent *The Ten-Cent Plague: The Great Comic-Book Scare and How It Changed America*.) It was low art made by even lower people crammed with morally subversive content between the covers. It was threatening because it was so popular, beloved, and influential. Kids and adults loved the horror, the thrills, the shocks, the subtle middle finger to the fear-mongering conservative establishment. From the beginning, comics were a pop cultural medium often made by outsiders for outsiders disrupting the system. Comic book writers were often the promethean mutants, society's morlocks deemed unworthy of being protagonists of the American narrative. Is it really surprising that some of the most notable comics creators have been Jewish?— Jerry Spiegel, Joe Shuster, Stan Lee, Jack Kirby, Will Eisner, Joe Kubert, Art Spiegelman.

Growing up I was often chided by my peers and Pakistani immigrant elders for indulging in this childish nonsense. But, that never stopped me from running around the house wearing a white towel around my neck pretending I was Superman and Batman. When I was a kid, my grandfather used to pick up Spiderman comics for me at the San Jose Flea Market. I always devoured whatever I could find sitting in the rack at the local Barber shop waiting for grandfather and father to finish their haircuts. Around fifth grade, my elder carpooler Jason Larson decided he was "too old" for comics and gifted me his entire collection which included mostly Marvel superheroes. It was amazing. I went through the entire box over a weekend. I needed more. Every two weeks my father took me to the local comic book store, Comics Pendragon in Milpitas, where I could get only five comics. I was judicious but consistent. My collection grew. My parents assumed the growing boxes would be worth money someday and I'd sell them and get college money. (They were wrong, but God bless them for their wishful thinking.)

Fast forward two decades and my son is now wearing Spiderman jammies and earlier this week he just chose a pair of glowing Teenage Mutant Ninja Turtles sneakers. (The turtles in a half shell were originally comic book heroes.) Every day he walks me out as I leave for work and right before closing the door he says, "Look, Baba! My muscles. I'm Hulk!!!! Arrrgh!!!" Then he shuts the door.

Far from being silly stories with forgettable characters in spandex, comic books are a multibillion dollar industry. Stories of Gods, villains and heroes, mortal men and women rising to battle injustice, being selfless in the pursuit of goodness have animated human stories, religions and shaped our values for thousands of years. It's basically the same grand cosmic opera now happening on illustrated panels, cartoons, and big screens.

The highest grossing movie of 2017 as of July is Marvel's *Guardians of the Galaxy* and Warner Bros.' *Wonder Woman*. In particular, the latter will flirt with $400 million domestically. A big budget movie directed by a woman and featuring a female lead character will gross more than the big boys who appeared in *Batman v. Superman.*

Three lessons can be learned from this:

1. Don't underestimate the universal, global appeal of comic books. "The 10 cent plague" has evolved into an influential, billion dollar enterprise.
2. Don't underestimate the power of diverse representation. If you tell a story well with a diverse cast, or feature a minority lead, they—the "ethnic" and "mainstream" audiences alike—will come.
3. Don't underestimate women, 51 percent of the population.

Growing up as a Muslim man and son of Pakistani immigrants, I could only dream of having a brown superhero. Where was the Muslim version of Peter Parker, a good, awkward dude trying to wield power responsibly while also juggling high school? Where was the Pakistani version of Captain America, a model of leadership, strength, and duty who commanded the Avengers, Earth's Mightiest Heroes?

They didn't exist.

So, instead, I lived vicariously through the web-slinging adventures of Spiderman and the space theatrics of Green Lantern and imagined they ate *daal* with their hands like me during their down time.

Indeed, one of the glaring blind spots in American pop culture has been the erasure of minorities, people of color and women. They are either tokens, ridiculous caricatures or mere footnotes. Muslims, the most diverse religious communities in America, numbering nearly 1.7 billion worldwide and following a faith tradition for over 1400 years, are barely visible. When we do make an appearance, it's often as a violent, angry antagonist. Sophia Rose Arjana's *Muslims in the Western Imagination* traces the origins and creations of this detrimental image that goes back to the Crusades and directly informs and shapes the toxic policies of the current White House administration. (Read that book after this one). The great, pioneering academic Jack Shaheen, who just passed away, documented how Hollywood exploited and Otherized these diverse narratives for nearly a century, reducing all of Islam, Muslims, and the Middle East to something foreign, hostile, villainous.

Black Jokers with big beard and zero smiles. Arab Penguins with hooked noses and kufis. Brown Riddlers sporting turbans and Kalashnikovs.

Within the realm of comics, perhaps no other minority has had it worse than women. These fellow humans who just happen to have ovaries suffered at the hands of a mostly male-dominated industry which reduced them as objects of lust. They are either anatomically ridiculous creatures fighting evil in skimpy clothes and bulging breasts or damsels in distress. This does not take away a rich legacy of strong, inspiring female characters such as Wonder Woman, Storm, Mystique, Jean Grey, as well as women creators who have tried to counter these images and negative trends.

Remember, comic books are mostly for boys, right? Women don't show up, yeah? Well, tell that to the global audience of *Wonder Woman*. (At least $400 million domestic box office take, in case you forgot.) But in 2017, why is *Wonder Woman* the unicorn, the rare big budget production featuring a female superhero lead? There should have been more—many more—that were green lit, made, released, and subsequently celebrated and embraced. And what about comic book stories featuring women of color? We have *Black Panther* coming out next year, but where's our *Storm* movie? Oh, and what about Muslim women? Don't hold your breath. The complexity, diversity, beauty, and identity of Muslim women seem to be singularly reduced to the hijab—an article of clothing that is simultaneously exploited and fetishized, commodified and penalized.

However, something glorious has happened after the 9/11 tragedy and Trump victory, which to many heralds the inevitable clash of civilizations between "Islam" and the "West." (By the way, if you ever meet "Islam" and the "West" please tell me where you found them and what they look like. Also, tell Islam he owes me $5.) The mutants, the outsiders, the morlocks have decided to bum rush the show. They're picking up the pen and the paintbrush and deciding to become protagonists of the American narrative. People of color, LGBTQ, women, and Muslims who grew up reading, inhaling, loving comic book pop culture have entered the mainstream and are creating characters that look like them and represent their story.

My friends G. Willow Wilson and Sana Amanat, both Muslim women born in the United States, cocreated *Ms. Marvel*, a universal story told through a culturally specific lens of Kamala Khan, a New Jersey teenager who gets superhero powers after being exposed to the Inhumans' terrigen mist. Oh, she's also Muslim and the daughter of Pakistani immigrants. We also have Simon Baz, an Arab-American Muslim who wears the Green Lantern ring. There's Nightrunner, an Algerian Muslim who's part of Batman's international squad. Across the Atlantic in Pakistan, Burqa Avenger dispenses justice to promote literacy and Bloody Nesrine is a violent vigilante cleaning up corrupt streets of Karachi.

The characters, the stories, and the storytellers keep growing. More and more, across the globe, folks are thirsting to see their communities as heroes not just the mortals on the ground looking up at the sky and cheering on their white saviors. Last year I was in Dhaka, Bangladesh, organizing a creative hackathon for Facebook and Google to come up with digital tools and initiatives that can promote pluralism. The winning team was a group of young comic book artists and storytellers, all still in college. They love U.S. pop culture and comics, but they were tired of seeing White, American heroes. "We want to see stories and heroes that look like us. That reflect our culture and our stories. We want Bangladeshi heroes."

We now have Bangladeshi heroes. Pakistani heroes. Black heroes. Latino heroes. LGBTQ heroes. Muslim heroes.

And these characters are for universal audiences, being accepted by the mainstream. I saw women of different ethnicities dress up in Ms. Marvel cosplay at pop culture convention in Washington, D.C. A Muslim-American woman of Pakistani descent is actively embraced as a positive role model and empowering hero by women all around the world. Amazing.

Going full meta, Ms. Marvel also showed up on San Francisco buses protesting hate-filled, anti-Muslim posters publicized by Islamophobes. She was also a symbol of resistance at the Women's March that brought over 3 million people out to the streets—the largest mass protest in U.S. history.

In the following pages, Sophia Rose Arjana shows you we got to this wonderful, weird, exciting place. It's an academic book, but well written and engaging; smart without being pretentious; accessible without being dumbed down; well researched, well argued and ultimately uplifting. She traces the journey of Orientalist stereotypes and how they've been used primarily as a suppressive women against Muslim women. She explores the strange fixation on the hijab and how Muslim feminists have reclaimed their faith tradition and cultures to fight back against misogyny and Western feminists who want to "save brown women from brown men." She highlights how Muslim storytellers have used comic books as a pop cultural medium to introduce bold, disruptives narratives, visions, and characters of what it means to be Muslim and woman and how we can all emerge as heroes for a new generation that is comfortable wearing spandex in public and praying toward Mecca a few times a day.

I'm fortunate to be alive to see such days. But, more importantly, I'm grateful my daughter will grow up seeing her skin color, her religion, and other formerly excised parts of her American story reflected in illustrated comic panels, the big screen, plastic action figures and pajamas that her friends wear during their slumber parties.

And who knows? Maybe a few years from now her friends' parents will have a giant painting hanging in their family room featuring their daughters as a superhero, standing tall, proud, fierce, and heroic wearing a Ms. Marvel costume.

Introduction

Discourse about Islam is largely a journey of the imagination. As Edward Said wrote, "Just as none of us is outside or beyond geography, none of us is completely free from the struggle over geography. That struggle is complex and interesting because it is not only about soldiers and cannons but also about ideas, about forms, about images and imaginings."[1] These tensions are often recorded in written and visual texts that tell competing stories about who Muslims are. This book is about some of those narratives; in particular, the stories of Muslim women as told through graphic, visually rich texts—comics and animated cartoons.

My book focuses on *Muslimah* (Muslim female) superheroes, who often, but not always, practice veiling. They are located in distinct social and cultural spaces—Kuwait, the United States, Pakistan, and Egypt. However, they are often global figures, familiar to fans who frequent comic book stores and festivals like Comicon. From *Ms. Marvel* to *Burka Avenger*, these are figures known "transnationally among other world comic cultures."[2] Even though comic superheroes are an American invention, they are, at the same time, universal. Female Muslim superheroes are often strongly political characters, challenging patriarchy on numerous fronts. As Deena Mohamed, the creator of *Qahera* (an Egyptian superhero) has remarked, the *Muslimah* superhero provides a way to counter both Islamic and Western misogyny. "As such, there was a certain enjoyable irony in creating an Egyptian, Muslim female character as a superhero, a genre distinguished by its numerous white male characters."[3]

The comic is the primary source for the material in this book. It is a text organized in panels and within this unit, three kinds of language are typically used—narration, dialogue, and sound effect (often through the *suggestion* of sound, such as loud noises—think of the BAM! POW! of the old Batman comics).[4] While the relationship of these elements is not a focus of this book, it is important to note that in many comics, the narration, dialogue, and imagery all work together to create a story. There are also comics that are largely pictorial, with little or no dialogue. My main point of analysis is the characters themselves; and in particular, what their bodies, costumes, words, and actions communicate. However, I do include discussion of certain artistic techniques, such as the positioning of a Ms. Marvel doll in Kamala Khan's bedroom, and the use of black, white, and gray in *Qahera*.

Comic art influences numerous other art forms, including the animated cartoons and filmic adaptations it inspires, which are also examined in this book. Filmmakers like Federico Fellini and Orson Wells have "explicitly acknowledged their indebtedness to comics in one respect or another," as has Paul McCartney, who counts comics as one of his inspirations for lyrics.[5] The superheroes of comics are also important cultural icons, representing social values and in more recent decades, confronting political issues. The casting of villains in superhero stories is often tied to the problems of the day. As one scholar writes, "The travelling superhero now finds hunger in Appalachia, corrupt politicians and public officials, cultists working to inflame race-war, victimized American Indians and superpatriotic—and right-wing—actors in Hollywood Westerns."[6] Like the superheroes of the past, *Muslimah* superheroes are powerful beings, fighting crime, corruption, poverty, and other social evils, all with the help of superpowers and special gifts. As scholars have pointed out, the artistic techniques used in comics help the expression of these special powers. "This objectification is especially problematic for women characters' depictions, because in using these techniques, their objectification is also a prominent sexualization of their characters."[7] Unlike most female superheroes, the *Muslimah* superhero is not physically objectified.

The overwhelming majority of depictions of Muslims in Western popular culture are negative and feature sultans, oil sheiks, concubines, and terrorists. Appearing on everything from movie screens to advertising, Muslims have provided a source of entertainment for Americans situated in stereotyping that is communicated in a violent and sensual imagery. For a long time, Muslims have functioned as commodities in the marketplace.

> Advertisers, recognizing an overall American association of sensuality with Muslims, used images of Arabs/Muslims and Arab/Muslim-associated places and objects to market their products. Camel cigarettes, with the eponymous camel standing in front of pyramids, best illustrates this, although other early cigarette brands included Fatima, Mecca, Medina, and Omar brands. Advertisements often suggested "romance, self-indulgence, or sexual innuendo."[8]

Television and film have offered few positive portrayals of Muslim females, in part because popular media tends to focus on Muslim men. When female characters have appeared in television and film in recent years, they have been dominated by the post-9/11 anxieties surrounding Islam. The turn to themes of terrorism and homeland security is represented in narratives and characters focused on Muslim violence.

Threatened or actual attacks on shopping malls figure in *24* (Fox, 2001–2010) and *NCIS: Los Angeles* (CBS, 2009–), for example, both of which are action shows that hybridize crime and espionage conventions. In *Bones*, a cultural center is targeted, whereas in *Lie To Me*, bombers first target a bus, and then a mall, before further attacks are averted at three public locations, including the area in front of the White House. *Numb3rs* sees a Muslim terrorist cell planning to distribute sarin via the city water supply, whereas in *NCIS* (CBS, 2003–) terrorist action threatens to take out the power grid. Televisional terrorism thus affects ordinary life in extreme or violent ways—with the nation and its urban and civic spaces reportedly under attack.[9]

Rarely do portrayals of Muslims include physicians, engineers, police officers, teachers, or artists, demonstrating a radical disconnection between fantasies about Islam and the lives that Muslims lead in the world today. This is a result of the power of the cultural imaginary, the reality that we create about the Other and ourselves. In the case of Islam, our construction of Muslims must fit into a politically constructed vision of the world. As Edward Said has argued, "Local and concrete circumstances are thus obliterated. In other words, covering Islam is a one-sided activity that obscures what 'we' *do*, and highlights instead what Muslims and Arabs by their very flawed nature *are*."[10]

As scholars have noted, popular culture is a powerful tool that helps to form personal identity, ideals of nationhood, and beliefs about cultures and communities outside our own. "Popular culture, in other words, is one of the ways in which people come to understand their position both within a larger collective identity and within an even larger geopolitical narrative, or script."[11] Popular culture is also used to instruct the masses or to teach a lesson to a particular social group. As one example, the creators of the *Captain America* comic remarked that they seek to "create narratives that have a point, that entertain and seek to do something more, perhaps educate on some level."[12] In this particular comic book, the lesson is that Muslims are dangerous. "Islam, in particular, is given as an example of a civilization innately tied to religious violence."[13]

This frightening vision of Islam is often played out on Muslim bodies, producing an imaginary world that is replete with girls and women being harassed, sexually assaulted, mutilated, tortured, and killed. In the 2004

Dutch film *Submission*, four stories of physical and sexual violence are told, producing a vision of Muslim religiosity that is predicated on the "master-slave relationship" between God and females.[14] This discourse is one that "openly and unequivocally represents the 'true Islam' as a violent religion that leads to cruelty" toward females.[15] One proponent of this discourse is Ayaan Hirsi Ali, who generally equates all of Muslim experience with the practice of Wahhabism in Saudi Arabia. It is a presentation of Islam defined by "mutilation of limbs, beheading, stoning, veiling."[16]

While the patriarchy and violence Muslim women are subjected to is undeniable (and highlighted in places like Saudi Arabia and Afghanistan), Islam's misogynistic practices have good company. "The regulation of women and their sexuality is, after all, a common feature of all patriarchal societies, traditional or modern, and certainly not simply Muslim ones."[17] Yet, tales of honor killings and Daesh's mass rapes seem to override information about much of the violence women living outside of Muslim-majority countries experience. In the United States, every ninety-eight seconds a sexual assault occurs and each day three women are murdered by a current or former partner.[18]

The characters examined in this book represent a growing number of portrayals that have emerged in recent years that *don't* fit the vision of Muslim women as victims of sexual and physical violence. The superhero is, in fact, a character predicated on agency and vigilantism. Violence is often inflicted upon others *by* the superhero. As scholars have noted, the introduction of violent female characters, which includes superheroes and other vigilantes, is a symptom of postfeminism. As Lisa Coulthard has explained, postfeminism has "transferred attention toward debates about the presence of violent women in cinema and popular culture and away from women as victimized subject *to* violence."[19] One of the things this entails is an understanding of how feminism affects cultural production.

In this book, I include *Muslimah* superheroes from Pakistan, Kuwait, Egypt, and the United States that illustrate the diversity of Muslim experience in today's world. Despite efforts to cast Islam as a monolithic religious and cultural system, Muslims are diverse, ranging from the late American athlete and civil rights icon Muhammad Ali to the Pakistani educational activist Malala Yousafzai. As John Esposito has written, "With 1.5 billion followers, Islam is the predominant religion in some fifty-six countries and the second or third-largest religion in Europe and America."[20] The wide distribution of Muslims in the world today helps us understand why there are so many different articulations of the faith, from authoritarian and patriarchal to liberative and feminist. This study examines two areas of popular culture—comics (print and web comics) and animated cartoons—that offer alternative visions of Islam that challenge these anxieties and the stereotypes that uphold them. I am not denying that these anxieties exist or are groundless. However, in this project, I show that in the face of Islamist terror, Western anxieties, a history of colonialism, and the current popularity of Islamophobia, there is still space for presentations of Islam that reflect the realities of Muslim lived experience.

The *Muslimah* superhero is an understudied academic topic that merits serious attention. Studies of Muslim women are often focused on the themes of oppression, Orientalism, or sensuality. This book seeks to show positive characters—Muslim women who are independent, exercise power, and fight against injustice. The characters examined in this book include both superheroes with special powers, including Burka Avenger's ability to fly and Ms. Marvel's powers of self-healing, as well as individuals who have no such magical gifts, such as Raat and Bloody Nasreen, regular citizens who take justice into their own hands.

I first became interested in the topic of Muslim superheroes when I directed Kim Fox's MA thesis, a study of the role of liberation theology in the Pakistani animated television series *Burka Avenger*.[21] I am grateful to Kim for introducing me to this subject. As she argued in her thesis, Burka Avenger challenges the notions of the Muslim female as oppressed, subservient, and powerless through her use of dress, her career as a schoolteacher, and her superhero activism. As we shall learn, Burka Avenger's use of the veil is an especially important part of the character's strategy of liberation.

The veil (also commonly called *hijab*) is often, but not always, an important part of the Muslim superheroine's identity. Among the ways that Burka Avenger challenges both Western and Islamic expectations of the Muslim woman is through her use of veiling as a subversive tool against corruption, criminality, and violence perpetrated against men, women, and children. The veil is neither oppressive nor is it imposed upon her: her use of it is intentional and liberative. As such, it is an important symbol of agency, representing the sartorial choices that many Muslim girls and women make as an aspect of performing Islam.

This book includes characters who use veiling and unveiling in some unexpected ways. Burka Avenger is perhaps the best example of this, for she uses her veil as a disguise, and books and pens as her weapons, thus simultaneously using a tool of the Taliban (the *burka*) and an object they despise (the book) to defeat them. It is important to understand the larger significance of the veil in Islamic thought. The veil does not always refer to a piece of clothing, but can also be the veil that protects the inner secrets of mystical contemplation. Islam teaches that veiling is not only simply a piece of clothing, but is a quality found throughout the universe in all of God's creation. As Ibn al-'Arabi wrote, "Some creatures are curtains over other creatures. Although curtains are signifiers, they are signifiers by way of differentiation, for the cosmos, or rather, all of *wujud* [the cosmos], is a curtain, a curtained, and a curtainer."[22] Thus, veiling is not always physical, but can be silent, disguised, and even invisible—all indicative of Allah's own mysterious qualities that are only revealed to those he loves the most. In this way, the veiled heroines in this book demonstrate not simply sartorial expressions of Islam, but symbols of the faith values in Islam that are not visible to the naked eye.

Saba Mahmood argues that agency should be rooted in the understanding that Muslim women face efforts to control them from within their communities as well as from external colonial and feminist voices. As she has written,

> Agency, in this form of analysis, is understood as the capacity to realize one's own interests against the weight of custom, tradition, transcendental will, or other obstacles (whether individual or collective). Thus the humanist desire for autonomy and self-expression constitutes the substrate, the slumbering ember that can spark to flame in the form of an act of resistance when conditions permit.[23]

Mahmood's elocution of agency brings us to an important question asked by another scholar of feminism and Islam, Lila Abu-Lughod, who writes, "Can there be a liberation that is Islamic?"[24] Burka Avenger is one of many fictive characters examined in this project who answer this question with a resounding, "Yes!"

The characters in this study help to construct a narrative about Muslim women that is anti-colonial, feminist, and liberational. These are individuals whose control of their own bodies challenges the colonization of female bodies that is embedded in the history of Islam and the West, while also establishing a feminist voice that is unapologetically Islamic. In this way, the feminist ideal of "self-realization/self-fulfillment" is expanded far beyond the sexual freedoms most often identified with feminism in North America and Europe.[25]

For the purposes of this study, I work from an understanding of liberation that is theological. This move will avoid the tendency to focus on secular, political solutions of liberation and instead reflect on the fact that theology is contextual. As the scholar of social ethics and liberation Miguel de la Torre has written "Theologies of liberation are spiritual responses to unexamined social structures responsible for oppressing a marginalized majority so that a privileged powerful minority can live abundant lives."[26] As in other traditions, in Islam this often involves a set of choices that have the potential to liberate the individual. At times, the freedom to make these choices may take place within the individual's culture by denying the call, voiced by some, to reject Islamic norms for an alternative way of being in the world. As Saba Mahmood argues,

> Viewed in this way, what may appear to be a case of deplorable passivity and docility from a progressivist point of view, may actually be a form of

agency—but one that can only be understood from within the discourses and structures of its enactment. In this sense, agentival capacity is entailed not only in those acts that resist norms but also in the multiple ways in which one *inhibits* norms.[27]

Gayatri provides a useful framework for understanding the characters examined within this book with her concept of *epistemic violence*. She defines this as "the construction of a self-immolating colonial subject for the glorification of the social mission of the colonizer."[28] The *Muslimah* superhero challenges this violence by providing a counter-narrative to this discourse. In particular, the Muslim heroes highlighted in this study do not *need* saving. They are fully agentic characters who reject Western paternalism, white feminism, and Islamic sexism. When Burka Avenger uses the veil as a disguise and an expression of her Muslim identity, she is rejecting all efforts to colonize her body and her spirit, thus destroying the possibility of the epistemic violence Spivak points to, embracing de la Torre's definition of liberation. The second way in which Spivak informs this project is through her notion of *resistant mimicry*, which involves challenging and altering the master narrative from a position within, allowing the subaltern to emerge as the dominant voice.[29] In these cases, the *Muslimah* superhero is the subaltern who speaks.

The theoretical framing of this study is multi-vocal, in part because I am tackling a topic that involves theology, gender, agency, and the politics of representation. Amina Wadud is a dominant theological voice in this book. In her work on gender in Islam, she argues that men and women are equal moral agents, based on a Qur'anic view of the creation of the world that establishes men and women as complementary partners (*zawjan*).

Although the male and female are essential contingent characters in the creation of humankind, no specific cultural functions or roles are defined at the moment of creation. At that moment, Allah defines certain traits universal to all humans and not specific to one particular gender nor to any particular people from any particular place or time. The divine *ayat* [verse], in both their words of revelation and empirical forms in nature, are available to all. The empirical *ayat* can be perceived by every person anywhere and at any time. The specific *ayat* which Allah has revealed to a chosen few at particular times under particular circumstances are meant for all.[30]

The patriarchy imposed on girls and women in the Muslim context is, in Wadud's view, a violation of the universality of the Qur'an, a document that has the potential to bring liberation to all. Wadud sees her work as *tasfir*—the careful exegesis of the Qur'an that brings about an understanding of the text. It is important to understand that this is not a view that is outside Islam, externally imposed from an external ideology; rather, it is an internal approach which, in Wadud's view, requires understanding the "spirit" of the Qur'an and its "objective to act as a catalyst affecting behavior in society."[31] The society Islam calls for is ruled by justice, which the Qur'an points to in numerous chapters. This justice is what the *Muslimah* superheroes profiled in this book seek through both soft and hard violence.

Juliane Hammer describes Wadud's view of gender as one in which "men and women can only be equal, in interchangeable positions."[32] Influenced by Fazlur Rahman's double movement of Qur'anic principles and their realization in the world, Wadud's interpretation of theology requires that *tawhid* (the oneness of Allah) necessitates a horizontal model of relationships in the world today.[33] It should be noted that even while she frames her work as pro-feminist, Wadud does not identify as a feminist but as a Muslim theologian who prioritizes Islam and as someone who, as an African-American, has often been excluded by the feminist movement.[34] Wadud's work informs my work in several ways. Among the most important is her view of Muslim female agency, one that, quoting Wadud, is predicated on the "special link between the Creator, Allah, and the created, humankind" that assigns human individuals as *khalifah*, trustees of God "on earth."[35] This is not an agency that should be controlled, or restricted, by anyone else, including Muslim men, Western men, or Western feminists. It is truly "liberated" by the disciplinary practices of both religion and secularism.

The contemporary philosopher Judith Butler articulates a liberative view of gender identity that is queered in the sense that it violates popular norms about femininity. Butler argues that gender is a culturally constructed identity often strictly regulated by the enforcement of social norms. The norms regarding females support hegemonic masculinity—the idea that there is a particular way of being male that manifests itself in things like patriarchy and militarism. As Butler argues, this determines the female role. "Women are the 'Other' according to Beauvoir in so far as they are defined by a masculine perspective that seeks to safeguard its own disembodied status through identifying women generally with the bodily sphere."[36] The *Muslimah* superhero constructs her own identity by rejecting the norms of hegemonic masculinity from *both* Muslim-majority and Muslim-minority societies.

Butler's work informs my work through her writings on agency and identity. Butler argues that individuals have the right and agency to construct their own gender, which includes independent versions, or expressions, that do not necessarily accord with traditional notions of femininity or masculinity, and involve a variety of other identities including transgender and nonbinary. While I do not propose that the characters in this study are transgender or nonbinary (in fact, they all identify as female), I do believe that *Muslimah* superheroes embody Butler's notion of gender agency. As she has written, the body is a *cultural situation* that is a "field of interpretive possibilities," which results in the body becoming "a peculiar nexus of culture and choice, and 'existing' one's body becomes a personal way of taking up and reinterpreting received gender norms."[37] The characters examined in this book offer ways of "existing" that illustrate a challenge to both dominant Western and Islamic models of Muslim womanhood.

Ella Shohat is another feminist scholar whose work informs my approach to the characters examined in this book. In her piece titled "Gender and Culture of Empire: Toward a Feminist Ethnography of the Cinema," she argues that Western cinema is dominated by the "colonialist imaginary" and the "gendered Western gaze," which have formulated a particular view of the Muslim female.[38] These representations dominate other fields of media, including comics and animated cartoons. Shohat argues that "Although a feminist reading of (post)colonial discourse must take into account the national and historical specificities of that discourse, it is equally important also to chart the broader structural analogies in the representation of Third World cultures."[39] Like Shohat, this book challenges such representations by providing a feminist, postcolonial reading of *Muslimah* superheroes that is socially located, thus opening up the analysis to intersectionality. As Shohat has written, the tendency to rely on one vision of feminism is problematized by the tendency to construct binaries such as the "Middle Eastern women" or "Latin American gays/lesbians" that Shohat notes in her work, and that in her view ignores the fact that people do not exist as "hermetically sealed entities but rather as part of a permeable interwoven relationality."[40]

I would like to make two important points concerning the content of this book in respect to the lives of Muslim women. While Muslim comics are an emergent topic for academia, including for scholars of religion like myself, the focus tends to be on the ways in which these texts function in popular culture. While this is certainly an interest of this project, I am also interested in the political power contained in that oft-mentioned object—the veil. As Valerie Behiery has argued, the veil is an incredibly powerful device.

> If the stereotype or trope of the veil rooted in the colonial project continues to be reproduced in contemporary visual culture—in print media most particularly—the myriad representations of the veil in contemporary art unequivocally delineate complex views of the sign, both as a garment and as a representational strategy, that have yet to be properly studied, despite the growing scholarship on art related to, or from, the Muslim world.[41]

This book is largely focused on these representational strategies, which allow for different articulations of feminism and Muslim identity.

The second point I want to make concerns the Islamic ethic of justice in respect to these characters. As I argue in later chapters, the *Muslimah* superhero serves as an example of moral behavior, and in particular, of the *jihad al-nafs*—the struggle against one's ego, also known as the *greater jihad*. This lifelong struggle of the Muslim is highlighted by the fight for social justice, which is the outer manifestation of the greater *jihad*. In these characters, we see how this struggle is expressed—in Ms. Marvel's moral decisions, in Burka Avenger's inner peace exercises, and in Qahera's social activism, among other places. Collectively, these characters also represent the chivalric values attached to spiritually developed individuals—the end result of this inner struggle against the ego, which balances the person and allows for the development of proper *adab* (Muslim values). The *jihad al-nafs* and its influence on *adab* are seen in the exemplary behavior of the *Muslimah* superhero. In this way, these characters who serve as excellent role models for Muslim audiences, especially young children, at whom many of these graphic texts are directed.

Chapter 1 provides a historical survey of the dominant representations of Muslim females in comics, cartoons, film, and other popular media, as well as some of the ways in which the characters examined in this book provide a counter-narrative to these images. This lays the groundwork for the rest of the book by illustrating why *Muslimah* superheroes represent such a radical departure from the dominant discourse about Muslims. As I argue, the visual consumption of colonized bodies, and in some cases formerly colonized bodies, is challenged by characters who reject outsiders' efforts to control them. One way this is achieved is through the actions of the *Muslimah* superhero who is more powerful than those who seek to dominate her. Of course, Muslim women are not alone in being cast as subsidiary characters to men. In comics, females often play subsidiary roles to men, even in cases where the superhero is not white. *Kaliman*, the Mexican superhero comic, features "elements of the Mexican stereotypes of the 'good woman,' or chaste, honorable woman and the 'bad woman,' or sexually active slut."[42] As I detail in this chapter, the comic is a representational form that often contains powerful messaging about gender.

Chapter 2 focuses on the veil and the harem and in particular their use in imagery that features Muslim girls and women. I illustrate the contrasts between the older and more dominant representations of Muslim women and the newer, arguably fairer treatments that challenge these images. These tensions are examined by looking at two texts—Frank Miller's *Holy Terror* and Naif Al-Mutawa's *The 99*, which provide radically different presentations of Muslims. This discussion illustrates how visual texts can serve as powerful instruments that offer competing political and cultural values.

Chapter 3 focuses on the American superhero Kamala Khan/Ms. Marvel, who faces careful negotiations that involve her faith as a Muslim and her social status as an American teenager. As the new *Ms. Marvel*, she joins a long tradition of feminist comix, which Sheri Klein describes as being typified by realism, social problems, and "the realities of women."[43] Ms. Marvel communicates important teachings and values that are central to the superhero's identity as a Muslim. She represents a departure from the majority of Muslim comic characters, who are cast as villains, terrorists, and mad scientists. Even in recent years, comics and their filmic adaptations have featured the most negative sorts of Muslims. Three *Iron Man* films and two Avenger films followed the comic's storyline featuring al-Qaeda. Jon Favreau, the director of the first two Iron Man films, "believes the popularity of the genre is a result of 9/11 but as escapism that does not require any responsibility to address reality."[44] As pointed out earlier in this introduction, this is yet another example of the commodification of Islam and the tropes attached to Arab bodies that mark much of American representations of Muslims. Nicholaus Pumphrey rightly states, "As a result, writers recapitulated dangerous stereotypes of Muslims in order to sell comics and to sell movie tickets."[45] Ms. Marvel challenges this and, as I shall show, represents a new kind of superhero—one that is Muslim, immigrant, and female.

In chapter 4, I shift my focus from the comic form to animation. The Pakistani animated television series *Burka Avenger*, as noted earlier, inspired this project. The title character is a powerful figure who merits special attention. *Burka Avenger* is a *Muslimah* superhero who fights for education and gender equity by using a clever disguise, the veil (specifically, a *niqab*), and her weapons are her body, as well as books. Her use of the *niqab* is important because it represents the coercive use of clothing that is assumed to be oppressive. *Burka Avenger* offers a superhero who deploys her body in unexpected ways.

Chapter 5 examines the topic of violence through characters that exist in the world of print and web comics—*Qahera*, *Raat*, and *Bloody Nasreen*. Qahera represents the street culture of Cairo following the 2013 uprisings against the Egyptian government, which included graffiti murals, music, and theater productions focused on social justice. Qahera has limits on the violence she inflicts upon others. Raat is one of two Pakistani superheroes examined in this chapter. She is more violent than Qahera, but not as extreme as Bloody Nasreen, who uses excessive violence. Where Qahera reflects the Islamic principle of mercy, Raat and Bloody Nasreen take a very different approach, reflecting a more militant form of action that echoes the current political situation in Pakistan. Both of these characters—one a superhero, the other a vigilante—represent the challenges made to the modern state when it fails to protect its citizens.

In the Conclusion, I reflect on the characters in this book and situate them in a larger discussion of Muslim female superheroes, Islamic feminism, agency, and the performance of gender. This chapter provides a lengthy discussion of Islamic feminism, including the numerous perspectives that have been voiced by Muslim intellectuals and the ways in which these perspectives differ from the dominant views of feminism in North America and Europe. The chapter voices the concerns of contemporary scholars whose work focuses on issues related to Muslim women, feminism, colonialism, and agency. These various perspectives show us that women's bodies, while often objects of contestation, are also powerful vehicles through which to exert agency, independence, and political power. The final chapter also suggests that Islamic chivalry offers a way for us to understand the *Muslimah* superhero in the context of Islamic values. This is important, because although *Muslimah* superheroes have broad appeal, they are situated in Islamic values, and we must not lose sight of this lest they be co-opted as emblems of types of feminism that do not give credit where it is due.

NOTES

1. Edward Said, *Culture and Imperialism* (New York: Vintage Books, 1993): 7.

2. Karline McClain, *India's Immortal Comic Books: Gods, Kings, and Other Heroes* (Bloomington: Indiana University Press, 2009): 23.

3. Deena Mohamed, "On Translating a Superhero: Language and Webcomics," in *Translating Dissent: Voices From and With the Egyptian Revolution,* ed. Mona Baker (New York: Routledge, 2016): 140.

4. Lawrence L. Abbott, "Comic Art: Characteristics and Potentialities of a Narrative Medium," *The Journal of Popular Culture* 19, no. 4 (1986): 156.

5. Max J. Skidmore and Joey Skidmore, "More Than Mere Fantasy: Political Themes in Contemporary Comic Books," *The Journal of Popular Culture* 17, no. 1 (1983): 84.

6. Skidmore and Skidmore, "More Than Mere Fantasy: Political Themes in Contemporary Comic Books," *The Journal of Popular Culture* 17, no. 1 (1983): 85.

7. Karen McGrath, "Gender, Race, and Latina Identity: An Examination of Marvel Comics' *Amazing Fantasy* and *Araña*," *Atlantic Journal of Communication* 15, no. 4 (2007): 272.

8. Peter Gottschalk and Gabriel Greenberg, *Islamophobia: Making Muslims the Enemy* (Lanham: Rowman and Littlefield, 2008), 35–36. Gottschalk and Greenberg quote Holly Edwards, "A Million and One Nights: Orientalism in America, 1870–1930," in *Noble Dreams, Wicked Pleasures: Orientalism in America, 1870–1920,* ed. Holly Edwards (Princeton: Princeton University Press, 2000): 43.

9. Yvonne Tasker, "Television Crime Drama and Homeland Security: From Law and Order to 'Terror TV,'" *Cinema Journal* 51, no. 4 (2012): 45.

10. Edward Said, *Covering Islam: How the Media and the Experts Determine How We See the Rest of the World* (New York: Vintage Books, 1997), xxii.

11. Jason Dittmer, "Captain America's Empire: Reflections on Identity, Popular Culture, and Post-9/11 Geopolitics," *Annals of the Association of American Geographers* 95, no. 3 (2005): 626.

12. Ibid., 627.

13. Ibid., 639.

14. Iveta Jusová, "Hirsi Ali and van Gogh's Submission: Reinforcing the Islam vs. Women Binary," *Women's Studies International Forum* 31 (2008): 153.

15. Ibid.

16. Adam Yaghi, "Popular Testimonial Literature by American Cultural Conservatives of Arab and Muslim Descent: Narrating the Self, Translating (an) Other," *Middle East Critique* 25, no. 1 (2016): 91.

17. Saadia Toor, "The Political Economy of Moral Regulation in Pakistan: Religion, Gender and Class in a Postcolonial Context," in *Routledge Handbook of Gender in South Asia*, ed. by Leela Fernandes (New York: Routledge, 2014): 140.

18. Alanna Vagianos, "30 Shocking Domestic Violence Statistics That Remind Us It's An Epidemic," *The Huffington Post*, October 23, 2014, http://www.huffingtonpost.com/2014/10/23/domestic-violence-statistics_n_5959776.html (accessed February 24, 2017).

19. Lisa Coulthard, "Killing Bill: Rethinking Feminism and Film Violence," in *Interrogating Postfeminism: Gender and the Politics of Popular Culture*, ed. Yvonne Tasker and Fiane Negra (Durham: Duke University Press, 2007), 154. Quoted in Yuko Minowa, Pauline Maclaran, and Lorna Stevens, "Visual Representations of Violent Women," *Visual Communications Quarterly* 21, no. 4 (2014): 217.

20. John L. Esposito, *Islam: The Straight Path* (New York: Oxford University Press, 2011): ix.

21. See Kimberly E. Fox, "*Burka Avenger*: On Agency, Education, and Equality in Pakistani Popular Culture," (master's thesis, Iliff School of Theology, 2014).

22. William C. Chittick, *The Self-Disclosure of God: Principles of Ibn al-'Arabi's Cosmology* (Albany: State University of New York Press, 1998): 104.

23. Saba Mahmood, *Politics of Piety: The Islamic Revival and the Feminist Subject* (Princeton: Princeton University Press, 2004): 8.

24. Lila Abu-Lughod, *Do Muslim Women Need Saving?* (Cambridge: Harvard University Press, 2013): 45.

25. Saba Mahmood, 13.

26. Miguel De La Torre, "Introduction," in *Introducing Liberative Theologies*, ed. Miguel de la Torre (Maryknoll, NY: Orbis Books, 2015): xx.

27. Saba Mahmood, 15.

28. Gayatri Chavravorty Spivak, *A Critique of Postcolonial Reason: Toward a History of the Vanishing Present* (Cambridge: Harvard University Press, 1999), 127.

29. Valerie Behiery, "Alternative Narratives of the Veil in Contemporary Art," *Comparative Studies of South Asia, Africa and the Middle East* 32, no. 1 (2012): 138.

30. Amina Wadud, *Qur'an and Woman: Rereading the Sacred Text from a Woman's Perspective* (New York: Oxford University Press, 1999), 26.

31. Amina Wadud, *Qur'an and Woman,* 5.

32. Juliane Hammer, "Gender, Feminism, and Critique in American Muslim Thought," in *Routledge Handbook of Islam in the West*, ed. Roberto Toppoli (London: Routledge, 2014): 401.

33. Ibid., 399.

34. Aysha A. Hidayatullah, *Feminist Edges of the Qur'an* (New York: Oxford University Press, 2014): 14.

35. Amina Wadud, *Qur'an and Woman,* 26, 23.

36. Judith Butler, "Variations on Sex and Gender: Beauvoir, Wittig, Foucault," in *The Judith Butler Reader*, ed. by Sarah Salih (Malden: Blackwell Publishing, 2004): 28.

37. Judith Butler, "Variations on Sex and Gender," 28–29.

38. Ella Shohat, "Gender and Culture of Empire: Toward a Feminist Ethnography of the Cinema," in *Visions of the East: Orientalism in Film*, ed. by Matthew Bernstein and Gaylyn Studlar (New Brunswick: Rutgers University Press, 1997), 20.

39. Ibid., 57.

40. Ella Shohat, "Area Studies, Gender Studies, and the Cartographies of Knowledge," *Social Text 72,* 20, no. 3 (2002): 68.

41. Valerie Behiery, "Alternative Narratives," 130.

42. Harold E. Hinds, "Kaliman: A Mexican Superhero," *Journal of Popular Culture* 13, no. 2 (1979): 236.

43. Sheri Klein, "Breaking the Mold with Humor: Images of Women in the Visual Media," *Art Education* 46, no. 5 (1993): 63.

44. Nicholaus Pumphrey, "Avenger, Mutant, or Allah: A Short Evolution of the Depiction of Muslims in Marvel Comics," *The Muslim World* 106, no. 4 (2016): 788–789.

45. Ibid., 789.

Chapter 1

Muslim Women in Western Popular Culture

In the Western imagination, Muslim women represent the exotic and the erotic. The promise of gratification associated with the East, as Sarah Graham-Brown writes, is nowhere "more evident than in the Orientalists' vision of women in the Middle East."[1] The seductive eyes behind the veil and the delights of the harem are but two of many representations of Muslim girls and women found in everything from advertising campaigns to Hollywood film. This chapter examines the dominant ways in which Muslim females have been represented—and continue to be represented—in American (and European) popular culture. A genealogy of these images helps us to understand why *Muslimah* superheroes are so revolutionary. As Deena Mohamed, the creator of the popular web comic *Qahera*, puts it, "Superheroes are by definition powerful and outspoken characters, a concept at complete odds with the image of an oppressed, subjugated Muslim woman."[2]

Orientalism has been defined in many ways. It is "the work of the orientalist and a style or quality commonly associated with the East, but also a body of knowledge, an instrument of power and a collection of stereotypical images of the other—as backward, mysterious, irrational, unchanging, despotic and inferior."[3] The dogmas that make up this system include: the West is superior to the East (most often represented in the white person vs. the Arab); Muslims are anti-modern (hence the need to colonize Islamic territories); the Muslim is incapable of defining or helping him- or herself (making the study of Islam a Western occupation); and Muslims are to be feared and/or subjugated (hence the rationale for occupation, colonialism, and imperialism).[4] These concepts deeply influence the imagery attached to Muslim girls and women, who are often seen as tools of subjugation that make the pacification of Muslim men necessary. Often termed *gendered Orientalism*, this system of domination highlights "the brightness of Western freedom amid the despotisms of the East."[5]

Orientalism utilizes a powerful symbolic system that is embedded in politics, entertainment—the focus of this chapter—and the economy. All three of these institutions instruct, maintain, and influence each other in complex ways.

While the classical orientalist mode of representations were fashioned by specialized literary modus operandi *narratives* including philology and anthropology, the new tropes of orientalist discourse have largely become a form of mass discourse disseminated in public forums and mass media platforms, and function as a masquerade that provides a moral legitimacy for American/western neo-imperial designs in the Islamic world.[6]

The Muslim functions as a dominant symbol in the network of powerful corporate interests that include the control of oil, land, and human capital. This capital includes Muslim girls and women.

MUSLIM BODIES AS CAPITAL

Women (and girls) are *visually consumed* by men, other women, and a market culture that commodifies the body. In earlier eras, non-white women were subjected to what Anne McClintock has described as a double conquest of the body.

As the slaves, agricultural workers, houseservants, mothers, prostitutes and concubines of the far-flung colonies of Europe, colonized women had to negotiate not only the imbalances of their relationships with their own men but also the baroque and violent array of hierarchical rules and restrictions that structured their new relations with imperial men and women.[7]

To some extent, this remains true today. Females' consumption by the audience is still taking place, even in cases where the viewer is challenged to see Muslims in a different light.

Historically, Muslim bodies have been used to commodify Islamic culture and make money for colonial powers. This often took the form of Oriental products. In some cases, the consumptive practices were literal, such as the mass production of fashion or home products. "In other cases, it was metaphorical, such as viewing harem photographs or an Orientalist painting of a nude Muslim female."[8] While these products were not always overtly sexual, they still suggested access—economical, territorial, sexual—to Muslims. Historically, the bodies of Muslim women and men have been featured in a variety of products as a way to communicate this idea, often promising tourists and other consumers the possibility of purchasing, or being (sexually) gratified, by foreign bodies.

Commodification has been an extensive practice that goes far beyond entertainment and includes "Arabic fabrics, clothing, jewelry, cigarettes, cosmetics, interior decorations, and design motifs."[9] Muslim girls and women have often been part of the visual arsenal in these images, either as decorative devices or as objects associated with popular symbols of the Orient such as the desert or the camel. Today, this is seen in the harem girl, concubine, or other female "accessory" who plays a supporting role to the male-centered narrative. Even in the *13th Warrior* (1999), a film that offered a sympathetic portrayal of an Arab traveler (likely inspired by the life of Ibn Battuta), the one instance in which a female Muslim appeared was in a face veil—as the seductive, beautiful girl who causes the main character's exile and life-threatening adventures in northern Europe.

Muslims have been an important part of American (and European) popular culture in the past and continue to be powerful figures in the present. In most cases, Muslim characters and images do not represent reality; rather, they express fantasies about Muslims that originated in the medieval period, are validated by Orientalism, and are sustained by neoliberalism, colonialism, imperialism, and white supremacy. In Europe and the United States, this attitude finds expression in a gendered form of Islamophobia that "recycles the colonial doxa that positions white European men (and sometimes women) as protecting brown Muslim women from their brown overlords."[10] This powerful doxa results in the creation of Muslim characters that do not correspond to the realities of Muslim lives.

We might ask ourselves why there is such a disconnect between fictive Muslims and the realities of Muslim lives. Talal Asad has argued that the acceptance of Muslims into Western societies will be difficult because Islam is so essentialized that its deconstruction requires that Islam be represented as a "carrier civilization which helped to bring important elements into Europe from outside," thus erasing a good bit of the civilizational difference on which the Us/Them paradigm rests.[11] This may be true, but this proposal casts Muslims to the periphery—as foreigners, immigrants, and perpetual outsiders, ignoring the communities of Muslims who have lived in Europe and North America for centuries.

Print media is one of many places where Muslim bodies have often functioned, and largely continue to function, as foreign or subaltern subjects of the white colonial gaze. This casting of Muslim as "Other" takes many forms, some of them quite prurient. The perverse use of the bodies of Muslim women is seen in many forms, including contemporary French pornography, where films featuring veiled women communicate a debased view of Muslim women that utilizes a pious symbol of the religion of Islam. As Annelies Moors writes, quoting a French source, "France is 'the contemporary leader and innovator of hijab porn—pornographic films where the women only wear a *niqab* (as a means of defiling it).'"[12]

The veil is the principal symbol of the exotic Muslim woman. As such, it dominates the visual discourse in the West about Islam. As Myra Macdonald has written, "Expressions of surprise, even in the twenty-first century, that veiled women can appear as Olympic athletes, 'suicide bombers,' feminists, politicians, musicians or even comedians, underline the tenacity of beliefs that Islamic veiling is intrinsically incompatible with women's agency in the construction of their identities."[13] The veil is also one of the primary symbols—along with the harem—of Orientalism.

Hijab porn is a postmodern expression of something that has taken place for centuries. Muslim bodies often function as objects of sexual consumption. In particular, the colonized body is often used this way, a fact numerous scholars have pointed to. Examples of this include the Turkish seraglio, which was "the locus of European gaze, obsession, and distortion," a "place where power and sensuality collided, providing Europeans with infinite subjects of tyrannical sultans, bloodthirsty guards, deformed slaves, and imprisoned concubines."[14]

Not all images of veiled women portray a state of undressing or subjugation. Muslim women can be presented in ways in which they are not sexualized or oppressed subjects. The *Muslimah* superheroes discussed in this book are examples of the third way; as such, they remind us that Muslim girls and women are not objects for men to admire, conquer, and enjoy, nor are they agents of Islamism. In the words of one Muslim feminist speaking about patriarchy, "we have a surprise for them: we're going to beat them at their own game."[15]

The characters examined in this study are part of a genre of liberational texts that have challenge the stereotype of Muslim females as weak and sensual. However, *Muslimah* superheroes are not simply entertaining; they are part of a larger movement challenging patriarchy, colonialism, and Islamism, elements that act upon the Muslim female in different ways. As this book illustrates, comics and cartoons can be places where efforts to control and discipline girls and women meet real resistance.

One challenge posed by this representation of Muslim girls and women as human subjects with agency is that Muslims are typically represented as products of a meta-culture that is arrested in time. The power of this *imaginaire* about Islam, which is embedded in culture and politics, makes the enforcement of a counter-narrative difficult. As one scholar argues, "the terms for entering into discussions of the Orient and of Muslims or Muslim women already have been determined discursively. Therefore, there is no pure space from which we can begin to create counter-narratives that capture the complexity obscured and denied by recurrent archetypes."[16] This book represents an effort (*jihad*) to create some of this pure space, but first we need to look at the common stereotypes of Muslim women.

THE COMIC AND THE GRAPHIC NOVEL

The comic is often identified as an American art form. In reality, it has numerous antecedents, including the illuminated manuscripts found in Islam and in Europe during the Middle Ages, the graphic narration traditions of South Asia, and the graphic narratives found in Japan such as the *Tale of Genji* (11th century). Scholars have also argued that the comic form can be found in the ancient world. As one scholar notes, "The comic is an interesting cultural product. It is an art form that has historical roots in ancient cultures like Egypt with its sequential juxtaposed panels."[17]

In its modern form, the comic has a 200-year history in the United States. Scholars frequently point to the serialized fiction appearing in literary magazines during the nineteenth century as early examples of the comic strip that led to the Sunday "Colored Supplements" in Pulitzer's *New York World* and Hearst's *New York Journal*.[18] These texts later evolved into the political cartoons we are familiar with in the newspaper as well as the comics supplement often included in the Sunday edition. Comics have frequently been sources of entertainment, often of a lighthearted nature. *Calvin and Hobbes*, *The Far Side*, and *Charlie Brown* are examples of this sub-genre that sometimes include more serious messaging.

In some cases, comics have functioned as social texts—commentaries on society and political life. The popular comics of the nineteenth century created by artists like Richard Felton Outcault and George Benjamin Luks often focused on issues like poverty and class, touching on the political issues of the day.[19] Today, political cartoons, comics, and graphic novels address war, feminism, racism, and other social issues. Political cartoons depicting Islam, Muslims, and, in particular, Arabs depict themes like oil, the Arab-Israeli conflict, the 1979 Iranian revolution, and Islam.[20]

The comic has European and American antecedents, but other cultures also have a long history of pictorial forms that include long narratives. As Raminder Kaur reminds us, "Too often the West is seen as the originator and everywhere else ('the rest') as the terrain of copies."[21] Kaur's point is well taken, and in fact when one looks at the origins of visual texts that might be classified as forms of the comic, they are situated in a large variety of cultures. India has a strong tradition of comics—a result in part of the deep roots of graphic narration in India that dates to the seventh century.[22] Kalamkari pen-work, Phad and Pata paintings, and other traditional art forms are deep-rooted cultural influences on the modern Indian comic, which dates to the 1950s.[23] Indian comics are also influenced by American comics, including the use of colorism to denote moral character, which include depictions of the Mughal ruler Akbar (a Muslim) as a "light-skinned king."[24]

This question of origins is rooted in debates surrounding how we define the genre of the comic, which is an ongoing topic among art critics, scholars of popular culture, and other intellectuals. Hayman and Pratt offer a definition that relies on a pictorial account that constitutes a narrative, either alone or with text.[25] However, some comics are non-narrative—they fail to tell a story at all—and other art forms are narrative in style, but it would be hard to call them comics. In his review of the definitional problems surrounding the genre, Aaron Meskin proposes that the art is what matters, what he calls the "artistic possibility of the form."[26] Scott McCloud also proposes a very open definition of the comic that includes a wide variety of forms of cultural production from comic books to illustrated children's books. For the purposes of this book, I am adopting his definition, which allows us to look at an expansive number of pictorial representations of Muslim women that includes comics but goes beyond a narrow classification of the genre. While I am not arguing that animation is a form of comics—clearly it is something different—it does rely on the power of pictorial representations.

This book looks at texts from Pakistan, Egypt, Kuwait, and North America, which illustrates that the comic is not simply a North American or Western medium. It is popular worldwide and often has numerous influences— cultural, social, and religious. In Indonesia, the *wayang* manga comic is hugely popular, representing elements of Javanese Hindu (shadow-puppet theater) and Muslim (religious themes) influences, U.S. comics and, importantly, *manga* aesthetics from Japan.[27] As we have seen, India has a rich comic tradition of its own, featuring Hindu gods and personalities, as well as contemporary storylines that are focused on politics. Raminder Kaur points out that comics focusing on the atomic age—and India's proliferation of nuclear weapons—are popular with both children and adults. In many of these texts, the hero is pitted against a super-powerful and sub-human villain, who often is a Muslim.[28]

In American comics, the comic superhero has typically been a white male, often representing nationalist attitudes and a powerful vision of hegemonic masculinity. Heterosexuality is often expressed in female desire for the male superhero and the threat of female sexuality to men. "Thus, a constant expression of male power in the genre is the woman's defeat and sometimes humiliation—teaching her a lesson—and the recuperation of male supremacy over would-be female empowerment."[29] However, this is only part of the story of comics. Scholars have also argued that comic book superheroes can represent homosocial themes, for instance, in *Captain Marvel*, in Superman's escapes from marriage, and in the Batman-Robin duo.[30]

Minorities and women also hold an important place in comic books, reflecting the somewhat subaltern status of the genre. As Alexander Abad-Santos has written, "Comics, as a medium, are a place to break free from the mainstream and empathize with characters who are either minorities, out-casts or otherwise different from the white-bread norm. Hence the plethora of robots, mutants, shape-shifters, aliens, amazons, and yes, women."[31] This tongue-in-cheek reference to the acceptability of women and minori-ties points to the ways in which comics and other graphic narratives offer spaces unavailable in other genres to those who aren't white, male, and hetero-normative. As Jeffery A. Brown points out, these characters function in a larger cultural conversation with the traditional gender framework at the core of American culture, which is defined vis-à-vis females. "In general, masculinity is defined by what it is not, namely 'feminine,' and all its associ-ated traits—hard *not* soft, strong *not* weak, reserved *not* emotional, active *not* passive."[32] Female superheroes often embody these same characteristics—strength, bravery, and power.

Superheroines like Batgirl, Wonder Woman, and Supergirl occupy an important place in American popular culture, appearing in comics, on tele-vision, and in a variety of products ranging from lunchboxes to t-shirts. These superheroines are often strongly sexualized, with curvy features and body-hugging costumes or disguises. The *Muslimah* superhero differs from these portrayals. Yet, it is important to remember that the representation of females in texts is always problematic because girls and women are popular subjects of the male gaze. In genres like painting and comics, women are often arranged, or presented, as available and passive objects existing for the voyeur (who is usually male).[33]

Graphic texts both reflect and create social meaning. Political comics, Sunday newspaper serials, graphic narratives, and other forms of the genre often reflect the social, cultural, and political milieu of the time. In some cases, comics have contributed to the enforcement of dominant social con-cerns. Such is the case of Marvel Comics in the 1950s, "rehabilitating the image of the nation's scientists" through characters like Reed Richards in *The Fantastic Four*.[34] In other instances, comics challenge the dominant social conventions of the time, existing as countercultural texts that may be feminist, queer, or anti-colonial. Underground comics generally known as "comix," have at times pushed subversive political agendas. Gay and lesbian comics began with Tom Finland's openly gay male comics of the 1940s and later included Mary Wing's *Come Out* comix released in 1972.[35] However, not all comix are gender-bending or liberal. Scholars have pointed to the sexism in underground comics, which eventually led to the reactionary genre known as "feminist comics."[36]

Orientalism, which includes a rich imagery of the "East" and costuming, has a long history in comics. Even in cases with no Muslim character, we often find the Orient playing a prominent role. In the Mexican comic book *Kaliman: El Hombre Increible*, the title character is a superhero with powers that come from his Hindu identity (he is protected by Kali) and Tibetan background. He wears a Nehru jacket and a turban, and his adventures "always take place in exotic settings," most notably the "Far and Middle East."[37]

Muslims are not new to cartoons and comics. Political cartoons and comics featuring Muslims have been a feature of American newspapers for most of the twentieth century. Many would assume that the oil crises and 1979 hostage ordeal marked the beginning of these images. It is true that caricatures of the greedy oil sheik and Ayatollah Khomeini are common political symbols of the 1970s and 1980s. But American anxieties surrounding Islam and Muslims have been present since the founding of the republic when the pirates of the Barbary Coast entered the popular imagination through dime store novels, board games, advertisements, and other media.[38] After 9/11, caricatures of oil sheiks were replaced with more frightening images of terrorists and wide-scale violence.

The presence of Muslim women in political cartoons is secondary to the menacing Muslim men featured in the genre. However, the depictions of Muslim girls and women as submissive and weak still support the presentation of Islam as a violent, oppressive, and backwards religion. As discussed in the following chapter, the veil is the dominant trope associated with Muslim females. Images of veil-less Muslim women are exceedingly rare. In the words of Peter Gottschalk and Gabriel Greenberg, "cartoonists almost never symbolize Islam or Muslims with images of women."[39] The veil is the dominant symbol of Islam that renders the Muslim female powerless. "In other words, it is the invisibility of a woman, seldom her presence, that symbolizes Islam."[40] Her visibility is one of the qualities that makes the *Muslimah* superhero so striking.

Most comics, animated cartoons, and other graphic narratives exclude Muslim females. The focus on Muslim men, who are in most cases cast as violent individuals, represents the exclusion of Muslim girls and women from much of the popular media. Scholars call this symbolic annihilation—the silencing of a group through their visual or textual exclusion. Debra Merskin has defined it as "the way cultural production and media representations ignore, exclude, marginalize, or trivialize a particular group."[41]

As discussed in detail in the following chapter, the veil can be liberative or oppressive depending on the context. The Islamist policing of female bodies includes the imposition of dress codes in Saudi Arabia, Afghanistan, and Iran. However, in other contexts the veil functions as an anti-colonial symbol, "a symbol of contest, as well as a marker of self-authored difference and authenticity."[42] In recent years, the development of Islamic fashion has led to the veil's inclusion in high fashion—Dior, Alberta Ferretti, and Nina Ricci have all designed *abayas*.[43] The complexities of the veil, and in particular, its numerous meanings, are important to keep in mind when looking at images of Muslim women in comics and other graphic narratives.

In subsequent chapters, we look at how the veil can function as a subversive tool. In *Burka Avenger*, the veil—in this case, a ninja-style *niqab*—is the *Muslimah* superhero's disguise, her weapon against detection and punishment by villains, including the Taliban, who attack schoolchildren and other innocent victims in her village. Since the era of colonialism, the veil has functioned as a symbol of Islam's repressive and misogynistic ideology. Today, it functions as "an over-determined signifier constantly deployed to illustrate the 'clash of civilization,' women's oppression in Islam, the fundamentalist peril and the pitfalls of multiculturalism."[44] *Burka Avenger* shows that the veil can simultaneously be used to uphold and challenge dominant models of "tradition."

The representations of Muslims found in graphic narratives are largely pejorative. In Sunday comic strips focused on Islamic themes, even those geared for children, Muslim men are portrayed as nefarious villains. In one *Little Orphan Annie* comic, an Arab named Bahd-Simel kidnaps Annie and holds her ransom for nuclear secrets; in a 1983 *Brenda Starr* comic, the title character is held ransom for a memory chip that will give the Muslim villains world domination.[45] Rescue narratives where foreign (non-white) men kidnap white women and girls represent an "essentializing discourse" that functions as an important part of white American male identity. Whether the villain is African, Native American, Mexican, or Muslim, the American myth of racial and cultural superiority is maintained in these narratives, "Thus while the victim of captivity is joined by the bold heroic protector, the exhortations about backsliding and weakness, and the association of violence with progress remain key themes in Americans' mythical understandings of their mission and purpose."[46] Male characters are typically primary in these comics while Muslim females are secondary (victims) or absent altogether. This erasure helps to maintain focus on the male villain.

Arab villains are especially popular in comic books in series like *Conan the Barbarian*, *Tarzan*, and *Heavy Metal*. In a *Heavy Metal* 1982 edition, a harem escapes from a nefarious sultan, who vows to capture the women and "feed their flesh to vultures."[47] Jack Shaheen's 1994 study of Arabs in comic books provides a nice survey of these portrayals, which include oil sheiks, bandits, and a variety of crooks and other villains. The Arab woman is typically portrayed as having no agency, "Voiceless, featureless and mindless, she is devoid of personality."[48] As in other areas of popular culture—film, television, and fiction—Muslim females play a secondary role to the Arab or other Muslim male character, who is usually a villain.

Since September 11, 2001, some comic storylines have adopted the civilizational conflict thesis espoused by Samuel Huntington and other conservative intellectuals. One example is found in *Captain America*, in which innocent American lives are juxtaposed with the lives of their killers, a portrayal "consistent with the idea of American exceptionalism, whereby American innocence is protected by its isolation from the rest of the world."[49] At the same time, this comic series features a battle between the hero and four children "in stylized Arab costumes, armed with daggers and hatchets," who have prosthetic limbs, a condition caused by American interventionism and weapons.[50] This shows how comics can function as a subversive, countercultural art form sending mixed messages about social and political issues as racism, colonialism, American power, and capitalism.

THE *MUSLIMAH* SUPERHERO

The *Muslimah* superhero emerged in the past decade and much of the academic literature frames her as a post-9/11 phenomenon. However, Muslim superhero characters predate 9/11. Although few in number, these characters voice alternative narratives that stand in stark opposition to media forms that vilify Muslims and Islam. Early Muslim comic superheroes include Kismet (1944), an Algerian Muslim "who wears a Fez and thanks Allah and the Prophet for granting him the power of freedom"; Black Tiger (1976), a religious leader whose identity is assumed by several people wearing the same disguise; and Arabian Knight (1981), who sealed away Gog and Magog and other demons.[51] More recent (and post-9/11) Muslim superheroes include The Doctor, also known as Habib ben Hassan (2005), a Palestinian would-be suicide bomber who is saved by The Doctor's powers and becomes a superhero; and G. W. Bridge (1991), an African-American Muslim.[52] The Nightrunner (Bilal Asseleh), who first appears in 2011 in DC Comics, is an Algerian-French superhero who lives in Paris. Also appearing in 2011 is Buraq (Yusuf Abdullah), a Muslim superhero who runs a relief organization to help those in need.[53]

Comics have often addressed social issues, as seen in the *Green Lantern* (1960s) where the plight of Native Americans and other social issues were addressed.[54] The inclusion of religion as a theme in comics is more recent, dating from the 1980s. This includes characters like William Stryker from the *X-Men* series, a pastor whose good deeds are motivated by Biblical texts; and Daredevil, whose Catholicism plays a central role in the narrative. Comics and religion has even become a topic in the classroom, with courses on superheroes as well as a focus on foreign comics such as those from India, which often are based on the Hindu epics.[55]

In recent years, *Muslimah* superheroes have begun appearing in American comics. DC Comics featured a *Muslimah* superhero in 1993 named the Iron Butterfly (Kahina Eskandari), who was a Palestinian. Marvel Comics has featured several *Muslimah* superheroes. One of the most interesting of these is Monet St. Croix, also known as "M." She is from Algeria, and although not overtly Muslim in the early years, it was revealed in a 2011 issue of *X-Factor* that she is indeed a *Muslimah* superhero.[56] Her religious identity is revealed when she fights protesters at an anti-Muslim rally. As Nicholaus Pumphrey has pointed out, she is not assumed to be Muslim because her costuming—which is provocative and highly sensual—deviates from the image of Muslim women as veiled.

> Based on this understanding, readers could not process her Muslim heritage because she did not exhibit any stereotypical signs, and as a result, the part of her canon that originally expressed she could have a Muslim background is ignored. Instead, the accepted Muslim characters for Marvel readers before 9/11 were Orientalist stereotypes.[57]

In chapter 5, which includes an analysis of the Pakistani character Bloody Nasreen, we have another example of an independent, sensual Muslim super-hero who also doesn't veil. Like Monet, her Muslim identity is not predicated on Islamic clothing.

Storm is an *X-Men* character who has Muslim influences, although her biography reveals nothing definitive. From Cairo, where her American father and African mother lived until they were killed in an airstrike during the 1956 Suez crisis, Storm was raised in a street gang led by the Muslim Achmed el-Gibar.[58] Dust, also known as Sooraya Qadir, is also part of the *X-Men* world. She represents post-9/11 anxieties about Islam, and in particular, Afghanistan. Dust appears momentarily in several storylines, but she is a minor character in the world of Marvel. The character is first introduced in the New X-Men Issue #133, when she is rescued from a slave trader in Afghanistan by Wolverine. When she transforms into a dust form, she strips the flesh from people's bones.[59]

As scholars have pointed out, while Dust is a prominent *Muslimah* super-hero, she is portrayed through the lens of American politics. "Dust's struggles are depicted, however, by a creative team who craft stories that view her religion through the lens of Western civilization in general, and American culture in particular."[60] Dust is very different from someone like Ms. Marvel, whose identity is American. Dust is problematic, for she is cast as foreign, different, and exotic. In one storyline, Wolverine carries Dust back to the X-Men headquarters in India. As one scholar puts it, "apparently, there aren't any X-Men headquarters in Muslim countries like Afghanistan and Pakistan."[61] Such a division reinforces old Orientalist prescriptions about Islam; in this case, Dust must be removed from the Islamic territory in order to be safe. The creators of Dust also missed the mark on details of this character's story, revealing the continuation of Muslim stereotypes. Her superpowers include controlling sand and transforming into a sand cloud, but Afghanistan is largely a mountainous region quite unlike Arabia. Her use of language is even more troubling. She speaks Arabic, and only one word, *turaab*, which means dust.[62] Arabic is not a language normally spoken in Afghanistan (except in the performance of certain religious rituals). Most Afghans speak Dari (a dialect of Persian), Pashto, Uzbek, or Tajik.

In other cases, *Muslimah* superheroines are portrayed in more positive ways, even assimilated in a European or American society. Such is the case of Excalibur, also known as Faiza Hussain. Her British Muslim identity is central to the narrative and she gains her powers through alien technology, after which she proves her worth by claiming a magical sword.[63] Later in the series, her costume and weapon make it clear that she is simultaneously British and Muslim; after all, the armor (which functions as a form of *hijab*) and the sword she uses are British cultural icons.[64]

Numerous other Muslim superheroes are found in American comics. While this study examines only a few of them, it is important to point out that outside of a few articles on *The 99*, few studies on these characters exist. According to one study, "There is a dearth of Muslim characters, superheroes or otherwise, from such places as Albania, Chechnya, Malaysia, or Indonesia, which have predominately Muslim populations."[65] This study challenges this statement a bit, and while the Marvel universe has a number of Muslim characters, they do not erase the importance of Qahera, the *Muslimah* superheroes in *The 99*, or other characters that exist outside North America.

The current Ms. Marvel is perhaps the best-known *Muslimah* superhero in the American context. This character is focused on in detail in a later chapter, but as an introduction, it is important to note that she is immensely popular, found in cosplay, children's Halloween costumes, and featured on a variety of products including buttons and t-shirts. The quality that makes Ms. Marvel, also known as Kamala Khan, most relatable—and radically different from Dust—is her American identity. As one scholar put it,

> The emphasis on relatability has the effect of positing a kind of universal teen experience which critics suggested was being fulfilled by the character. Rather than focusing on the specificity of Kamala's female-teen-American-Muslim subjectivity, critics concentrated on how the themes of the book fit into their experiences.[66]

This aspect of Ms. Marvel does not erase her Muslim identity, allowing her to be both Muslim and American.

Ms. Marvel is published in single comic issues, and also as a trade paperback in a long-form comic, much like a graphic novel, but is not one—it is a comic. However, it should be pointed out that the comic and graphic novels are closely related. Like the comic, the genre of the graphic novel is difficult to define. Often described as a longer, linked version of the comic, the graphic novel shares similarities with children's books and other genres. The origins of the graphic novel may be the comic, but as we have seen, forms of graphic narratives have existed for many centuries and often influence the renderings of superheroes found in print. The graphic narrative is a diverse medium that resists categorization due to the often fluid interaction between the verbal and the visual. Because these texts are diverse, the term "graphic novel" is at times contested.[67]

Whether these texts stand apart from the "comic" or are an extension of it, *graphic texts* (an even broader term) feature stories that vary from the comedic to the tragic (or, like *Maus* and *Persepolis*, are both funny and tragic), offering a space in which the underdog, in some cases Jewish, Muslim, Indian, or African-American, can be developed as a complex character in a longer form. Jennifer Ryan has argued that the African-American graphic novel is a medium that can challenge racial and cultural stereotypes, "This type of fiction [the graphic narrative] attempts to reconcile the stereotype and truth, absence and presence."[68] This is also true of graphic novels that deal with religious themes, including those focused on Islam. Although few in number, they tend to complicate the overly simplistic picture of Islam that is common in other media forms.

To date, the majority of graphic novels dealing with Islamic subjects have been autobiographical. Among these, Toufic El Rassi's *Arab in America* (2007) addresses the issue of identity through a male character who is constantly being judged by non-Arabs. One of the ways this is communicated is through the sketch-like appearances of other characters, who do not stand out in contrast to the Arab, with his signature beard (a signifier of Muslim identity that is a focus of the comic).[69] Dara Naraghi's *Lifelike* (2007) documents that author's experiences as an Iranian-American, providing vignettes from his life.[70]

Marjane Satrapi's *Persepolis* is perhaps the best-known graphic narrative that focuses on Muslim girls and women. The reception of this memoir, which was in general overwhelmingly positive, has received scholarly attention in recent years. Of the many concerns voiced about Satrapi's work is its reliance on exoticism, its harsh critiques of Shi'i practices, and the presentation of an East/West division that lacks subtlety. Other scholars have questioned whether Satrapi's work is post-colonial or Orientalist. The "exotica of Islam" is a central part of what is clearly a beautiful drawn, both funny and tragic narrative about female adolescence in which the main character rebels against a variety of systems of domination.[71] In part because the novel is a critique of Islam, Muslim girls and women, including the main character, are depicted in ways that are fairly one dimensional—unhappy, oppressed, and often veiled. As one study notes,

> Because Marji and her mother are shown as having no amount of respect for the religion and scoff at everything Islamic, there is no space for leaving a good impression about Islam in Western readers. Muslim men and women, usually revolutionary guards, are portrayed as brutal and having a savage personality. The male and female Muslim characters are depicted the same in her drawings as always having a frowning expression: men have beards and women are covered head-to-toe.[72]

There are other graphic novels (sometimes called comic book novels) with Muslim characters. The majority of these are centered on political conflicts; for instance, Joe Sacco's *Palestine* (1996), *Safe Area Gorazde: The War in Eastern Bosnia 1992–1995* (2000), and *Footnotes in Gaza: A Graphic Novel* (2010); and Leila Abirached's graphic narrative on Lebanon, *A Game for Swallows: To Die, to Leave, to Return* (2012). The female characters in these narratives, while they have important roles, are not superheroes.

ANIMATED CARTOONS, FILM, AND TELEVISION SERIES

Animated cartoons, which are often inspired by comics, include racist and Orientalist Disney productions featuring Arab characters, veiled females, and other Orientalist tropes as well as other examples that communicate a number of themes found in films in animated cartoon form. At times, comics have inspired animated cartoons; however, the consensus of most scholars is that comics and animated cartoons are two distinct forms of narrative. As Robert S. Petersen writes,

> It is critical to distinguish the artistic qualities of graphic narratives from animated cartoons because even when they share a common visual style, they use different visual codes to tell the story and are different in the way the audience experiences them. With graphic narratives, the pace reading the story is more like reading a book than watching a movie or a television show, where the narrative pace is dictated by the medium. But unlike the reader of a book, the reader of a graphic narrative does not always read the story in a linear fashion.[73]

Muslim characters appear in several early black-and-white animated cartoons, perhaps most famously in the 1932 Disney production "Mickey in Arabia." In this seven-minute cartoon, Mickey saves Minnie from a sultan who has kidnapped her and is attempting to sexually assault her. In addition to an Arab villain, the animated short film is full of Orientalist and anti-Muslim imagery—camels, turbans, veiled females, cobras, and lots of violence. The violence associated with Islam is portrayed through the weaponry of Arabs, which includes knives, swords, and daggers, as well as the aggression of the sultan and other Arabs. While Mickey's adventures may seem innocent, they communicate ideas about Muslims that include dangerous men and helpless women. Arabs dominate the Muslim characters who appear in animated cartoons and are typically cast as the villainous man. Ali Baba, the Mad Dog of the Desert, is one of the better known of these characters. As in other forms of media and entertainment, Muslim females are often less visible or completely invisible, obscured by a veil or peripheral to the story.

The treatment of Islam in cinema is closely tied to the European and American fascination with the East, typically expressed in an Orientalist language. A few positive portrayals and narratives, what Foucault called interstitial moments, exist in recent films, perhaps most famously in the historical adventure film *The 13th Warrior* (1999) and in the historical drama *Kingdom of Heaven* (2005). In the first of these films, a male action piece with an Arab hero, women are not particularly important. The only Muslim female appears at the beginning (in a face veil with heavy black eyeliner, thus fulfilling the Orientalist vision of the Muslim woman), when she seduces the main character (played by Antonio Banderas), causing him to be expelled from the Islamic empire. Female characters in *Kingdom of Heaven* are not much more prominent, unsurprising given Hollywood's preference for male-centered storylines.

An unfortunate consequence of Orientalism is the portrayal of Muslims as fantastical characters far removed from the lived experiences of individuals in diverse communities stretching around the globe. Jack Shaheen's work on the portrayal of Arabs in Hollywood includes a survey of films over the past century, illuminating the prevalence of Arab men and women as negative characters in Hollywood film. Shaheen's study of this problem is important in helping us understand how Arabs are portrayed (here, the Arab is synonymous with the "Muslim" in the West). This identification is one of Said's "final terminals," reductive prescriptions of the Arab and the Oriental and Islam that co-identify them in one entity, "staked upon the permanence of the whole Orient," which is static and unchanging.[74] In his work, Shaheen discusses how Arab females appear in a series of "B" roles as "bosomy bellydancers," "Beasts of Burden," "Bundles of Black," "Black magic vamps," and "Bombers."[75] These stock characters are marked by sensuality and violence, intertwined with conventions such as the veil, harem, or other sign of Eastern exoticism. The majority of these characters are oppressed Muslim women—a harem girl, imprisoned princess, dancer, or other damsel in distress.

One of the more interesting female character types that deviates from the maiden is the vampire or monster, which illustrates the essential trope connected with Islam—violence—while granting Muslim females some agency. In the 1966 film *Beast of Morocco*, the vampire Marisa terrorizes the main character and his (French) girlfriend.[76] Other female monsters identified as Arab include the mummy, popularized by the Egyptomania seen in both European and American popular culture during the nineteenth and twentieth centuries. Theda Bara initiated the Muslim vamp role and her name, according to one scholar, was "an anagram of 'Arab death.'"[77] Although the filmic Muslim female monster is not what we could call "positive," in terms of agency she contrasts with the oppressed, imprisoned women more typically associated with Islam in cinema. As Ella Shohat has shown, the women of the Third World, and the Orient in particular, "allowed the imperial imaginary to play out its own fantasies of sexual domination."[78]

Muslim females continue to function in the celluloid fantasies Shohat alludes to. One example is found in the Liam Neeson film *Taken* (2008), the first in a trilogy of violent movies centered on a white American hero who fights foreign villains threatening white women. In the first installment, the main character kills thirty-five people, culminating in the death of a wealthy oil sheik who purchased Neeson's character's daughter from a white slavery ring.[79] *Taken*, like many other films, is structured within old discourses of "historic sex panics in which violence and repression were seen as essential to protect white women against dark-skinned predators."[80]

Television also has a history of presenting Muslim females in negative ways. The title character of *I Dream of Jeannie* is an "apologue in which representatives of the two worlds—American technology (the astronaut) and the erotic energy of eastern magic (the genie)—coexist in domestic bondage."[81] The genie does have some subversive agency, but she is also dependent on the Orientalist fantasy of women, which is enforced through clothing and decoration. Although blonde, she dresses like a Western fantasy of a sex slave in a harem, wears the appropriate costume, and calls her husband "master." This show, although sexist and Orientalist, was more lighthearted than portrayals of Muslim females, characters that appear as helpers to terroristic Muslim men or in other cases, as the victims of rape, sexual slavery, or murder.

In television, Muslim female characters are few in number and as in film, they are typically cast as subsidiary characters. In Amir Hussain's study of Muslims on North American television, which includes the shows *Oz*, *Lost*, *24*, and *Sleeper Cell*, the majority of characters are male—terroristic and violent in all but a few cases—and Muslim females are few. Among them are the terrorist Mina (who carries out a suicide bomb attack at a Las Vegas hotel) and the wife of another terrorist.[82] The one television show that features positive female Muslim characters is the Canadian comedy *Little Mosque on the Prairie* (2007–2012). While some critics have argued that the female characters on the program were not diverse enough—they all subscribed to a single reading of Islam that is moderate and did not represent the variety of Muslim practices and rituals that exist—the show portrayed Muslim women as intelligent, funny, decisive, and educated.[83] Since the show ended in 2012, there has not been a comparable show on either Canadian or American television that has such positive portrayals of Muslim girls and women. As we shall learn, Ms. Marvel, Burka Avenger, Qahera, and other *Muslimah* superheroes take up where this show left off.

NOTES

1. Sarah Graham-Brown, *Images of Women: The Portrayal of Women in Photography of the Middle East 1860–1950* (New York: Columbia University Press, 1988): 5.

2. Deena Mohamed, "On Translating a Superhero: Language and Webcomics," in *Translating Dissent: Voices from and With the Egyptian Revolution*, ed. Mona Baker (New York: Routledge, 2016): 140.

3. Alexander Lyon Macfie, "My Orientalism," *Journal of Postcolonial Writing* 45, no. 1 (2009): 83.

4. Mahmood Mamdani, *Good Muslim, Bad Muslim: America, the Cold War, and the Roots of Terror* (New York: Pantheon Books, 2004): 32.

5. Reina Lewis, *Gendered Orientalism: Race, Femininity and Representation* (New York: Routledge, 2013): 217.

6. Mazhar Al-Zo'by, "Representing Islam in the Age of Neo-Orientalism: Media, Politics and Identity," *Journal of Arab & Muslim Media Research* 8, no. 3 (2015): 218.

7. Anne McClintock, *Imperial Leather: Race, Gender and Sexuality in the Colonial Contest* (New York: Routledge, 1995): 6.

8. Sophia Arjana, *Muslims in the Western Imagination* (New York: Oxford University Press, 2015): 103.

9. Hsu-Ming Teo, *Desert Passions: Orientalism and Romance Novels* (Austin: University of Texas Press, 2012): 2.

10. Robert Stam and Ella Shohat, *Race in Translation: Culture Wars Around the Postcolonial Atlantic* (New York: NYU Press, 2012): 150.

11. Talal Asad, "Muslims and European Identity: Can Europe Represent Islam?" *Cultural Encounters: Representing "Otherness"* ed. Elizabeth Hallam and Brian V. Street (New York: Routledge, 2000): 17.

12. Annelies Moors, "NiqaBitch and Princess Hijab: Niqab Activism, Satire and Street Art," *Feminist Review* 98 (2011): 132.

13. Myra Macdonald, "Muslim Women and the Veil: Problems of Image and Representation," *Feminist Media Studies* 6, no. 1 (2006): 132.

14. Nasser Al-Ta'ee, *Representations of the Orient in Western Music: Violence and Sensuality* (New York: Routledge, 2010): 3.

15. Nayereh Tohidi, "Muslim Feminism and Islamic Reformation: The Case of Iran," in *Feminist Theologies: Legacy and Prospect,* ed. by Rosemary Radford Ruether (Minneapolis: Fortress Press, 2007): 109.

16. Jasmine Zine, "Muslim Women and the Politics of Representation," *The American Journal of Islamic Social Sciences* 19, no. 4 (2002): 18.

17. Caryn E. Neumann and Lori L. Parks, "The Fan and the Female Superhero in Comic Books," *Journal of Fandom Studies* 3, no. 3 (2015): 297.

18. Daniel Stein, Christina Meyer, and Micha Edlich. "Introduction: American Comic Books and Graphic Novels," *Amerikastudien/American Studies: A Quarterly* 56, no. 4 (2011): 509.

19. Ibid.

20. Christina Michelmore, "Old Pictures in New Frames: Images of Islam and Muslims in Post World War II American Political Cartoons," *Journal of American and Comparative Cultures* 23, no. 4 (2000): 38.

21. Raminder Kaur, "Atomic Comics: Parabolic Mimesis and the Graphic Fictions of Science," *International Journal of Cultural Studies* 15, no. 4 (2011): 330.

22. Dipavali Debroy, "The Graphic Novel in India: East Transforms West," *Bookbird: A Journal of International Children's Literature* 49, no. 4 (2011): 33.

23. Ibid.

24. Radhika E. Parameswara and Kavitha Cardoza, "Immortal Comics, Epidermal Politics: Representations of Gender and Colorism in India," *Journal of Children and Media* 3, no. 1 (2009), 23.

25. Aaron Meskin, "Defining Comics?" *The Journal of Aesthetics and Art Criticism* 65, no. 4 (2007): 370.

26. Meskin, "Defining Comics?" 376.

27. Meghan Downes, "Hybridities and Deep Histories in Indonesian *Wayang* Manga Comics," *Situations* 8, no. 2 (2015): 23.

28. Raminder Kaur, "Atomic Comics: Parabolic Mimesis and the Graphic Fictions of Science," *International Journal of Cultural Studies* 15, no. 4 (2011): 338.

29. Mark Best, "Domesticity, Homosociality, and Male Power in Superhero Comics of the 1950s," *Iowa Journal of Cultural Studies* 6 (2005): 85.

30. Best, "Domesticity, Homosociality, and Male Power," 83.

31. Alexander Abad-Santos, "Marvel Dismisses Female Superheroes," *The Atlantic*, September 18, 2013, https://www.theatlantic.com/entertainment/archive/2013/09/marvel-dimisses-female-superheroes/310923/ (accessed September 18, 2013).

32. Jeffrey A. Brown, "Comic Book Masculinity and the New Black Superhero," *African American Review* 33, no. 1 (1999): 26–27.

33. Sheri Klein, "Breaking the Mold with Humor: Images of Women in the Visual Media," *Art Education* 46, no. 5 (1993): 61.

34. Robert Genter, "'With Great Power Comes Great Responsibility': Cold War Culture and the Birth of Marvel Comics," *The Journal of Popular Culture* 40, no. 6 (2007): 960–961.

35. Devon Greyson, "GLBTQ Content in Comics/Graphic Novels for Teens," *Collection Building* 26, no. 4 (2007): 131.

36. Matthew P. McAllister, Edward H. Sewell, and Ian Gordon, "Introducing Comics and Ideology," *Comics and Ideology*, ed. Matthew P. McAllister, Edward H. Sewell, and Ian Gordon (New York: Peter Lang, 2001): 8–9.

37. Harold E. Hind, "Kaliman: A Mexican Superhero," *The Journal of Popular Culture* 13, no. 2 (1979): 230–232.

38. See Paul Baepler (editor), *White Slaves, African Masters: An Anthology of American Barbary Captivity Narratives* (Chicago: University of Chicago Press, 1999).

39. Peter Gottschalk and Gabriel Greenberg, *Islamophobia: Making Muslims the Enemy* (Lanham: Rowman & Littlefield Publishers, 2008): 54.

40. Ibid.

41. Debra Merskin, "Sending Up Signals: A Survey of Native American Media Use and Representation in the Mass Media," *Howard Journal of Communications* 9: 335.

42. Sirma Bilge, "Beyond Subordination vs. Resistance: An Intersectional Approach to the Agency of Veiled Women," *Journal of Intercultural Studies* 31, no. 1 (2010): 20.

43. Annelies Moors, "Fashion and Its Discontents: The Aesthetics of Covering in the Netherlands," *Islamic Fashion and Anti-Fashion: New Perspectives from Europe and North America*, ed. Emma Tarlo and Annelies Moors (New York: Bloomsbury, 2013) 248.

44. Bilge Sirma, "Beyond Subordination," 10.

45. Laurence Michalak, "Cruel and Unusual: Negative Images of Arabs in American Popular Culture," *American Arab Anti Discrimination Committee Issue Paper* 15 (Washington: ADC Research Institute, 1988): 13.

46. Catharine V. Scott, "Bound for Glory: The Hostage Crisis as Captivity Narrative in Iran," *International Studies Quarterly* 44, no. 1 (2000): 181.

47. Laurence Michalak, "Cruel and Unusual," 14.

48. Jack Shaheen, "Arab Images in American Comic Books," *Journal of Popular Culture* 28, no. 1 (1994): 129.

49. Jason Dittmer, "Captain America's Empire: Reflections on Identity, Popular Culture, and Post-9/11 Geopolitics," *Annals of the Association of American Geographers* 95, no. 3 (2005): 637.

50. Jason Dittmer, "Captain America's Empire," 640.

51. Fredrik Strömberg, "'Yo, rag-head!': Arab and Muslim Superheroes in American Comic Books after 9/11," *Amerikastudien/American Studies* 56, no. 4 (2011): 579.

52. Fredrik Strömberg, "'Yo, rag-head!,'" 588–589.

53. Nour Sheety, "10 Muslim Superheroes That Totally Beat Batman," *Stepfeed*, March 17, 2017, http://stepfeed.com/10-muslim-superheroes-that-totally-own-superman-7496 (accessed March 17, 2017).

54. Bradford W. Wright, *Comic Book Nation: The Transformation of Youth Culture in America* (Baltimore: John Hopkins University Press, 2003): 226–227.

55. Jeffrey Brackett, "Religion and Comics," *Religion Compass* 9, no. 12 (2015): 493–500.

56. Pumphrey Nicholaus, "Avenger, Mutant, or Allah: A Short Evolution of the Depiction of Muslims in Marvel Comics," *The Muslim World* 106, no. 4 (2016): 785.

57. Ibid.
58. Ramzi Fawaz, "'Where No X-Man Has Gone Before!': Mutant Superheroes and the Cultural Politics of Popular Fantasy in Postwar America," *American Literature* 83, no. 2 (2011): 371.
59. Grant Morrison, Ethan Van Sciver, and Norm Rapmund, *New X-Men #133* (New York: Marvel, 2002), n.p.
60. Julie Davis and Robert Westerfelhaus, "Finding a Place for a Muslimah Heroine in the Post/9–11 Marvel Universe: New X-Men's Dust," *Feminist Media Studies* 13, no. 5 (2013): 801.
61. Jehanzeb Dar, "Holy Islamophobia, Batman! Demonization of Muslims and Arabs in Mainstream American Comic Books," *Counterpoints* 346 (2010): 107.
62. Pumphrey Nicholaus, "Avenger, Mutant, or Allah," 789–790.
63. Fredrik Strömberg, "'Yo, rag-head!,'" 591.
64. Fredrik Strömberg, "'Yo, rag-head!,'" 591.
65. Davis and Westerfelhaus, "Finding a Place for a Muslimah Heroine in the Post-9/11 Marvel Universe: New X-Men's Dust." *Feminist Media Studies* 13, no. 5 (2013): 804.
66. Miriam Kent, "Unveiling Marvels: Ms. Marvel and the Reception of the New Muslim Superheroine," *Feminist Media Studies* 15, no. 3 (2015): 524.
67. Stein et al., "Introduction: American Comic Books and Graphic Novels," *Amerikastudien/American Studies: A Quarterly* 56, no. 4 (2011): 516.
68. Hillary L. Chute and Marianne DeKoven, "Introduction: Graphic Narrative," *Modern Fiction Studies* 52, no. 4 (2006): 776.
69. Adrielle Anna Mitchell, "Distributed Identity: Networking Image Fragments in Graphic Memoirs," *Studies in Comics* 1, no. 2 (2010): 267.
70. Frederick Luis Aldama, *Multicultural Comics: From Zap to Blue Beetle* (Austin: University of Texas Press, 2010): 10.
71. Esmaeil Zeiny Jelodar, Noraini Md. Yusof, and Ruzy Suliza Hashim, "Muslim Women's Memoirs: Disclosing Violence or Reproducing Islamophobia?" *Asian Social Science* 10, no. 14 (2014): 220.
72. Jelodar, Yusof, and Hashim, "Muslim Women's Memoirs: Disclosing Violence or Reproducing Islamophobia?" Asian Social Science 10, no. 14 (2014): 220.
73. Robert S. Petersen, *Comics, Manga, and Graphic Novels: A History of Graphic Narratives* (Santa Barbara: Praeger, 2010), xiv.
74. Edward Said, *Orientalism* (New York: Vintage Books, 1979): 239.
75. Jack Shaheen, *Reel Bad Arabs: How Hollywood Vilifies a People,* (New York: Olive Branch Press, 2001): 22–23.
76. Ibid., 87.
77. Antonio Lant, "The Curse of the Pharaoh, or How Cinema Contracted Egyptomania," in *Visions of the East: Orientalism in Film*, ed. Matthew Bernstein and Gaylyn Studlar (New Brunswick: Rutgers University Press, 1997): 90.
78. Ella Shohat, "Gender and Culture of Empire: Toward a Feminist Ethnography of the Cinema," in *Visions of the East: Orientalism in Film*, ed. Matthew Bernstein and Gaylyn Studlar (New Brunswick: Rutgers University Press, 1997): 47.

79. Casey Ryan Kelly, "Feminine Purity and Masculine Revenge-Seeking in Taken (2008)," *Feminist Media Studies* 14, no. 3 (2014): 1.

80. Ibid., 2.

81. Michael Beard, "Review: Between West and World (Review of Orientalism by Edward Said)," *Diacritics* 9, no. 4 (1979): 9.

82. Amir Hussain, "(Re)presenting Muslims on North American Television," *Contemporary Islam* 4 (2010): 75.

83. Faiza Hirji, "Through the Looking Glass: Muslim Women on Television—An Analysis of *24*, *Lost*, and *Little Mosque on the Prairie*," *Global Media Journal* (Canadian Edition) 4, no. 2 (2011): 41.

Chapter 2

The Muslim Body, Veiling, and Contestations of Islam

MUSLIM BODIES

When I published *Muslims in the Western Imagination* in 2015, many readers were surprised at the extent to which the West has imagined Muslims as non-human creatures, in particular the large number of fictive male characters that have been cast as monsters. While my study includes a few Muslim female monsters such as the Saracen cannibals of the medieval period and Gothic horror characters like Bram Stoker's harem of female vampires (*Dracula*, 1897) and his Lady Arabella (*The Liar of the White Worm*, 1911), a serpentine creature who consumed her victims alive, these characters are few in comparison to the hypermasculine, violent, and homicidal men that populate much of the Western *imaginaire* about Islam. As I argue in my study, "For centuries, Muslim men have been characterized as monstrous beings, exhibiting many of the qualities portrayed by contemporary Orientalism."[1]

As shown in the previous chapter, the Western presentation of Muslim men as homicidal sultans and terrorists is different from representations of Muslim women (and girls) as victimized, oppressed, and sensual beings. This set of oppositional stereotypes functions in a symbiotic relationship. As Juliane Hammer has argued, "The pervasive representation of Muslim women as oppressed, silent, and hidden behind veils (by Muslim men and Islam) is only rivaled in its mediatized power by the arguably more recent image of Muslim men as inherently violent (towards other societies as terrorists and towards their own women and children as abusers)."[2]

The realities of Muslim life, both historically and contemporaneously, are much different than these representations would suggest. While Islam has a history that includes sexual servitude, enslavement, and harems, practices largely situated in "the premodern acceptance of a male owner's

23

sexual access to his female slaves," its history also includes Muslim scholars, queens, and political leaders.[3] In her 1993 monograph on the subject, Fatima Mernissi made the following comment on the individuals she encountered in her research:

> Just as in a fairy-tale, queens, malikas, and khatuns emerged little by little from the soft crackle of yellowed pages in old books. One by one they paraded through the silent rooms of the libraries in an interminable procession of intrigues and mysteries. Sometimes they appeared in twos or threes, passing the throne from mother to daughter in the faraway isles of Asiatic Islam. They were called Malika 'Arwa, 'Alam al-Hurra, Sultana Radiyya, Shajarat al-Durr, Turkan Khatun, or, more modestly, Taj al-'Alam (Crown of the Universe) and Nur al-'Alam (Light of the Universe). Some received the reins of power by inheritance; others had to kill the heirs in order to take power. Many themselves led battles, inflicted defeats, concluded armistices. Some had confidence in competent viziers, while others counted only on themselves. Each had her own way of treating the people, of rendering justice, and of administering taxes. Some managed to stay a long time on the throne, while others scarcely had time to settle down. Many died in the manner of the caliphs (either orthodox, Umayyad, or Abbasid)—that is, poisoned or stabbed. Rare were those who died peacefully in their beds.[4]

Of course, Muslim women in history did not rule over kingdoms, but not all of them were slaves either. Hence this project, which rejects these binaries and, using popular culture, offers a way to see Muslim girls and women as the complicated humans they are.

Popular culture can be both a reflection of and an influence on society. In the case of feminism and its backlash, scholars have shown how women's anxieties are mediated through popular television serials and movies. In some cases, feminism is presented as a restraint to romantic or "traditional" desires, such as the *Bridget Jones* franchise. As Angela McRobbie argues, "These popular texts normalize post-feminist gender anxieties so as to re-regulate young women by means of the language of personal choice."[5] In other cases, popular culture influences the way the public sees the world and, in some cases, it helps individuals construct the world. As Jeffery Mahan argues in his work on religion and popular culture, "New media do more than simply provide access to a wider range of information about religion. Instead, media model and encourage a constructionist way of building knowledge and articulating identity."[6]

This book does not claim that *Muslimah* superheroes flip the script, but it does contend that visual narratives offer an alternative space in which we can see Muslims through a different lens that more accurately reflects reality. Unlike the majority of academic studies of Muslim females, this study

Figure 2.1   Mannequin with hijab and evening gown. Photo courtesy of the author.

focuses on a different type of portrayals—those that are largely pictorial and supplemented with text or other narratives, and those that are positive. The power of these images is a critical part of this project, and one that this chapter focuses on; in particular, I discuss those topics related to the Muslim woman's body—the veil, the body as an object of consumption, and the different ways in which Muslim bodies function in the current political economy.

Historically, the inclusion of women in comics and other visual media has upheld visions of male power. Often expressed in the narrative or plot, women are seen as threatening to men. Sexual dominance and the fear of female sexuality are common themes. In the Batman universe, sensual dominance and monstrosity are expressed in villains like Poison Ivy, Harley Quinn, and Batwoman, who are "seen as a threat and must therefore be controlled or otherwise diminished by men."[7] In other cases, graphic narratives reify white masculinity and female weakness, expressed in the relative importance of the superhero. In Batman, "While Harley and Catwoman are both portrayed as monstrous, they are still anchored to the men around them, who make them weaker."[8] Women also function as characters who desire the superhero, who may rebuff their advances or refuse to make a commitment. For Superman, "just the prospect of marriage—even when initiated by the super-hero himself—results in heavily gendered chaos."[9] This is yet another place in which female sexuality is seen as threatening. Like Batman's female villains, other characters express the dangerous nature of the female, which often culminates in her defeat by the male hero. One example is Warrior Woman, an Axis villain in the *Captain America* comic of the 1960s.[10]

The bodies of superheroes and superheroines are an important part of the aesthetic of graphic narratives. Some superheroines possess characteristics usually assigned to men—bravery, strength, and power. This is true of Wonder Woman, for example, whose historical location formulated her superheroine qualities. "Wonder Woman originates in an era that saw the entirety of America mobilize for the war effort, making possible a superheroine who was comparable, if not quite equal, to her male counterparts in her assertiveness, strength, and independence."[11] Historically, comics have used the body and dress to reflect the sexual desires of men. This has been achieved through displaying the female body in a partially undressed state with a tight-fitting costume that shows a lot of skin. Wonder Woman's "hypersexualized body" is perhaps the best example of this; in some cases appearing in scenes of sexual bondage and torture, "Wonder Woman is forever being tied up, bound with ropes and chains, and tortured, as well as rescuing other women from the same scenarios with her famous golden lasso."[12]

Superheroines are, of course, a work in progress. Characters found in interwar American comics expressed the more conservative beliefs of that time. Supergirl is one example, "She lives in Superman's shadow, and is understood by many to be simply a Superman for girls, using her superpowers to fly kites ('Supergirl's Greatest Victory' 135/1–2) and rescue burning dinners ('Supergirl's Darkest Days' 147/2): she is derivative, uninteresting, and an inferior and instrumentally complicit kind of Wonder Woman."[13] This type of portrayal is only part of the story, of course. Over the past half-century, comics and other graphic genres have expanded the ways girls and women are presented, including independent, strong, and intelligent individuals. However, even when female superheroes are portrayed as muscular, strong, and powerful, they are still sexually objectified through scant costuming.[14] This fact makes the *Muslimah* superheroes profiled in this book quite different.

Print media in the West has often functioned as a space for the consumption of female bodies. As Sheri Klein points out, "The spectator is always assumed to be male, and the ideal woman is always assumed to be there to flatter them."[15] The presence of the male gaze is a problem for the white female subject, as Klein points out. The colonized female is subjected to the male gaze, thus enforcing gendered Orientalism and other colonial systems of domination. In colonial fiction about Africa, for example, the land functions as a kind of territorial imagining of the woman's body. "Thus as the 'aerial view' is the imperialist gaze of desire, its object here is the vision of a gigantic recumbent woman, veiled in sleep and complete with breasts and snow-covered nipples."[16]

The veiled heroines that are the focus of this study are more closely aligned with feminist graphic narratives, but they differ from the superheroines many of us are familiar with such as Wonder Woman and Supergirl. The *Muslimah* superhero is not typically sexualized. The sexual desire often attached to super-heroines is downplayed through artistic techniques that minimize body curves and breast size, often through the use of veiling. This represents a radically different presentation of the superheroine, a point Kecia Ali makes here. "Western media present the Muslim woman as a figure whose oppression is inextricably linked to her sexuality; her oppression is a particularly sensual one, symbolized by fanatical concern with women's bodies, 'the veil,' and female seclusion."[17]

Muslim girls and women were often the subject of Orientalist paintings in which they appeared nude, posing in bathhouses, bedrooms, and other intimate locations for the male to enjoy. Photography is another medium in which the female body has been subjected to the colonial male gaze. In Algeria and other colonized territories, young girls and women were often photographed in pornographic poses, disrobed, exposing their intimate body parts—a symbolic embodiment of the French occupation. "The most explicit versions of this sub-eroticism were produced mostly in the cities of North Africa and Egypt; they were more rarely seen in Turkey, Lebanon, Iran and Iraq, and seldom in Syria and Lebanon."[18]

Today, Muslim women are almost always portrayed in Western media as veiled. When they are unveiled, it is a consequence of Western political liberation, suggesting once again that Muslim women have no personal agency and that their lives can only be improved by outside intervention. As Lila Abu-Lughod has pointed out, this object of clothing is often the last thing women in oppressive political situations are worried about. She poses the question, "Could we only free Afghan women to be 'like us,' or might we have to recognize that even after 'liberation' from the Taliban, they might want different things than we would want for them?"[19] The question she asks illustrates that "liberation" is often a cover for cultural imperialism.

In contrast to the Orientalist visions of Muslim girls and women as sexual objects, Islamic patriarchal systems do not represent Muslim women in this way, but often articulate a form of patriarchy that restricts girls and women from exerting agency. Sexual politics in Islam is very complicated, even in the case of an Islamic state like Iran. As Fatemeh Sadeghi has argued, the effort to protect women's honor is historically located.

> The moment of revolution was liberating for women in the sense that being appropriately feminine did not mean having to avoid political activities. Unlike during the period of the Pahlavis, in which women's perfect femininity was defined as their being sexually desirable, the revolution made women feel they were not sexual objects but political agents.[20]

This is seen in a variety of ways, including advertising and public service campaigns. In post-Revolutionary Iran, women have at times been visually erased as a strategy to negate their former objectification. In an advertisement for the clothing store *Yashar* (2004), an eye with prominent lashes and a drawn female figure stands in for a model, "Thus, pictorial synecdoche is another strategy in the post-revolutionary period to compensate for the lack of actual pictures of women."[21]

What is the response when Muslim women who wear a *hijab*, or a veil, do exert agency? One case where the imposition of patriarchal controls—or efforts to control—was very apparent was in the Muslim "Happy" video, which featured Muslim women dancing, smiling, and laughing to the tune of Pharrell's hit song. Among the responses some voiced condemnation of Muslim females dancing to music and appearing to violate their faith, which met a response by one of the participants—Aminah, a model—that these critiques were attempts at "taking away the agency and power" of Muslim women.[22] This example illustrates that the efforts to control Muslim females is not limited to dress, but also to other choices related to the body.

The disciplinary regimes imposed by colonialism and patriarchal expressions of Islam put Muslim women in a difficult position in which all choices may be criticized and disapproved by one party or another. I do not deny this reality, but hope to show there are also possibilities for the interstitial moments that Foucault argues are possible, even if the moments are only fleeting. In the texts examined in this book, the actions of the female characters are independent of their relationship to men, or at least not predicated on them. This is radically different from the typical presentations of Muslim women as "the trademark of Islam's repression."[23] As we shall see, Muslim women can be the captain of their own destinies rather than the focus of the desires of Western and Muslim men.

The following section delves more deeply into issues regarding the Muslim female body—its symbolic use in colonialism, the complicated ways in which Muslim females use the veil (or headscarf), variations of the veil, and the ways in which the bodies of Muslim girls and women are used in colonialist and Islamist ideological programs. All of these are necessary to understand the larger issues involved with Islam, feminism, and agency that are critical junctures in this book. Burka Avenger, Ms. Marvel, Qahera, and other *Muslimah* superheroes are not productions of colonial or Islamist powers but they are important voices responding to these systems of domination.

THE VEIL

The harem and the veil are among the most popular tropes of Islam in the West. In a variety of places including travel narratives, paintings, novels, and films, they work together to frame Muslim women as subjugated. As part of the legacy of Orientalism, these images are so common that disentangling discussions about Islam from gender is challenging. As other scholars have noted, the focus on Muslim female bodies is a fixation, seen in the legislative efforts in Europe and North America to control sartorial choices; the growth in the number of assaults on women wearing the veil; and the use of the veil as a symbol of Muslim cruelty and deprivation, often displayed visually in Western publications and in media productions focused on the abuse of girls and women. The veil functions as the most powerful symbol of Islam, "an all-encompassing symbol of repression, and its dominant association with Islam (with equivalent Jewish, Christian, or Hindu practices written out of the script) reinforces the monocular representation of that religion."[24] As we shall see, it plays an important role in the *Muslimah* superheroes that are the subject of this book.

The harem has been a popular focus of Western anxiety—and fascination—since the beginning of Orientalism. The efforts to control colonized bodies were frustrated by the harem, which often hid Muslim girls and women from the eyes and hands of strangers. The harem is typically portrayed as a site of sensuality revolving around the practice of polygamy. The sexual fantasies that white colonial agents imposed on the harem were in part, a response to the restricted access they had to these private spaces. I am not the first scholar to suggest that the interest in the harem is deeply embedded in fantasies of sexual conquest and power. The restrictive quality of the harem, in fact, provoked fantasies among those who did not have access, resulting in a long list of desires: "the lure of a sybaritic world where women could be imagined through the male voyeur's eyes as seductive, languorous and available for sexual fantasies, including those of lesbian dalliance."[25] While it is true that harems included the sultan's large cadre of sexual servants (and slaves), in other cases they were simply the part of the home where girls and women resided. In these cases, while the harem was restricted from public purview; activities there were quite mundane. These domestic harems also varied greatly, even within one community. As Fatima Mernissi writes in her memoir detailing her childhood growing up in her home's harem, "given a choice, I would have used different words for Yasmina's harem and our own, so different were they. Yasmina's harem was an open farm with no visible high walls. Ours in Fez was like a fortress."[26]

The veil typically accompanied presentations of Muslim women in the harem. Like the fantasies imposed on the harem, the veil, as we have seen, has been subject to the sexual desires of the colonizer. Fanon is one of many who have linked the efforts to unveil to those of other types of conquest, including sexual conquest and rape. In the past, the bodies of girls and women, much like today, have functioned as sites of contestation and of violence. "Around the metaphoric linking of control of territory and control over the women's body hovered unspoken connotations of rape."[27]

While the literature on Islamic dress is too large to survey here, it is important to note that veiling is not an eponymous practice among Muslim girls and women. Covering one's hair and face are practices determined by numerous factors including local culture, ethnic or regional style, politics, colonialism, and socioeconomic status. Practices of veiling include wearing a headscarf that covers part of one's head, a common style seen on the streets of Tehran, the *jilbab* (which covers the hair, but never the face) popular in Indonesia, and the all-encompassing *niqab* often seen in Arabian Gulf states. There is a great variety of styles of veiling, including special occasion *hijabs* worn for weddings and birthdays, national holidays, and other occasions and *couture* versions sold by Paris fashion houses and in the shopping malls of Jakarta and elsewhere.

The veil has incredible social power. Its religious history, role in colonialism, and status as a cultural icon are important factors in the ways it is used today, including its role as a powerful symbol of agency. In France, which subjects Muslim women to the institution of republican unveiling, thus effectively controlling the bodies of girls and women, the act of veiling is a way that individuals can act as "active critical agents."[28] In Iran, the veil is a mandated form of dress, required for citizens and tourists. Due to these sorts of disciplinary actions on Muslim bodies, the role of the veil in society and, in particular, in defining Muslim women's lack of—or expression of—power, is an aspect of this topic that cannot be ignored.

Despite these complexities, white (predominantly North American and European) feminists have largely adopted the point of view that the veil is necessarily oppressive, an example of the "feminist fundamentalism" that requires all women to accept Western body norms. This includes a style of dress that, in their view, equalizes the genders. Unfortunately, this isn't the case, "Western democracies which are premised on universalist ideals of liberty and equality," under scrutiny, "in practice are generally sexist and racist."[29] One of the ways we know this is true is by the reactions of non-Muslims to Muslim dress. While contemporary feminism espouses agency for individual women, it in fact relies on very narrow ideals of liberation that are largely focused on sexual and bodily freedom. The veil bothers many Western feminists because it creates a "dissonance of [the] imperialist feminist gaze" and defines Muslim women as "total, abject, and irreconcilable."[30]

The clothing and costume of the characters examined in this book constitute an important part of the power of the *Muslimah* superhero. The veil's function is multivalent in these characters, much as it is for many Muslim women. For Burka Avenger, it defines her religious identity as a Muslim fighting corruption and crime. It also functions as a disguise and a weapon that deflects the villains' attacks. In the case of Ms. Marvel, the absence of the veil (she wears a loosely tied scarf around her neck) is a part of Kamala's reckoning of her identity as a Muslim, an American, and a superhero.

The veil has always had multiple meanings. The practice of veiling among Muslims has its origins in early Islamic history when, according to Islamic texts, the female relatives of Prophet Muhammad wore the veil as a sign of piety, or perhaps as a way to disguise themselves from the enemies of Islam. The Qur'an and *hadith* (the sayings and actions of Prophet Muhammad) are used to argue both that veiling is a required act and that it is optional. Some Islamic scholars, including those who follow conservative schools of Islamic law, have stated it is an optional act. Today, some Muslim women veil to emulate early Muslim women as a public display of piety, while others cover their hair (or entire body) as a political statement.

The problem of how to define the "veil" is one that scholars have focused on in great detail. *Hijab*, the Arabic word that literally means "partition," is used colloquially to refer to a head covering. Girls and women who wear the veil are often called *muhajibat*, but in Muslim slang, the word *hijabi* is often used, as well as numerous other words in local language. In one study of contemporary Muslim veiling, this type of modest dress was varyingly termed the *khimar, dishdash, smagh, salwaar kamiz, shash, maro, shayla, buknuk, niqab, burka, kaftan, thobe*, and *galabiyya*.[31]

The power attached to the veil often overshadows the achievements of Muslim girls and women, both historically and currently. As Leila Ahmed writes,

> That so much energy has been expended by Muslim men and then Muslim women to affirm or restore it [the veil] is frustrating and ludicrous. But even worse is the legacy of meanings and struggles over issues of culture and class with which not only the veil but also the struggle for women's rights has become inscribed as a result of this history ad as a result of the cooption by colonialism of the issue of women and the language of feminism in its attempt to undermine other cultures.[32]

In the West, the veil is often seen as a disruption to white, secular space. Numerous scholars have written about this issue, including those who have argued that Muslim bodies, and in particular women wearing the veil, are used to define notions of citizenship. Called sexual democracy, this is a way of determining membership in the modern state based on bodily appearance and adherence to secular sartorial practices, or dress. In particular, this is an issue in Europe, as the French example shows us. "Indeed, these sexualized republican values have been epitomized in the recurrent debate on the so-called Islamic veil: while it first erupted in 1989 in terms of cultural difference, it was reformulated in sexual terms for the new millennium, leading to the 2004 law that excludes 'conspicuous signs' of religion from public schools."[33]

The veil also can support Islamic systems of domination. At the same time that Muslim girls and women are challenging Western articulations of feminism, they are also faced with disciplinary efforts in their own communities to control their bodies and voices. Islamism, the belief that Islam should be part of governance in a modern state, often involves patriarchal impositions on its populations. Under the Taliban, women were beat in public for violating the dress code and subject to daily indignities and abuses, which included public floggings and executions. Several scholars have argued that these impositions on women's dress are efforts to "negate the fear of female sexuality."[34] Islamism, perhaps quite accidentally, has encouraged Muslim women (who may or may not subscribe to Islamist ideologies) to find a textual basis for the political and social rights they are seeking. As Margot Badran reminds us, this is even taking place in Iran, which uses the Qur'an as the foundation of its constitution.

> In their studies, Iranian scholars Afsaneh Najmabadi and Ziba Mir-Hosseini have presented the Islamic feminist rereadings of the Quran underway in the Islamic Republic of Iran since the early 1990s in which the non-gender egalitarian and misogynist constructions of Islam are being dismantled through interpretive methodologies that include classical Islamic and modern (secular) social science approaches.[35]

Like the work of Najmabadi and Mir-Hosseini, the texts and characters examined in this book articulate a vision of Islam that is independent of norms established by Western feminists and patriarchal Islamists. While the majority of the characters in my study wear some form of the veil, the ways in which it is worn, or not worn, speaks to the great diversity within Islam and the choices available to Muslim women. These choices include using the veil in political activism, as seen in the example of *Princess Hijab*, the French street artist who is most famous for hijabizing models on Paris billboards, acts she sees as resistance against the "'visual terrorism' of the advertising industry" and an expression of her "physical and mental integrity."[36]

The fact that *Muslimah* superheroes exert agency in their clothing choices does not mean that the veil does not function as a source of oppression; in many other cases, it represents the real choices that many Muslim girls and women have. Many Muslims choose to wear the *hijab* (in all its various forms). Critics of Islam often assume that this is impossible (that they must be coerced), but the work of anthropologists like Lila Abu-Lughod has proven that their claims are erroneous. As she argues, "Veiling must not be confused with, or made to stand for, lack of agency. Not only are there many forms of covering, which themselves have different meanings in the communities where they are used, but veiling has become caught up almost everywhere now in a politics of representation—of class, of piety, and of political affiliation."[37]

In this discussion, I have tried to show that the veil is a complicated object, implicated in history, politics, colonialism, and sexual agency. Its qualities are dependent not just on the wearer, but on her larger social milieu. Muslim women are often political agents and in these contexts the veil has been, and can be, a subversive tool. The iconic film *Battle of Algiers* (1967) included this use of the veil in its presentation of the Algerian revolution against the French occupiers. As Sohail Daulatzai writes in his recent book, "The film's portrayal of Zohra, Hassiba, and Djamila, three women who 'looked' as though they had embraced European values of modernity—only to pass through a checkpoint without being searched and then successfully plant bombs among French settler-civilians—revealed the veil, and, more important, Western feminist values, to be overdetermined, and, ultimately, a ruse."[38] The subversive use of the veil is not limited to anti-colonial political struggles. Islamic fashion, and in particular the manipulation of the veil, is one way in which Muslim girls and women are challenging social norms— imposed from all directions—that they are uncomfortable with.

Muslimah superheroes can be understood within the larger context of an ongoing Muslim reformation in which Islamism has failed, colonialism is being challenged, and the *ummah* (the worldwide community of Muslims) are tech savvy, young, and often living in diasporic communities around the world. Elsewhere I have argued that Islamic reform does not necessarily involve the changing of tradition, but rather is a return to the ethos of Islam that characterizes the religion's nascent period. "A central message of the Qur'an is that humans have strayed and must return."[39] Omid Safi calls this the Muhammadi Revolution, which brought about a "full-scale social and political transformation of Arab society" through an "interior affair, a trans- formation of the heart (*qalb*)."[40] The *Muslimah* superhero is the expression of these foundational Islamic morals in modern clothing.

MUSLIM BODIES: MONSTERS AND ANGELS

Muslim bodies are subjected to numerous disciplinary practices in the modern world. As I documented in my 2015 book, the control of Muslim male bodies includes extrajudicial arrest, detainment, and in some cases, torture and death.[41] In the United States, Muslim men are often policed, a symptom of how

> race and religion have comingled to form indispensible aspects of an othered identity which is not only clearly outside of the nation's mainstream, but one that has been criminalized by the state. What has resulted is a phenomenon in which visible religious identity becomes the determining factor which renders individuals vulnerable to the phenotypically based social degradation—and potential violence—normally reserved for racialized minorities in this nation's history.[42]

For women, this takes place both in Muslim-majority countries in which the legalization of dress code "establishes a strong sexual hierarchisation" and in Muslim-minority countries where the "effect of these disciplinary practices has reverberations not only among male and female Muslims, but also throughout entire populations."[43] These acts also take place in fictional worlds, including those areas of popular culture this book is focused upon. As one scholar put it, "Visual practices survey, discipline, and marginalize bodies."[44]

In the following pages, I shift to the subject of *Muslimah* superheroes. As I have suggested, the pejorative images of Muslims and, in particular, representations of girls and women do not tell the entire story. Before turning to these superheroes, I would like to contrast two sets of texts that illustrate the divide between the colonial/imperial presentations of Muslims and the Muslim voices that challenge them. As I illustrated in the previous chapter, Muslims are represented in many different areas of American popular culture, including characters that appear in comics, graphic novels, film, and television. These representations are overwhelmingly negative, supporting the colonial and imperialist visions of the world that have dominated Western media for over a century. Ella Shohat and Robert Stam have described the world these images create as the "imperial imaginary." Although their focus is on cinema, it is worth noting the larger process by which colonization took place:

> The colonial domination of indigenous peoples, the scientific and aesthetic disciplining of nature through classificatory schemas, the capitalist appropriation of resources, and the imperialist ordering of the globe under a panoptical regime, all formed part of a massive historical movement that reached its apogee at the beginning of the twentieth century.[45]

In the case of Islam, the imperial imaginary includes those images, narratives, and characters that have populated texts, including comics, animated cartoons, and others, for close to a century. In an essay reflecting on his childhood and the way these images helped to create imaginary worlds for him, Alexander Lyon Macafie writes,

> Such a litany would not exhaust the catalogue of oriental influences we were subjected to in my childhood and youth. Like everyone else in that period, I was from time to time made aware that the Orient was gorgeous (Milton), dangerous (the "black hole of Calcutta"), seductive (Cleopatra), mysterious (Shangri-La), and despotic (Ghenghis Khan, Tamberlaine).[46]

One of the reasons these texts are important is that they function in the larger field of popular culture that influences the way that people see the world. As Shohat and Stam have argued, the colonized subject is often part of this visual world, subjected to the power of the viewers, "armchair conquistadors" who affirm their own sense of superiority while framing the Other as "spectacle."[47] Frank Miller's graphic novels, and the films they are based on, certainly fit this description.

Frank Miller's graphic novels *300* and *Holy Terror* present a terrifying vision of the East and of Muslims. Miller's graphic novel *300* (1998) was made into a film in 2007. As I have written elsewhere, this is a story about Islam, not about ancient Greece. "Remember, *300* is not about an ancient battle—it's about the victory of the West's advanced and modern civilization over Islam's backward and brutal culture."[48] Among the most memorable scenes from the film is the episode in which Xerxes lords over an orgy in his harem, which includes disfigured lesbians and other monstrous figures from the East.

In 2014, a sequel to the film was released titled *300: Rise of an Empire*, also based on Miller's graphic narratives. Among the most interesting scenes in this film is the transformation of Xerxes, the ancient Persian king who defeated the Spartans, from a mortal to a monster through his immersion in a mysterious liquid located in a pool in a cave. He emerges as an eight-foot-tall God-king. The voiceover during this interlude includes the comment "no human part of Xerxes survived," and he returns to the capital to mobilize his "monster army." If it wasn't clear enough in the first filmic adaptation of Frank Miller's graphic novel, this scene makes it evident that Xerxes represents the monstrosity of Islam—homoerotic, giant, racialized, and mutilated.

Xerxes is the villain in these graphic narratives and films. He is the celluloid threat to the Spartan superheroes who, as Tom Holland has written, are executed in beautiful fashion. "Nevertheless, the representation of Spartan phalanx as a compound of glistening bronze shields and no less glistening naked flesh is a stunning one, and made all the more so by the visualization of ancient combat as a kind of balletic *danse macabre*."[49] In contrast to these heroes, the Persians are portrayed as an army of monstrous villains who, although historically located in the ancient world, are in fact Muslim.

> Regardless of nationality, ethnicity, or race, the foot soldiers wear prototypical Arab headwear and tunics, and to differentiate regular soldiers from messengers and emissaries, messengers wear caps and helmets with scarves draped around their necks and heads and flowing tunics under light armor. Furthermore, they are differentiated from the Spartans because they cover themselves from head to toe.[50]

Holy Terror, published in 2011, presents Muslims not as Persian monsters attacking heroic Spartans but as homicidal villains decapitating their victims, flying planes into skyscrapers, and wreaking havoc on the American landscape. No academic studies of *Holy Terror* exist, but the graphic novel is clear in its sentiments about Islam. Frank Miller has publicly described Muslims as terroristic villains with no qualifications,

> For some reason, nobody seems to be talking about who we're up against, and the sixth century barbarism that they actually represent. These people saw people's heads off. They enslave women, they genetically [sic] mutilate their daughters, they do not behave by any cultural norms that are sensible to us.[51]

Miller's beliefs are displayed on the pages of his 2011 graphic novel. They include Muslim female characters who are suicide bombers, including one who responds to a question about what she wears under her coat with, "Paradise," then blows herself and helpless victims to pieces.[52] This is the vision of Muslim women presented to Miller's readers.

The 99 stands in stark contrast to Miller's vision of Muslim women as disfigured lesbians and suicide bombers. Created by Naif al-Mutawa of Kuwait, this comic book and animated television show feature Muslim superheroes who represent the ninety-nine qualities of God. "From Hadya (the Guide) from England whose brain works like a GPS system, to Fattah (the Opener) from Indonesia who can create rifts in time and space, the characters don't lack for variety."[53] Al-Mutawa was inspired to create *The 99* because of the poor public reception Islam has among many Westerners as well as the dearth of role models in popular culture available for Muslim children. As he explained in a 2010 Ted Talk,

> An entire generation of Muslims is growing up believing that Islam is a bad thing. They are put in a situation to defend the indefensible. My thinking was, how can I expand the boundaries of what Islam is, talk about stuff that all human beings share together, and not allow people to sabotage and hijack Islam?[54]

The 99 is different from the other texts explored in this book because its characters are what scholars call a *supergroup*. Rather than focus on an individual character, this comic features a group of heroes. As scholars have noted, the supergroup often includes female characters, which are often translated to animation for children.[55] *The 99*'s heroes represent the global flavor of Islam, with members of the group featuring "a wide swath of super-heroic characters from across the globe."[56] These characters, coupled with the popularity of the series in places like North America, reflect the transnational quality of many comic book characters.

In comics and other graphic narratives, the superhero usually has a special power, which is granted to him (or her) through a miraculous or magical event. In *The 99*, the Noor Stones, which were forged in 1258 by the librarians of Baghdad's Dar al-Hikma (the greatest library of the era), seek "out their bearers," who are all young Muslims with "pure hearts."[57] *The 99* is filled with Islamic symbols, themes, and teachings, of which the stones are but one example. In Issue 13, a character remarks, "The Noor Stones cannot be used like blunt tools. Like axes and guns. They are living repositories of wisdom. And they seek out their own human partners."[58] The back story to the stones is important, for their magical content is composed of Islamic wisdom. As the great library is set afire by invading Mongols, the librarians find a way to preserve the knowledge within it.

> As the librarians cannot escape and take the books with them, they discover instead a way to capture the books' spirit. Using the knowledge of alchemy found in the library, they prepare a secret potion called the "King's Water," whose properties "were attuned to the very fibers in the parchments, scrolls and maps that lay stacked" on the shelves of the library. With the potion they create, they hope "to distill the sum total of knowledge contained within the tomes" and instill it into ninety-nine gemstones that had been "crafted to absorb the very light of reason, the very depths of a culture's collective soul."[59]

In al-Mutawa's vision of Islam, the tools of the superhero and superheroine are activated through an individual's Muslim character. The youth of these heroes is critical, for they have not had time to stray from the path of Islam or to sever their ties from Allah and violate *tawhid*. *The 99* includes numerous *Muslimah* superheroes, some who wear the *hijab* and others who do not. The first female character introduced in the series is Dana Ibarhim/Noora, who with the help of a Noor stone is able to see light and darkness in people.[60] This ability to see the truth is reflected in her name Noora, which is a homage to the Arabic word *Nur*, a reference to the Divine Light held by Prophet Muhammad and other holy figures. Like the images of *Nur Muhammad*, where the Prophet is shown with light emanating from his face and fingertips, Noora has this ability as well, as she is often shown with "outstretched arms, poised to spread light."[61]

This power links her to the Prophetic ideals al-Mutawa highlights in his work. The stones are tools that activate the inner qualities of each individual

Figure 2.2   Noora of *The 99*. Photo courtesy of Naif al-Mutawa.

hero. They are used in *The 99* as a rhetorical device to show how Islam is present in all parts of the world, including the United States, Asia, and Europe. This is the way to argue that Islam is not a divisive religion, but a global one. As the story goes,

> The stones were separated with the fall of Granada in 1492. Christopher Colum-
> bus unknowingly carried 33 stones to the New World on the Niña, Pinta, and
> Santa Maria. Another 33 stones were carried along the Silk Route and hidden in
> Asia. The remaining 33 gems were hidden throughout Europe.[62]

The *Muslimah* heroes in *The 99* communicate other Islamic values and traditions, oftentimes without appearing in a *hijab* or veil. Hope Mendoza, a character from the Philippines, becomes Widad, "The Loving One," and is vested with the power of convincing people to donate to her causes.[63] The Islamic practice of *zakat*, or giving to charity, is reflected in this character. Amira Khan, a Pakistani Londoner, is another prominent *Muslimah* superhero in the series. She becomes "The Guide," and has the power to visualize places she has never seen, essentially drawing a map in her mind with the use of a Noor stone set in a medallion she wears as a necklace.[64] Her name Hadya is derived from *Al-Hadi*, or guide, an attribute of God that refers to guiding one on the right path—the ethical path mandated by Islam.[65] Her power of sight is also reflective of the visions of Sufis well known to Muslims, which include travel to far-off locations, meetings with prophets and saints, and the ethereal voice (*hātif*) that reminds the individual of the reality of "all creation as replete with divine 'signs.'"[66]

Batina, who wears a *niqab*-like face covering, is perhaps the most promi-nent veiled *Muslimah* superhero in the series. Her name comes from the attri-bute of God that means hidden (*Al Batin*), and she is quiet, curious, and able to scramble electronic equipment with the aid of her Noor stone.[67] What is perhaps most interesting about Batina, whose background is Yemeni, is that her use of the veil is agentic—representing the choices Muslim women can, and do, make about their body. As one study notes, "Significantly, Batina's powers, and her own personal struggles, powerfully reflect the choice of Muslim women behind the veil who nevertheless make consistent, if unac-knowledged, contributions to society."[68]

The vastly different presentations of Islam seen in the works of Frank Miller and Naif al-Mutawa help to introduce the characters that serve as the focus of the rest of this study. *The 99* is not the only graphic narrative to reflect Islamic values, but it represents an important foundational step in the ongoing contestation of how Muslims are presented in popular media. As we shall see in the following chapters, Muslim superheroes and superheroines answer a theological question posed by al-Mutawa: "How upset must God

Figure 2.3 Hadya of *The* 99. Photo courtesy of Naif al-Mutawa.

Figure 2.4 Batina of *The 99*. Photo courtesy of Naif al-Mutawa.

be over how far Muslims had strayed from the values of compassion, intelligence, and generosity that Islam was supposed to extol."[69] The answer to this question is found in the *Muslimah* superheroes, who, as I shall illustrate, symbolize these values.

NOTES

1. Arjana Sophia Rose, *Muslims in the Western Imagination* (New York: Oxford University Press, 2015): 11.

2. Juliane Hammer, "Gender, Feminism, and Critique in American Muslim Thought," in *Routledge Handbook of Islam in the West*, ed. Roberto Toppoli (London: Routledge, 2014): 396.

3. Kecia Ali, *Sexual Ethics and Islam: Feminist Reflections on Qur'an, Hadith, and Jurisprudence* (Oxford: Oneworld, 2006): xvi.

4. Fatima Mernissi, *The Forgotten Queens of Islam*, trans. Mary Jo Lakeland (Minneapolis: University of Minnesota Press, 1993): 3.

5. Angela McRobbie, "Post-Feminism and Popular Culture," *Feminist Media Studies* 4, no. 3 (2004): 262.

6. Jeffrey Mahan, *Media, Religion, and Culture: An Introduction* (New York: Routledge, 2014): 27

7. Shannon Austin, "Batman's Female Foes: The Gender War in Gotham City," *The Journal of Popular Culture* 48, no. 2 (2015): 286.

8. Shannon Austin, "Batman's Female Foes," 293.

9. Mark Best, "Domesticity, Homosociality, and Male Power in Superhero Comics of the 1950s," *Iowa Journal of Cultural Studies* 6 (2005): 83.

10. J. Richard Stevens, *Captain America, Masculinity, and Violence: The Evolution of a National Icon* (Syracuse: Syracuse University Press, 2016): 120.

11. Alex Link, "The Secret of Supergirl's Success," *The Journal of Popular Culture* 46, no. 6 (2013): 1185.

12. Mitra C. Emad, "Reading Wonder Woman's Body: Mythologies of Gender and Nation," *The Journal of Popular Culture* 39, no. 6 (2006): 978, 981.

13. Alex Link, "The Secret of Supergirl's Success," *The Journal of Popular Culture* 46, no. 6 (2013): 1177.

14. Margaret Robbins, "Female Representation in Comics and Graphic Novels: Exploring Classroom Study with Critical Visual Literacy," *SIGNAL Journal* (Fall 2014/Winter 2015): 12.

15. Sheri Klein, "Breaking the Mold with Humor: Images of Women in the Visual Media," *Art Education* 46, no. 5 (1993): 61.

16. Rebecca Stott, "The Dark Continent: Africa as Female Body in Haggard's Adventure Fiction," *Feminist Review* 32 (1989): 79.

17. Kecia Ali, *Sexual Ethics and Islam: Feminist Reflections on Qur'an, Hadith, and Jurisprudence,* xiv.

18. Sarah Graham-Brown, *Images of Women: The Portrayal of Women in Photography of the Middle East 1860–1950* (New York: Columbia University Press, 1988): 44.

19. Lila Abu-Lughod, *Do Muslim Women Need Saving?* (Cambridge: Harvard University Press, 2013): 43.

20. Fatemeh Sadeghi, "Negotiating with Modernity: Young Women and Sexuality in Iran," *Comparative Studies of South Asia, Africa and the Middle East* 28, no. 2 (2008): 252.

21. Mohammad Amouzadeh and Manoochehr Tavangar, "Decoding Pictorial Metaphor: Ideologies in Persian Commercial Advertising," *International Journal of Cultural Studies* 7, no. 2 (2004): 164–165.

22. Huma Mohibullah and Kristi Kramer, "'Being True to Ourselves . . . Within the Context of Islam': Practical Considerations in *Hijab* Practice Among Muslim American Women," *Practical Matters* 9 (2016): 12.

23. Jasmin Zine, "Muslim Women and the Politics of Representation," *The American Journal of Islamic Social Sciences* 19, no. 4 (2002): 2.

24. Myra Macdonald, "Muslim Women and the Veil: Problems of Image and Voice in Media Representations," *Feminist Media Studies* 6, no. 1 (2006): 8.

25. Myra Macdonald, "Muslim Women and the Veil," 11.

26. Fatima Mernissi, *Dreams of Trespass: Tales of Harem Girlhood* (Boulder: Perseus Books, 1995): 39.

27. Myra Macdonald, "Muslim Women and the Veil," 9.

28. Inés Valdez, "Nondomination or Practices of Freedom? French Muslim Women, Foucault, and the Full Veil Ban," *American Political Science Review* 110, no. 1 (2016): 22.

29. Floya Anthias, "Beyond Feminism and Multiculturalism: Locating Difference and the Politics of Location," *Women's Studies International Forum* 25, no. 3 (2002): 278.

30. Jasmin Zine, "Muslim Women and the Politics of Representation," 13.

31. Heather Marie Akou, "Building a New 'World Fashion': Islamic Dress in the Twenty-First Century," *Fashion Theory* 11, no. 4 (2007): 405, 407, 414, 416.

32. Leila Ahmed, *Women and Gender in Islam: Historical Roots of a Modern Debate* (New Haven: Yale University Press, 1992): 167.

33. Eric Fasson, "National Identities and Transnational Intimacies: Sexual Democracy and the Politics of Immigration in Europe," *Public Culture* 22, no. 3 (2010): 514.

34. Jasmin Zine, "Muslim Women and the Politics of Representation," 8.

35. Margot Badran, "Understanding Islam, Islamism, and Islamic Feminism," *Journal of Women's History* 13, no. 1 (2001): 50.

36. Annelies Moors, "NiqaBitch and Princess Hijab: Niqab Activism, Satire and Street Art," *Feminist Review* 98 (2011): 134.

37. Lila Abu-Lughod, *Do Muslim Women Need Saving?* 39.

38. Sohail Daulatzai, *Fifty Years of "The Battle of Algiers": Past as Prologue* (Minneapolis: University of Minnesota Press, 2016), 75.

39. Sophia Rose Arjana, "Returning to the One: Postcolonial Muslim Liturgy," in *Liturgy in Postcolonial Perspectives: Only One Is Holy*, ed. Claudio Carvalhaes (New York: Palgrave Macmillan, 2015): 27.

40. Omid Safi, *Memories of Muhammad: Why the Prophet Matters* (New York: HarperOne, 2010): 98–99.

41. Arjana Sophia Rose, *Muslims in the Western Imagination*, 178–183.

42. Jaideep Singh, "A New American Apartheid: Racialized, Religious Minorities in the Post-9/11 Era," *Sikh Formations: Religion, Culture, Theory* 9, no. 2 (2013): 123.

43. Angeles Ramirez, "Control Over Female 'Muslim' Bodies: Culture, Politics and Dress Code Laws in Some Muslim and Non-Muslim Countries," *Identities: Global Studies in Culture and Power* 22, no. 6 (2015): 682.

44. Michelle Aguayo, "Representations of Muslim Bodies in *The Kingdom*: Deconstructing Discourses in Hollywood," *Global Media Journal—Canadian Edition* 2, no. 2: 45.

45. Ella Shohat and Robert Stam, *Unthinking Eurocentrism: Multiculturalism and the Media* (New York: Routledge, 1994): 100.

46. Alexander Macfie, "My Orientalism," *Journal of Postcolonial Writing* 45, no. 1 (2009): 88.

47. Shohat and Stam, *Unthinking Eurocentrism: Multiculturalism and the Media* (New York: Routledge, 1994), 104.

48. Sophia Rose Arjana, *Muslims in the Western Imagination*, 161.

49. Tom Holland, "Mirage in the Movie House," *Arion* 15, no. 1 (2007): 178.

50. David C. Oh and Doreen V. Kutufam, "The Orientalized 'Other' and Corrosive Femininity: Threats to White Masculinity in *300*," *Journal of Communication Theory* 38, no. 2 (2014): 156.

51. Oh and Kutufam, "The Orientalized 'Other' and Corrosive Femininity: Threats to White Masculinity in 300." *Journal of Communication Inquiry* 38, no. 2 (2014): 155.

52. Frank Miller, *Holy Terror* (Burbank: Legendary, 2011), n.p.

53. Meha Ahmad, "Islamic Superheroes Out to Change the World," *Islamic Horizons* 40, no. 5 (2011): 44.

54. Avi Santo, "'Is It a Camel? Is It a Turban? No, It's *The 99*': Branding Islamic Superheroes as Authentic Global Cultural Commodities," *Television and New Media* 15, no. 7 (2014): 680.

55. Kaysee Baker and Arthur A. Raney, "Equally Super?: Gender-Role Stereotyping of Superheroes in Children's Animated Programs," *Mass Communication and Society* 10, no. 1 (2007): 28.

56. Winona Landis, "Diasporic (Dis)Identification: The Participatory Fandom of Ms. Marvel," *South Asian Popular Culture* 14, nos. 1/2 (2016): 39.

57. James Clements and Richard Gauvain, "The Marvel of Islam: Reconciling Muslim Epistemologies through a New Islamic Origin Saga in Naif al-Mutawa's *The 99*," *The Journal of Religion and Popular Culture* 26, no. 1 (2014): 38, 54.

58. Clements and Gauvain, "The Marvel of Islam: Reconciling Muslim Epistemologies through a New Islamic Origin Saga in Naif al-Mutawa's *The 99*." *The Journal of Religion and Popular Culture* 26, no. 1 (2014): 56.

59. Mary-Jane Deeb, "*The 99*: Superhero Comic Books from the Arab World," *Comparative Studies of South Asia, Africa and the Middle East* 32, no. 2 (2012): 394.

60. Mary-Jane Deeb, "*The 99*: Superhero Comic Books from the Arab World," 400.

61. Shirin Edwin, "Islam's Trojan Horse: Battling Perceptions of Muslim Women in *The 99*," *Journal of Graphic Novels and Comics* 3, no. 2 (2012): 175.

62. Fahmida Rashid, "99ers Power," *Islamic Horizons* 35, no. 4 (2006): 43.

63. Mary-Jane Deeb, "*The 99*: Superhero Comic Books from the Arab World," 402.

64. Mary-Jane Deeb, "*The 99*: Superhero Comic Books from the Arab World," 404.

65. Shirin Edwin, "Islam's Trojan Horse," 176.

66. John Renard, *Friends of God: Islamic Images of Piety, Commitment, and Servanthood* (Berkeley: University of California Press, 2008): 83.

67. Shirin Edwin, "Islam's Trojan Horse," 182.

68. Ibid.

69. Avi Santo, "'Is It a Camel? Is It a Turban? No, It's *The 99*,'" 681.

Chapter 3

Ms. Marvel, Islam, and America

Muslimah superheroes are characterized by their Muslim identity, superpowers (such as shape-shifting, flying, and instantaneous healing of injuries) and at times, a deeply embedded theology that guides their heroic actions. *Ms. Marvel* features a sixteen-year-old Muslim Pakistani-American teenager named Kamala Khan as the title character. She is highly intelligent, brave, independent, and has a great sense of humor. The supporting characters include Kamala's parents, who many immigrants would recognize as their own—hard-working, patriotic, and upwardly mobile. It is important to note the significance of this series in the context of post-9/11 media productions about Muslims. After 9/11, many comics featured storylines about "real-life" superheroes like firemen and often expressed tolerance for Muslims and other religious minorities, "The characters often called for tolerance of ethnic groups that lived in the United States, especially Arab-Americans."[1] In some cases, the defense of Muslims—and their rights as Americans—played a central role in a series, such as in new editions of *Superman* and *Captain America* produced after 9/11. "Captain America, in the first issue of the new line, fought off skinheads who were threatening the life of an Arab-American merchant in New York, then made a point of noting that there has to be a distinction between those who look different, and those who think differently and want to do the U.S. harm."[2] These storylines, which featured white male heroes who rescued Muslims or defended American diversity, often portrayed Muslims with little power or agency. *Ms. Marvel* changes this by offering a superhero who is both Muslim and American. What is equally significant is that before the Muslim Ms. Marvel, superheroines coming out of the Marvel company were still the subjects of sexual objectification. As Keith Edmunds argues,

Marvel's heroines tended to be clad in skimpy, highly sexualized outfits, substituting their position of love interest for another character with that of being a love interest for the reader, as it is widely assumed that males account for between 80 and 95 percent of superhero comic readership.[3]

In *Ms. Marvel*, Muslim themes also play a central role, including numerous references to classical Islamic texts. In an early scene from the first issue, Ms. Marvel is shown in the clouds, surrounded by birds and other Marvel superheroes. The use of parallel appearances by other characters is popular because it ensures the production of various Marvel publications. "To maintain themselves, comic serials must have reliable content-generating potential, since mass market serial comic titles need a constant supply of stories. In other words, Marvel needs numerous characters, temporal frames, and settings to feed its multiple titles."[4]

The text accompanying the cloud scene includes lines from a poem by Amir Khusro, an Indian Sufi poet from the thirteenth century whose prolific writings in Persian and Hindi numbered in the hundreds.[5] The presence of birds suggests Attar's famous text, which is centered upon the mystical quest for God told through the travels of a group of birds. In Seyyed Hossein Nasr's classic writing on the subject titled "The Flight of Birds to Union: Meditations upon 'Attar's *Mantiq al-tayr*," he writes,

All those who are not completely at home in this world of fleeting shadows and who yearn for their origin in the paradisal abode belong to the family of the birds, for their soul possesses wings no matter how inexperienced they might be in actually flying towards the space of Divine Presence.[6]

This scene in the comic represents Ms. Marvel, a teenager and a superhero, as someone embarking on a spiritual quest, much like Attar's birds. Ernesto Prigo has argued that we can see this scene as an expression of metamorphosis and transfiguration of both Kamala and Ms. Marvel, who both become something greater than their former selves.[7]

The series is populated with Muslims and other diverse characters that create a picture of America focused on the experiences of immigrants and minorities. Kamala's brother Aamir is religiously devout and at times comical in his intense religiosity, striking a note of familiarity with readers who have a politically or religiously conservative relative. One of Kamala's best friends Nakia, an African-American, is a fellow Muslim. She wears the *hijab* and often serves as a prominent Muslim voice in the series, reminding Kamala of her religious foundations. Her other best friend is an Italian-American named Bruno. Kamala's parents are proud immigrants who believe that America is the land of opportunity. The characters and storylines featured in

Ms. Marvel construct a vision of Islam in America that challenges Islamophobic discourse. In one exchange between Kamala and her mosque's imam, a man who recognizes Kamala's independence, "misconceptions about Islam, particularly those related to the severity of its teachings and its attitude toward young women" are dismantled.[8]

Ms. Marvel is significant because it features the first American *Muslimah* superheroine as the headline character. While other comics examined in this book, such as *The 99*, and characters like Marvel's Dust are important, *Ms. Marvel* represents a major shift in the industry's treatment of Islamic subjects, which have historically been largely negative. This entire chapter is dedicated to the series because it is a culturally important text. *Ms. Marvel* has seven volumes in print (which are collections of the individual comics), a large readership, and has won many awards. Marvel may have taken a risk in introducing a Muslim superheroine who is also a person of color (POC), but Ms. Marvel has outperformed expectations. "Despite the long odds, however, *Ms. Marvel* has exploded in popularity, thanks to the series' talented writer, G. Willow Wilson (herself a convert to Islam), and artist Adrian Alphona, *Ms. Marvel* #1 has been reprinted seven times, practically unheard of in the comic book industry."[9]

Fans have even brought Ms. Marvel into the real world, plastering her image over Islamophobic bus ads in San Francisco that equated Nazism with Islam.

> But San Franciscans soon grew tired of Hitler's mustache and the ridiculous claims that Muslims are Nazis. Soon, anonymous graffiti artists and activists responded to the right-wing Islamophobic campaign, pasting posters of super-powered Kamala over the bigoted bus ads. Suddenly, the newest *Ms. Marvel* was a resistance figure of a sort, speaking for the more just side of Islam, albeit in very American terms.[10]

This kind of vigilante activism mirrors the actions of the superhero. As one scholar suggests, "These are citizens inspired by the caped crusaders of comic book fame, dedicated to making the world a better place."[11]

The comic has also received numerous awards, including the Eisner Award for Best New Series (2015), the Hugo Award (2015), the Dwayne McDuffie Award for Diversity (2016), and the Angoulême Best Series award (2016). Enormously popular, *Ms. Marvel* fans include boys, girls, and adults, as well as scholars who may use the comic in the classroom as a teaching text. Because it is geared toward children and young adults, Ms. Marvel, as a superhero, uses limited violence on her enemies. As one scholar notes, "She is not traumatized by the death of a loved one, unlike Batman or Spiderman, and she has no interest in violence."[12]

This chapter relates the history of the series and the reception of the new Ms. Marvel by fans and critics. Comics like *Ms. Marvel* require "a different kind of literacy that combines images and text and requires active participation."[13] To aid in this literacy, I include a detailed discussion of each of the six volumes—characters and plotlines as well as Islamic symbols, themes, and issues. *Ms. Marvel* is focused on social and political issues. Among these is Islamophobia, which represents the long history of comics taking on issues concerning civil rights and bigotry. While in the 1950s comics often featured words like "darkie" to refer to African-Americans, just one of many slurs reserved for minorities, by the 1980s Luke Cage and other minority superheroes emerged as a symbol of a more conscious understanding of racial, ethnic, and gender hierarchies.[14] As I will show, Ms. Marvel also addresses these hierarchies, in ways that are quite revolutionary.

INTRODUCING MS. MARVEL

Marvel Comics deserves much credit for the popularity and success of Ms. Marvel. Over the past decade, they have taken the incentive of introducing a number of female and minority superheroes. In 2012, Marvel had no female-led comics and by 2016 they had sixteen, a change due in large part due to the leadership of editor in chief Axel Alonso.[15] The idea for a *Muslimah* superhero came from two editors at Marvel, Sana Amanat (who grew up in a Muslim family) and Steve Wacker, who with Amanat, approached G. Willow Wilson.[16] Wilson is the author of numerous books including the award-winning memoir *The Butterfly Mosque* (2010), the novel *Alif the Unseen* (2012), and the graphic novel *Cairo* (2007). An American convert to Islam, Wilson is careful in her presentation of Islam and stereotypes surrounding Muslim females, resulting in a title character who has a thoughtful and introspective relationship with her faith. As one article notes, Kamala's "actions, encounters, and relationship to Islamic faith openly question the stereotypes that surround Muslim Americans, especially Muslim-American women."[17]

It is not surprising that Marvel Comics introduced such a revolutionary series. Kamala Khan is one of the numerous minority superhero characters Marvel has created. Historically, the company is placed after first-generation and second-generation comics, and as such it is associated with a more politically progressive culture. As Ronald Schmitt has written,

By the Third Generation Comics (The Marvel Comics Group, Eroticomics and Underground Comics) The Fall is complete and comics are overtly political, sexual and even radical, insisting on a "relevance" in which even the most escapist comics involve themselves with social issues, often issues which are not "acceptable" to older generations who are used to the more innocent comics of previous years.[18]

Kamala Khan is a teenager. Her age plays a central role in the series, whether she is looking up to adults (other Marvel superheroes) or rebelling against them (her parents, the imam at her mosque). Teenage superheroes are not new. Spiderman is perhaps the most famous teen in the comic book canon. While he is an orphan with adoptive parents (his aunt and uncle), Kamala is not. "Wilson and Amanat create the same situation as Spider-Man, a young kid trying to deal with strict parents, being bullied at school, and being different. The major difference with Spider-Man and Ms. Marvel is that Kamala's parents are strict because they are Pakistani immigrants and her friends are constantly bullied because of their religion."[19]

Teenage superheroes first emerged in the 1960s, during what scholars have called the silver age of comics (which followed the 1950s "Golden Age").[20] As John Trushell explains, these superheroes expressed "an allegory of adolescent anomie."[21] Ms. Marvel is like these other teenage superheroes (who tend to be male) in her adolescent angst. She also resembles the dualities often seen in comic superheroes. Among these are the conflicts presented by her age and her family. "Kamala, like other superheroes, has many dualities in her identity. First of all, she has the typical teenage girl issue of trying to please both her family and her peers, and her identity as a Pakistani-American girl intensifies this challenge."[22]

Like Kamala, age plays a central role in Ms. Marvel's adventures. At times, she struggles to control her own superpowers, symbolizing the challenges adolescents have in negotiating their worlds. Kamala's body changes as a result of the effect of Terrigenesis (her inhuman parts are activated by a magical mist) and in the beginning, these changes are often beyond her power to manage. At one point, she shrinks when hearing someone's voice and in another case, she loses control of her body at school, thus symbolizing a lack of agency.[23]

Kamala Khan's home is Jersey City, across the river from Manhattan, and is also an important element of the comic series. Ms. Marvel is a comic about urban problems—crime, in particular. This location allows Ms. Marvel to have proximity to the place around which the Marvel universe revolves—New York City.[24] Jersey City also plays an important role in Kamala's life as an American Muslim, as well as her family's larger community of diasporic South Asians.

Kamala and her family live in Jersey City, a location marked by the strong South Asian immigrant presence, but also by its diversity more broadly. Kamala's high school contains teenagers from various backgrounds (many of them Asian judging from their last names). Not only does Kamala feel an affinity for and desire to defend her own city, but this city is also legible and recognizable for readers who identify with Kamala.[25]

The first issue in the series introduces Kamala to other superheroes in the Marvel world. Carol Danvers, the original Ms. Marvel, appears in later issues and plays a central role in the series. Her presence is tied into Kamala's nerdy love of comics, which includes being a fan of *Ms. Marvel* comics.[26] Her status as a fangirl is an acknowledgment of the growing importance of the fangirl, who in addition to representing a large consumer base of comics, is also present at Comic Con and other fan-based gatherings for comic books and the movies they inspire. The typical fangirl, like Kamala, often goes as far as to emulate her heroes in fashion. "Fangirls pay attention to clothing and style as well as the treatment of female characters. They are not just fanboys with different genitalia."[27]

Ms. Marvel is in many ways a traditional superhero, reflecting the qualities of earlier superheroes in American comics, including the most iconic character of all—Superman. As scholars have noted, Superman laid the groundwork for the superheroes that followed him. "The genre assumed its contemporary form with the introduction of Superman in the pages of *Action Comics* in the late 1930s, whose commercial success inspired the creation of hundreds of broadly similar characters whose exploits have subsequently provided content for a full spectrum of visual and print media."[28]

Superman is, in the words of one scholar, "about as American as it gets."[29] One of the ways this is communicated is through his costume—a red and blue emblem of justice. Ms. Marvel's costume is reminiscent of Superman's, with the addition of a yellow lightning bolt Instead of a cape she has a loosely worn scarf—a symbol of her Muslim identity. Superman and Ms. Marvel represent the colors associated with patriotism, but Kamala's Pakistani-American identity is expressed through numerous storylines, including interactions with her parents, friends, and others.

Kamala Khan's Pakistani immigrant identity is a central part of the narrative in the series. In one scene in the sixth volume, which takes place during the partition of India, Kamala's mom states that she does not feel they belong on Earth. This foreshadowing of Kamala's alien status is also found in Superman, who is an otherworldly immigrant. Many superheroes in the comic world come from other places and as such, they are immigrants. This gives them special qualities. As one scholar puts it, "All of these characters, despite their various powers and realms, have one thing in common—they are archetypal visions of 'the good guy.' Many are from faraway galaxies; they fight crime in the name of perfect justice."[30]

Ms. Marvel and Superman are both overtly religious characters. As this chapter discusses, Kamala often reflects on her religion as well as her identity as a Muslim. Superman is a very Jewish character, shaped by the Jewish identities of Superman's cocreators, Jerry Siegel and Joe Schuster, who were sons of refugees.[31] The refugee experience can be seen in the story of Superman, who is exiled. As one scholar notes,

> Sent across galaxies in a tiny spaceship by desperate parents from the doomed planet Krypton, Superman's back story invokes the almost four-thousand-year-old story of Moses. Similarly, Superman's otherworldly strength is reminiscent of Samson, whom the Old Testament describes as owing his power to long locks of hair.[32]

American exceptionalism is another theme that is identified in both Ms. Marvel and Superman. Kamala's family represents the success of the immigrant experience. While the Khan family has struggles, including a rebellious daughter and what the parents see as an overly religious son, their economic and social success is evident. Superman is a character who often emphasizes American exceptionalism. His adventures over the past seventy-nine years have included numerous cases of America being cast as special or even superior to the rest of the world. In one case, Superman's quest is to save the world by "trying to feed the entire human population in twenty-four hours by correcting a historic problem by bringing US surplus food to where it is most needed across the planet."[33]

Despite the ways in which she reflects Superman, Ms. Marvel is also revolutionary. She represents a diverse, socially progressive, and politically active youth culture. This is reflected both in the emergence of minority superheroes in recent years and in the fan base of series like *Ms. Marvel.* As Wilson has pointed out, the conversation surrounding the underrepresentation of minorities in comics has radically altered in recent years.

> I think that's because fandom has reached a critical mass of people who are minorities but who make up a higher and higher percentage of fandom. Nowadays, when you go to a convention, it's pretty much a 50–50 split between male and female attendees. You have more and more LGBT people who want better and more accurate representation, more and more people of color who are interested in comics.[34]

The intersectionality represented in recent comics is important. Historically, superheroes have often been predominately white men, but in recent years, there has been an explosion in minority lead characters. These include a female Thor; Miles Morales, the Latino/African American Spiderman; and a black female MIT student, Riri Williams, as the new Ironman.[35]

The myth of American exceptionalism is part of the appeal of Ms. Marvel. "The story of the immigrant overcoming fantastic odds and making good in a new land of opportunity is a contemporary and still very plausible democratic fairy tale which is highly translatable to other cultures with similar ideals."[36] There are critiques of this narrative including one that argues, "But the cookie cutter immigrant story here is not so revolutionary."[37]

Another, perhaps more serious critique is that Kamala's questioning of her faith reifies Islamophobic sentiments about Islam, that Islam a religion that always needs to be questioned. Meher Ahmad argues that this is a serious problem in the series, one that misrepresents the lived realities of Muslim-American life.

> Leaving her faith as merely a sub-identity, as with any other Marvel character, won't do. She's Marvels' first Muslim American lead, and it seems that one can't be Muslim in America, fictional or not, without questioning the religion's legitimacy or struggling with some sort of internal crisis regarding the faith. It would be more realistic—albeit less exotic—if Kamala took Islam for granted, as so many American Muslims do.[38]

This opinion is not shared by the majority of scholars, who see Ms. Marvel as a strongly Muslim character. As the next chapter illustrates, this is communicated in a number of ways in the series. For *Ms. Marvel*'s fan base, which includes Muslims, this comic speaks to the experiences of their lives. It can be argued that it even falls in the emerging genre of the Muslim comic, a text that highlights cultural and religious themes.

> When reading *Ms. Marvel* through this culturally specific lens, one can see that, although on the surface her story is heroic and fantastic entertainment, her Muslim readers may also already be attuned to the political messages beneath the surface though their cultural and (trans)national readership practices. Just as with Indian comics, *Ms. Marvel* recognizes an existing, but often overlooked group of comic book consumers by crafting a superhero who moves beyond a purely Western context and location.[39]

ADVENTURES OF AN AMERICAN MUSLIM SUPERHEROINE

At the time this book was written, Marvel had published seven trade paperback volumes of *Ms. Marvel*, comprising the first twelve issues.[40] Kamala, although Pakistani and Muslim, does not appear to be Muslim in a stereotypical way. Unlike the vast majority of other Muslim comic book characters, she has no turban, or scimitar. As we have seen, Orientalist fashion has often identified Muslim characters. Nicholaus Pumphrey has said,

> There were figures such as Sinbad, the typical orientalist pirate with which most Americans are familiar. He often wore a turban, pointy shoes, and rescued

damsels, dressed like belly dancers, from monsters and jinn. Another was the Arabian Knight, Abdul Qamar, who also wore a turban, Turkish styled trousers, and pointy shoes. He was bearded, flew a magic carpet, brandished a large scimitar and was meant to be the Arab version of Nick Fury.[41]

Ms. Marvel is a very different kind of Muslim character. Her daily interactions with family and friends reveal a Muslim identity, but it is not an identity that relies on the stereotypes usually in force in graphic narratives. Islam plays a prominent role in the series, but it is presented as an integral part of Kamala, not as a costume or accouterment. Instead of presenting Islam as an accessory, or a series of tropes, Ms. Marvel instead offers nuanced, complex portrayals of Muslims.

Each of the six *Ms. Marvel* volumes focuses upon Kamala Khan's Muslim identity in different ways. At times, the theme of gender comes up, such as in Kamala's interactions with her brother, parents, and the imam at the local mosque. In other cases, a deep theological issue is woven within the narrative. The following discussion highlights some of the more prominent ways in which Islamic themes are presented in *Ms. Marvel*. I do not include every instance of a Muslim character, theme, or symbol, but we can see how the creators of Ms. Marvel interweave the concerns of the superhero with her religious identity.

The first volume of *Ms. Marvel* (2015) introduces the reader to Kamala, an American teenager living with her Pakistani family in Jersey City. The focus of this issue is on Kamala's transformation from a human to a superhero, an act that is predicated on her rebelliousness and independence. On the way home from a party she had snuck out of her house to attend, she is overcome with the magical mist that causes Terrigenesis. This moment activates the non-human part of her that has been latent since birth. Visually it is represented as a religious experience, complete with clouds, an Urdu poem, and references that are both Christological (the scene resembles the paintings of Jesus's assumption) and Islamic (the inclusion of birds has resonances of Attar's classic text on spiritual transformation).

However, *Vol. 1: No Normal* also includes other scenes in which Kamala struggles with her identity as an American, a Muslim, and a teenager. In the opening scene, Kamala leans over a case of sandwiches that include BLTs, and says, "Delicious, delicious infidel meat."[42] Her statement is met with disapproval from her Muslim friend Nakia, whom Kamala calls Kiki to annoy her. When Nakia protests, Kamala jokes, "Sorry Nakia. Proud Turkish Nakia doesn't need 'Amreeki' nickname. I get it."[43] Another scene takes place after her transformation into a superhero. She returns home and is confronted by her brother and parents (their parental titles are Abu and Ammi), who all disapprove of Kamala sneaking out at night to attend a party. At one point, her mother exclaims, "See how the children turned out? See? One sneaks out to parties with **boys** and the other dresses like a **penniless mullah**."[44]

Figure 3.1 Kamala and Ms. Marvel in the clouds, Issue #1. © Marvel.

These two scenes illustrate the ways in which Kamala and her family use humor to defuse challenging social situations. In the first case, Kamala pokes fun at her own identity as well as the rules surrounding what is *halal* (permissible) and *haram* (forbidden) in Islam. In the second case, Kamala's mother does the same by presenting two different expressions of Islam in her children—one that is liberative (Kamala) and another that is more traditional (Aamir). Wilson provides the reader with a way to access Kamala's world through humor, a common technique in comics. As scholars have argued, humor is often used to counter ignorance and bigotry.

> When the proximity of multiple ethnic groups engenders jokes displaying diverse perspectives and what Henri Bergson described as "corrective" satire, such jokes can help remedy racism and fear of the other. Taking a humorous or satirical stance allows artists and writers to explore alternatives to contemporary reality and to uncover truths overlooked or consciously elided by government and mass media discourse.[45]

The second volume of the series (*Ms. Marvel Vol. 2: Generation Why*) introduces the character Lockjaw, a giant bulldog-type canine creature who, like Kamala, is a member of the Inhumans. He is 1240 pounds, has superhuman strength, and can teleport. Lockjaw adds a healthy dose of comic relief to the comic, which is focused on Kamala's battle with a villain known as The Inventor. While Ms. Marvel's rescue of children from the clutches of this madman is the primary narrative at the center of this issue, there are several moments in which Islam is seen to be an important part of Kamala's life journey. Among these is the moment when she and Wolverine (a popular Marvel character from the *X-Men*) bid farewell after rescuing several children and surviving being crushed together in a giant trash compactor—an ode to the famous scene in *Star Wars* and its feminist princess Leia, who, like Kamala, saves herself in numerous dangerous situations. Kamala reflects on all that has just happened and thinks, "It occurs to me that Sheikh Abdullah was right. When the student is ready, the master will appear."[46]

Kamala's reflection on Sheikh Abdullah (the religious leader at her local mosque) is significant for two reasons. First, it reveals that despite her independent spirit, she recognizes the wisdom in the Islamic tradition. Second, and perhaps more importantly, the appearance of a master and the readiness of the student to learn from him (or her) is symbolized in her relationship with Wolverine, whom she looks up to. Wolverine is a powerful figure who resembles the Sufi sages in Islam in several ways. He has lived a long time, born in southern Alberta at the turn of the twentieth century.[47] He appears and disappears, offering guidance to Kamala and then leaving, much like the *awliya* (saints) in Islamic stories of the Friends of God.[48]

Kamala and Wolverine have important similarities. As scholars have noted, Wolverine is Canadian. He is an immigrant to the United States like Kamala and Superman. Similar to the presence of Pakistani culture in *Ms. Marvel*, Wolverine's Canadian origins are often referenced in the various storylines in which he appears. As Vivian Zenari has written, in one case, Logan (Wolverine's alias) describes Canada in nostalgic terms, "a vast beautiful place, with trees and lakes and mountains covered with snow . . . and clean, fresh air, and fantastic wild creatures, a place with beauties . . . and dangers, and all the wonders in nature."[49] (In the film *Logan* (2017), he dies near the Canadian border, signifying his attempt to return home). Both Kamala and Wolverine are mutants. As is revealed in the sixth volume, Kamala's origins are other-worldy, thus making her one of the Inhumans. Wolverine is a different kind of mutant, one born out of modern biotechnology.

> As the X-Men mythos goes, Wolverine is thought to be the product of military experimentation on humans, using biotechnologies to craft the ultimate fighting machine, with an anatomical structure fortified by a near-indestructible metal, and a biology designed to efficiently regenerate and repair itself in response to injury. Wolverine bears the markers of both industrial technology (his cyborg-like metallic claws) as well as contemporary biotechnology (the flesh wounds that we see healing right before our eyes).[50]

A third way in which Kamala and Wolverine are similar is that they both can heal themselves. In the first volume, Kamala heals herself from a fatal-seeming gunshot wound. Wolverine is a "rapid healer" whose bones are unbreakable.[51] The *X-Men* series, with Wolverine arguably the most popular character, has engendered numerous postcolonial readings. Scholars have pointed to the themes of inclusion, including the focus on anti-Semitism and LGBTQ issues. Like Kamala, the "mutant" status of the *X-Men* is about social inclusion—of Jews, queers, immigrants, and Muslims. As P. Andrew Miller argues, an "important aspect of the X-Men is its series-encompassing theme of prejudice and bigotry."[52] As one of the creators has remarked, "I wanted to spotlight a group of innocent people who were feared and shunned and later hunted and persecuted."[53] This is, of course, an apt description of the status of American Muslims in the age of Islamophobia.

The third volume of Ms. Marvel is titled *Crushed*, a reference to her ill-fated romance with Kamran, a striking young man her parents try to set her up with. At the outset, Kamala is smitten with him. He is handsome, smooth, romantic, and polite. However, by the end of this issue it is revealed that Kamran is not what he seems. He is, in fact, a villain who kidnaps Kamala and then blames her predicament on her own choices. What is most interesting about the final scenes between Kamran and Kamala is how they mirror the language of rape culture. At one point, Kamala says, "I never thought anything like this would happen! I thought—I thought it mean something else when we were together—something good." To this Kamran responds, "Who's gonna believe that? You got in my car of your own free will. As far as anybody knows, you chose to be here. **You** put yourself in this situation."[54] Blaming the victim of a criminal act (in this case, kidnapping) reflects the bias to which females—even female superheroes—are held.

In addition to the Muslim romance and heartbreak attached to Kamala in this issue, there are other moments when Islam plays an important role. In the first part of the issue Kamala, her brother Aamir, and Kamran are caught up in an attack. After it is over and Kamala is found safe, Aamir embraces her and exclaims, "Al-Hamdulillah!*" The comic includes an asterisk and a text box that says, "Praise be to God."[55] This is one of many moments in the series where an explanation or translation is provided for the reader. This particular episode communicates Aamir's thankfulness for his sister's safety, expressed in his thanking God. Both endearing and an example of religious literacy, the translation of the character's religious values here helps the reader understand Islam better.

Ms. Marvel Vol. 4: Last Days is a darker and more serious volume focused on the kidnapping of Aamir by Kamran and his rescue. Vol. 4 begins with Manhattan being overtaken by dark forces, then moves on to Aamir's kidnapping, poisoning, and near death—all at the hands of Kamala's former love interest, Kamran. Kamran knows that Aamir is an Inhuman and tries to transform him for his own purposes, but Aamir remains in control of his own powers. The rescue of Aamir also sets up an important encounter between Kamala and her close friend Bruno.

Up to this point in the series, Aamir is represented as the super-religious brother who lectures Kamala on her behavior and passes judgment on her moral choices. He leans toward the Salafi brand of Islam—attending mosque religiously, wearing traditional clothing, and choosing to wear a beard (an emulation of Prophet Muhammad). Aamir and Kamala represent the dichotomy between the "traditional" and "progressive" Muslim, which is a false division. It is revealed in this volume that Aamir is not just a religious "follower"; to the contrary, he is a leader and an Inhuman. When Aamir awakens from the coma Kamran has put him in, he stands up for his religious identity, his sister, and his family:

I'm a what? A religious freak? An MSA* nerd? A Salafi? Yeah. I'm all of those things. And I'm not ashamed of any of them. And if you think that means you can take advantage of my sister—that I'll blame **her** for whatever happened between you, while **you** sashay off into the sunset 'cause you're a guy and nothing is ever your fault. Well, my brother, you are **incorrect**.[56]

The message that Aamir's character expresses is that Muslims are often judged by their appearances. Just as Kamala appears to be "liberal" because she doesn't wear the veil, Nakia appears to be "religious" because she wears the veil. What this tells us, much like Aamir's Salafi presentation—through his dress and speech—is that Muslims in America are often judged in unfair ways. Indeed, Salafi Muslims are very misunderstood, both in the United States and other locations.

> Islam's devotional and mystical tradition, Sufism (*tasawwuf*), is commonly cast as antithetical to Salafi Islam. Self-identified "Salafism," with their ideological roots in anti-liberal strands of twentieth-century modernist Islam, commonly view Sufis as heretics propagating practices wrongly introduced in Islam centuries after the time of the pious ancestors (the Salaf). Yet the reformist zeal that fixes on the singular importance of the Salaf (particularly the Prophet Muhammad and his principal companions) as models for correct piety can also be found amongst Sufis.[57]

The other main storyline in Vol. 4 is the unrequited love between Kamala and Bruno. Kamala's true feelings for her best friend Bruno are revealed, as are his for her. Ultimately Kamala admits they cannot be together, not because of cultural and religious differences (he is Italian, she is Pakistani)—but because her responsibilities as a superhero are too great. A hero's focus on her duties at the cost of a personal relationship is a common theme in comics. Superman, Batman, Captain America, and Spiderman all end up single.

Vol. 4 also includes an important reference to Kamala's religious education at the mosque where once again, the sheikh's wisdom is highlighted. The issue begins with a long conversation between Carol Danvers—the original Ms. Marvel—and Kamala. While star struck, Kamala listens to Danvers' words intently, which include, "But **your** fate—what you decide to do right now—is still up to you. That's what I came here to tell you. The airlifts and the heroes and the money–they're not coming to Jersey City. You're **it**, Ms. Marvel. Today is the day **you** stand up."[58] Kamala's response to this is expressed in thought bubbles in the comic. "What she's saying–weirdly, it makes me think of one of Sheikh Abdullah's lectures." "We all face the end alone, he said, and we alone have to account for our time on earth." "The good and the bad." "'What will be in the book of your life?' He used to ask, 'How will you be remembered?'"[59]

These last lines are profound, representing one of Islam's central beliefs about moral conduct. The Islamic rules for moral conduct, called *adab*, are connected to obeying the Divine order.[60] One who has good *adab* will be judged accordingly at the end of their life. This is what the sheik refers to in the aforementioned episode. Kamala's recognition of the importance of right morality is a recognition of *adab*, which, as a *Muslimah* superhero, she represents. Like other superheroes, Kamala is a vessel of goodness, what one

Sufi master, quoting Prophet Muhammad, describes as, "God has shown His majesty to humankind through these virtues (*adab*). These virtues are through personal training, to light the flints to set a fire to a pure and virtuous life."[61]

Ms. Marvel Vol. 5: Super Famous uses a comedic formula centered upon Kamala multiplying numerous times after a mishap in the school science laboratory. The clones appear as zombie-like, and in one scene, they appear as an army of Kamalas, uttering phrases like "Easy pleasy" and "Shaadi mubarakbad!"[62] Much of the issue is focused on how to get rid of these clones. This predicament intersects with Aamir's engagement and marriage to an African-American Muslim, Tyesha. This is a key religious plotline in the series and touches upon difficult cultural issues. Tyesha's parents and Aamir's parents are equally uncomfortable with their children marrying each other, out of concerns surrounding compatibility. During their initial meeting at the Khans' home, one of Kamala's clones appears and at one point, melts because she is served chai. As Bruno and Kamala talk on the phone, both absent from her house, "Wait . . . you don't think your mom will try to serve it **chai**, do you?" Kamala answers, "Yeah, probably . . . why?" Bruno exclaims, "The golems can't ingest fluids! The outer skin is **waterproof**, but inside, they're totally **soluble!**"[63] At the engagement party a week later, a giant Kamala clone wreaks havoc on the celebrations.

Following the disastrous engagement party, a week later Aamir and Tyesha have a wedding party. In this scene, we see Aamir's insecurities expressed. He worries whether his relatives will accept Tyesha because she is not South Asian and more pointedly, because she is African-American. Kamala eases her brother's concerns and then, as the bride arrives, she is wearing a *shalwar kameez* to please her new husband. At the same time, he wears a *kurta*, which the text explains, is a "Traditional West African formal attire for men."[64] These gestures illustrate the love the two characters have for each other as well as the mixing of cultures that is often a part of American Muslim experience. The scene ends with the line, "Home is the most important thing in the world."[65]

The issue ends with a number of images of Kamala from various artists. The first is a full-page picture of Kamala, pushing the buzzer on her alarm clock. She has slept in her costume and in the background various framed photos of her life sit on the wall, including one where a girl, perhaps Kamala, wears a headscarf. On the corner of her bed lies a doll of Carol Danvers with blonde hair and in costume. This image expresses the conflicts in Kamala's life—she is Muslim, she is a female, she is a teenager, and she is a superhero. The look on her face is one of exhaustion and resignation.

Ms. Marvel Vol. 6. Civil War II is a powerful issue that includes current political content, the story of Ms. Marvel's origins as an Inhuman, and religious material. In one of its boldest political statements about Islam, the series makes clear the Muslim support for queer allies. This is expressed in the relationship between Zoe and Nakia. The relationship is intimated

Figure 3.2   Ms. Marvel #1 Variant, by Sara Pichelli and Justin Ponsor, Issue #6. © Marvel.

in earlier issues, when Zoe admits she is jealous of Kamala (presumably because of her close friendship with Nakia) and in one scene, in which Zoe refers to Nakia as "my baby."[66] In Vol. 6, it is clear than Zoe has feelings for Nakia, representing one of the few references to queer Muslim issues in popular culture.[67] In Issue 16, titled "Damage Per Second," it is revealed that Nakia does not share Zoe's feelings. However, instead of rejecting her friend (who has just professed her love to her), Nakia embraces Zoe—a symbol of the affection many Muslims feel for the LGBTQ people in their lives.[68]

The sixth volume of *Ms. Marvel* also includes strong political themes that involve the War on Terror. The topic of extrajudicial arrest and detainment dominates the issue. Kamala loses and finds herself in this volume. She initially supports the arrest of individuals who have not committed a crime but might do in the future, a policy supported by Carol Danvers. Danvers, along with a group of volunteers known as "Cadets," convinces Kamala that the threat of future and possible crimes justifies giving up one's liberties. An obvious meditation on the War on Terror and the U.S. Patriot Act, this story costs Kamala dearly when she loses Bruno's friendship.

This loss proves to be devastating for Kamala, who is heartbroken over the loss of her friend. It brings us to the penultimate subject in this issue, and arguably in the entire *Ms. Marvel* series, which involves Kamala's origins. In the middle of the volume, during a flashback to the time when Kamala's mother Muneeba was pregnant with her, we learn that she had a sense that there was something special about her heritage. Muneeba has a conversation with her mother, who has just put down Aamir for sleep, about the special sense she has. She says, "Sometimes I look up at the **stars** and I feel like I've **already** traveled thousands and thousands of miles . . . and when I'm carrying a **child**, I feel it even more. Is that strange? Is there something **wrong** with me?" Her mother responds, "No, *jaanu*. There's nothing wrong with you." The scene closes with Muneeba saying, "I've always thought that there is some . . . some **secret** we carry, a **strength** that is waiting to appear."[69]

At the end of the volume, after her disappointment with Carol Danvers and the loss of Bruno as a friend, Kamala visits her parent's homeland Pakistan. Here Ms. Marvel comes full circle, fulfilling the prophecy that her mother sensed was within her while pregnant with Aamir and Kamala—who it turns out, are both special. After meeting the handsome Kareem (who is staying at the same relative's house as Kamala) and beginning to adjust to her new environment, Kamala immerses herself in prayer and self-reflection. In one panel, she is shown at morning (*fajr*) prayer, and in another, riding horses. However, Kamala cannot escape her superhero identity and after several attacks by criminals and terrorists, and a failed attempt at a purely civilian life, she improvises a costume. It is composed of a red scarf, which she uses to cover her hair and face, a blue tunic with yellow decorative trim, and red leggings.

Figure 3.3 Ms. Marvel in Pakistan with face veil, Issue #12. © Marvel.

She meets another superhero—the Red Dagger, who is likely Kareem. The scene ends with Kamala reflecting on her identity. She muses on her time away from home, "I didn't find the missing pieces of my life in Karachi, because . . . The missing pieces aren't part of a **place**. They're part of **me**. They're things only **I** can figure out."[70]

MS. MARVEL'S BODY, SENSUALITY, AND THE VEIL

In the previous section, I tried to show how *Ms. Marvel* functions as an Islamic teaching text—one that presents Islamic values and difficult issues that affect American Muslims, and offers theology in the form of a graphic narrative. All of these strategies help to make Ms. Marvel a relevant superhero—one that is clearly Muslim, albeit in ways that are not stereotypical. In the last section of this chapter, I return to the subject of Kamala and in particular, to her body, for the body of the female superhero is a central theme of this book.

Because *Muslimah* superheroes are relatively new to American popular culture, they are not subjected to the same symbolic systems that Wonder Woman or Supergirl are. Typically, these latter characters are judged by their bodily curves. "Voluptuousness is the standard by which superheroines are measured."[71] Neither Kamala nor her alter-ego is voluptuous, and although strong and fit, this characteristic is compromised by her own body, her age, and the challenges posed by puberty. Kamala's struggles with adolescence include frustration, a feeling also seen in her superhero alter-ego. Ms. Marvel's ability to change shapes—she is a polymorph—is symbolic of Kamala's own reckoning with her changing body, emotions, and maturity.

Kamala is a nerd and this, coupled with her status as a Muslim teenage girl, renders her de-sexualized. She never expresses real desire and even her attraction to Kamran is not acted upon. Even her athleticism—a hallmark of superheroes like Wonder Woman—is downplayed. There is no Olympic body or "masculinized" form.[72] Other teenage female superheroes are presented as sensual, but *Ms. Marvel* deviates from this formula. As Karen McGrath has written, in the Latina teenage superhero Araña, "female desirability is depicted in her body type (thin waist, fuller hips, larger breasts) and its display," which includes her "willingness to objectify her own body" and her choice of costume, "that is age appropriate for the teenager she is, yet still accentuates her full breasts, slim waist, and fuller hips, which ultimately sexualize her for these voyeurs."[73] Ms. Marvel, in contrast, is portrayed with small breasts and a low apex; her stance is at times pigeon-toed, and in some cases she is drawn from the side and at a distance, making her body and features "cartoonish, thereby removing a great deal of the potential for sexualization."[74] Ms. Marvel, though confident in her moments as a superhero, persists in the role of a nerd. Scholars have called this the "ultimate androgyny of the superbody."[75]

Ms. Marvel's costuming is a creation of Kamala. Initially she makes herself into a blonde Carol Danvers, but quickly realizes that this is not who she is. Her bodysuit, as the above discussion suggests, is part of what de-sexualizes her. It is modest, even when it fits snugly on her body. It comprises a blue tunic with a yellow lightning design on the front, a red undergarment that resembles a leotard with long sleeves and leggings, and blue boots. Even when Ms. Marvel is drawn as a blonde superhero (a signification of her emulation of Carol Danvers), she is not like the sexed-up superheroines of past comic books. Ms. Marvel is an example of the "girl power" movement that is shaped by power feminism, but unlike many of the products tied to the movement, does exploit the female body.[76] The use of clothing, both on Kamala and Ms. Marvel, communicates modesty, independence, and respect for one's body. As Kristin Peterson has written, "When she is just a regular teenager, Kamala wears jeans, sneakers, and her comic book t-shirts, refusing to appear as a sexual object of attraction for men. She creates her Ms. Marvel costume in a way that shows pride in her religion, culture and comic book fandom."[77]

Kamala uses different types of veiling throughout the *Ms. Marvel* series. Most commonly Ms. Marvel's costume features a "deconstructed" veil, a scarf that appears as a long, red piece of fabric. It is worn tied loosely around her neck. In some panels, it is flowing behind her, such as in Vol. 5, where it shown waving in a breeze as Kamala walks down a street with Bruno and his girlfriend Mike. In other instances, such as in Vol. 2, it has a thin, yellow border and what appears to be a star outlined in yellow at one end. In a few cases, Kamala is shown wearing a traditional *hijab* or headscarf as part of a religious event or occasion. In the first volume of *Ms. Marvel*, Kamala attends a mosque service with her friend Nakia, wearing a headscarf that is the same color as Ms. Marvel's, suggesting that the costume of the superhero incorporates an important religious sign from Kamala's life. In Vol. 2, Kamala wears the same *hijab* when she meets with the sheikh, which, a few panels later, appears as part of Ms. Marvel's costume. This transition shows how the two lives—the Muslim teenager and the superhero—involve the translation of an object that gives power to its wearer. As I discuss in the last chapter of this book, veiling/unveiling is one way for Muslim girls and women to control their body. This is precisely what Kamala and her alter-ego Ms. Marvel do.

The transition from Kamala to Ms. Marvel is expressed in other ways. In Vol. 3, Kamala's headscarf doubles as a *hijab*. But even more interesting is what happens when she leaves the mosque.

When she is at the mosque, the red scarf that is used as a superhero cape doubles as a modest head covering for prayer. After prayer is over, Kamala puts on her

Ms. Marvel lightning bolt sweatshirt over her Pakistani tunic and drapes her scarf back over her neck. She is shown in one image, walking down the street with a unique combination of clothing items: her Pakistani-style tunic, a Ms. Marvel sweatshirt, and her superhero cape/modest headscarf for prayer.[78]

In addition to this double use of the scarf, Ms. Marvel shows an additional way Muslim women use clothing—in this case, to protect their identity. Perhaps the most "covered" Kamala appears is in *Ms. Marvel Vol. 6: Civil War II*, when she wears a headscarf when visiting her relatives in Pakistan as well as in her adventures as a superhero. At one point, when she appears as Ms. Marvel, she uses the scarf as a face veil to disguise herself. Like Burka Avenger, Ms. Marvel uses veiling in a way that hides her identity from the very people who would force her to veil against her will. This, *the subversive veil*, is the focus of the following chapter.

NOTES

1. Cord Scott, "Written in Red, White, and Blue: A Comparison of Comic Book Propaganda from World War II and September 11," *The Journal of Popular Culture* 40, no. 2 (2007): 336.
2. Cord Scott, "Written in Red, White, and Blue," 337.
3. Keith T. Edmunds, "Heroines Aplenty, but None My Mother Would Know: Marvel's Lack of an Iconic Superheroine," in *Heroines of Comic Books and Literature: Portrayals in Popular Culture*, ed. Maja Bajac-Carter, Norma Jones, and Bob Batchelor (New York: Rowman and Littlefield, 2014): 212.
4. Vivian Zenari, "Mutant Mutandis: The X-Men's Wolverine and the Construction of Canada," in *Culture and the State 3: Nationalisms*, ed. James Gifford and Gabrielle Zezulka-Mailloux (Edmonton: CRC Humanities Studies, 2003): 55.
5. Abdul Halim Jaffer Khan, "Hazrat Amir Khusro," *Journal of the Indian Musicological Society* 4, no. 2 (1973): 1, 19.
6. Seyyed Hossein Nasr, *Islamic Art and Spirituality* (Albany: State University of New York Press, 1987): 98.
7. Ernesto Priego, "Ms. Marvel: Metamorphosis and Transfiguration of the 'Minority' Superhero," *The Winnower* (May 11, 2016): 4.
8. Winona Landis, "Diasporic (Dis)Identification: The Participatory Fandom of Ms. Marvel," *South Asian Popular Culture* 14, nos. 1/2 (2016): 41.
9. Abigail Olcese, "Real Life, with Superpowers," *Sojourners* (2015): 39.
10. Molly Hannon, "Kamala Khan, Marvel Superhero Fights Real-Life Racism," *The Daily Beast*, February 15, 2015, http://www.thedailybeast.com/articles/2015/02/15/kamala-khan-marvel-superhero-fights-real-life-racism.html (accessed February 18, 2017).
11. Stephanie Juliano, "Superheroes, Bandits, and Cyber-nerds: Exploring the History and Contemporary Development of the Vigilante," *Journal of International Commercial Law and Technology* 7, no. 1 (2012): 44.

12. Caryn Neumann and Lori Parks, "The Fan and the Female Superhero in Comic Books," *Journal of Fandom Studies* 3, no. 3 (2015): 294.

13. Rae Hancock, "Comic Books in the Classroom," *Prep School* 85 (2016): 60.

14. Max Skidmore and Joey Skidmore, "More Than Mere Fantasy: Political Themes in Contemporary Comic Books," *The Journal of Popular Culture* 17, no. 1 (1983): 88.

15. Eliana Dockterman, "Behind Marvel's Decision to Create These Controversial Female Superheroes," *Time,* August 28, 2015, time.com/4014894/marvel-female-superheroes-thor-ms-marvel/ (accessed February 16, 2017).

16. Emine Saner, "Ms. Marvel: Send for the Muslim Supergirl!" *The Guardian,* January 1, 2014, https://www.theguardian.com/culture/2014/jan/01/ms-marvel-muslim-superhero-graphic-novel (accessed February 9, 2017).

17. Molly Hannon, "The Subversive and Liberating World of G. Willow Wilson," *Los Angeles Review of Books*, February 14, 2015, https://lareviewofbooks.org/article/subversive-liberating-world-g-willow -wilson/ (accessed February 13, 2017).

18. Ronald Schmitt, "Deconstructive Comics," *The Journal of Popular Culture* 15, no. 4 (1992): 155.

19. Nicholaus Pumphrey, "Avenger, Mutant, or Allah: A short Evaluation of the Depiction of Muslims in Marvel Comics," *The Muslim World* 106, no. 4 (2016): 791.

20. John M. Trushell, "American Dreams of Mutants: The X-Men—'Pulp' Fiction, Science Fiction, and Superheroes," *The Journal of Popular Culture* 38, no. 1 (2004): 153.

21. Ibid.

22. Margaret Robbins, "Female Representation in Comics and Graphic Novels: Exploring Classroom Study with Critical Visual Literacy," *SIGNAL Journal* (Fall 2014/Winter 2015): 13.

23. Catherine Clark, "'Holy Agency, Batgirl!': Evaluating Young Adult Superheroines' Agency in Gotham Academy and Ms. Marvel'" (Honors thesis, Trinity University, 2016): 33.

24. Dilshad D. Ali, "Interview: G. Willow Wilson on the Creation of the Newest Muslim-American Comic Superhero," *Patheos*, November 8, 2013, http://www.patheos.com/blogs/altmuslim/2013/11/interview-g-willow-wilson-on-the-creation-of-the-newest-muslim-american-comic-superhero/

25. Winona Landis, "Diasporic (Dis)Identifications," 37–38.

26. George Gene Gustines, "She's Mighty, Muslim and Leaping off the Page," *New York Times*, November 6, 2013: C3.

27. Neumann and Parks, "The Fan and the Female Superhero in Comic Books." *Journal of Fandom Studies* 3 no. 3 (2015): 293.

28. Matthew J. Costello and Kent Worcester, "Introduction. Symposium: The Politics of the Superhero," *Political Science* 47, no. 1 (2014): 85.

29. Michael Soares, "The Man of Tomorrow: *Superman* from American Exceptionalism to Globalization," *The Journal of American Popular Culture* 48, no. 4 (2015): 747.

30. Jamie A. Hughes, "'Who Watches the Watchmen?': Ideology and 'Real World' Superheroes," *The Journal of Popular Culture* 39, no. 4 (2006): 546.

31. Michael Soares, "The Man of Tomorrow," 748.

32. Michael Soares, "The Man of Tomorrow," 748.

33. Michael Soares, "The Man of Tomorrow," 751.

34. Abraham Riesman, "Meet G. Willow Wilson, the Muslim Woman Revolutionizing Superhero Comics," *Vulture*, March 20, 2014, http://www.vulture.com/2014/03/g-willow-wilson-ms-marvel-kamala-khan-interview.html (accessed March 9, 2017).

35. Molly Driscoll, "Meet the New Iron Man: A Black Female Teenager," *The Christian Science Monitor*, July 7, 2016, http://www.csmonitor.com/The-Culture/Arts/2016/0707/Meet-the-new-Iron-Man-a-black-female-teenager (accessed February 17, 2017).

36. Michael Soares, "The Man of Tomorrow," 758.

37. Meher Ahmad, "Muslim Girl Superhero," *The Progressive* 78, no. 4 (2014): 44.

38. Meher Ahmad, "Muslim Girl Superhero," 45.

39. Winona Landis, "Diasporic (Dis)Identification," 39.

40. At the writing of this book (March 2017), issues 13 through 16 were available as original single issues. They will be released as part of a trade paperback (Volume 7) in the summer of 2017.

41. Nicholaus Pumphrey, "Avenger, Mutant, or Allah," 785.

42. G. Willow Wilson and Adrian Alphona, *Ms. Marvel Vol. 1: No Normal* (New York: Marvel, 2014), 1, n.p.

43. Wilson and Adrian Alphona, *Ms. Marvel Vol. 1: No Normal*, 1, n.p.

44. Wilson and Adrian Alphona, *Ms. Marvel Vol. 1: No Normal*, 2, n.p.

45. Jill E. Twark, "Approaching History as Cultural Memory Through Humour, Satire, Comics and Graphic Novels," *Contemporary European History* 26, no. 1 (2017): 176. See also Henri Bergson, *Laughter: An Essay on the Meaning of the Comic*, ed. Cloudesley Brereton, trans. Fred Rothwell (London: MacMillan and Green Integer, 1999), 21.

46. G. Willow Wilson, Jacob Wyatt, and Adrian Alphona, *Ms. Marvel Vol. 2: Generation Why* (New York: Marvel, 2015), 7, n.p.

47. Zenari, "Mutant Mutandis," 57.

48. John Renard, *Friends of God: Islamic Images of Piety, Commitment, and Servanthood* (Berkeley: University of California Press, 2008), 80.

49. Vivian Zenari, "Mutant Mutandis," 58. Also, see *Wolverine* 1.25.

50. Eugene Thacker, "Bio-X: Removing Bodily Contingency in Regenerative Medicine," *Journal of Medical Humanities* 23, nos. 3/4 (2002): 240.

51. Ramzi Fawaz, "'Where No X-Man Has Gone Before!': Mutant Superheroes and the Cultural Politics of Popular Fantasy in Postwar America," *American Literature* 83, no. 2 (2011): 363.

52. P. Andrew Miller, "Mutants, Metaphor, and Marginalism: What X-actly Do the X-Men Stand For?" *Journal of the Fantastic in the Arts* 13, no. 3 (2003): 283.

53. Douglas Martin, "The X-Men Vanquish America," *The New York Times* August 21, 1994, 27, quoted in Miller, "Mutants, Metaphor, and Marginalism," 283.

54. G. Willow Wilson, Elmo Bondoc, and Takeshi Miyazawa, *Ms. Marvel Vol. 3: Crushed* (New York: Marvel, 2015), 15, n.p.

55. Wilson, Bondoc, and Miyazawa, *Ms. Marvel Vol. 3: Crushed*, 13, no p.n.

56. G. Willow Wilson and Adrian Alphona, *Ms. Marvel Vol. 4: Last Days* (New York: Marvel, 2015), 18, n.p. The author explains in a bubble that MSA is the acronym for Muslim Students Association.

57. Julia Day Howell, "Indonesia's Salafist Sufis," *Modern Asian Studies* 44, no. 5 (2010): 1029–1030.

58. Wilson and Alphona, *Ms. Marvel Vol. 4: Last Days*, 17, n.p.

59. Wilson and Alphona, *Ms. Marvel Vol. 4: Last Days*, 17, n.p.

60. Qamar-ul Huda, "The Light beyond the Shore in the Theology of Proper Sufi Moral Conduct (Adab)," *Journal of the American Academy of Religion* 72, no. 2 (2004): 470.

61. Huda, "The Light beyond the Shore," 471. Huda quotes Shaykh al-Suhrawardi's *'Awârif al-Ma'ârif* (Cairo: Maktabat al-Qâhira, 1973), 250.

62. G. Willow Wilson, Takeshi Miyazawa, Adrian Alphona, and Nico Leon, *Ms. Marvel Vol. 5: Super Famous* (New York: Marvel, 2016), 4, n.p.

63. Wilson, Miyazawa, Alphona, and Leon, *Ms. Marvel Vol. 5: Super Famous*, 5, n.p.

64. Wilson, Miyazawa, Alphona, and Leon, *Ms. Marvel Vol. 5: Super Famous*, 5, n.p.

65. Ibid.

66. Wilson, Miyazawa, Leon, and Alphona, *Ms. Marvel Vol. 5* (New York: Marvel, 2016), 5, no p.n.

67. In 2011, the CBS show *The Good Wife* featured a storyline about two gay lovers—an Arab and a Jew—in which one is killed in a jealous rage.

68. G. Willow Wilson, Takeshi Miyazawa, and Ian Herring, *Ms. Marvel #16: Damage Per Second* (New York: Marvel, 2017), n.p.

69. G. Willow Wilson, Adrian Alphona, Takeshi Miyazawa, and Mirka Andolfo, *Ms. Marvel Vol. 6: Civil War II* (New York: Marvel, 2016). 9, no p.n.

70. Wilson, Alphona, Miyazawa, and Andolfo, *Ms. Marvel Vol. 6*, 12, no p.n.

71. Aaron Taylor, "'He's Gotta Be Strong, and He's Gotta Be Fast, and He's Gotta Be Larger Than Life': Investigating the Engendered Superhero Body," *The Journal of Popular Culture* 40, no. 2 (2007): 353.

72. Aaron Taylor, "'He's Gotta Be Strong,'" 356.

73. Karen McGrath, "Gender, Race, and Latina Identity: An Examination of Marvel Comics' Amazing Fantasy and Araña," *Atlantic Journal of Communication* 15, no. 4 (2007): 274.

74. Sara Marie Kern, "Females and Feminism Reclaim the Mainstream: New Superheroines in Marvel Comics" (master's thesis, Middle Tennessee State University, 2015), 94.

75. Aaron Taylor, "'He's Gotta Be Strong,'" 346.

76. Rebecca C. Hains, "Power Feminism, Mediated: Girl Power and the Commercial Politics of Change," *Women's Studies in Communication* 32, no. 1 (2009): 107.

77. Kristin M. Peterson, "More Than a Mask, Burkini and Tights: Fighting Misrepresentations through Ms. Marvel's Costume," (unpublished paper, University of Colorado, December 17, 2015), 9.

78. Kristin M. Peterson, "More Than a Mask, Burkini and Tights," 22–23.

Chapter 4

Burka Avenger and the Subversive Veil

In 2010, the Pakistani pop music star Haroon began work on *Burka Avenger*, an animated children's television series. The show features the schoolteacher Jiya and the adventures of her alter ego, Burka Avenger, a *Muslimah* superhero who wears a black *ninja*-like costume when she fights criminal elements like the Taliban. Burka Avenger is a powerful character—visually arresting and extremely entertaining. She is not simply a children's character, but an icon of Pakistani and Islamic feminism. Burka Avenger does not resort to Western styles of dress or politics in her quest for liberation. Instead, she relies on her own religious and cultural foundations, which are strongly Islamic.

Burka Avenger is significant for several reasons. For one, it is a Pakistani production, not an imported series from Hollywood. Pakistan, like much of the world, has a large number of imported forms of entertainment from the United States, including some, like *Cartoon Network*, geared toward children. In the case of animated cartoons, Disney has a huge reach; their products are found all over the world. As one scholar has remarked, Disney has a history of featuring white characters in privileged positions. In *Pocahontas* (1995), even the title character is subjected to her white lover's power. "The exoticized body of Pocahontas tells us it is only through a white man's fantasy about her that a woman of color can become a heroine and can have a romance with a white hero."[1] *Burka Avenger* represents a departure from these sorts of productions, with a *Muslimah* superhero created by Muslims.

Burka Avenger is an animated series, and as such, it functions in a different way than a comic or other graphic narrative. As Darcy Orcutt has written,

Comics constitute "multimodal" texts, those necessitating and facilitating understanding through multiple approaches to meaning-making. While their sensory grounding is normally visual, comic narratives evoke such multi-sensory experiences.[2]

Animation is a medium that evokes many senses. In Pakistan, a country in which attempts are made to exclude women from public view through seclusion and enforced veiling, *Burka Avenger* is an effort to counter these practices. While girls and women are subjected to *symbolic annihilation* in public, this is challenged by the visibility of an enormously powerful *Muslimah* superhero. This is important because of the power the media has in society. "Symbolic annihilation in the media is of concern because it presents people with implied messages about what it means to be a member of a culturally valued group versus a member of a socially disenfranchised group (or 'out group')."[3]

Animation gives life to elements that would otherwise be on the page. The movement inherent in a show like *Burka Avenger* draws the audience into an imaginary world that looks alive. Cultivation theory argues that "media viewers' perceptions of social reality will be shaped by extensive and cumulative exposure to media-provided messages" like those seen in animated children's series, which are then used to "make decisions about how they will behave in real-world settings and situations."[4] *Burka Avenger* is intended to influence the beliefs of its viewership—Pakistani children and adults—on issues of gender equity. As scholars have pointed out, animation affects how we see the world. In the case of children's animated cartoons, males have often been privileged over females, resulting in stereotyping of girls and women as weak, submissive, and unintelligent. As studies show, this has improved over the past decades, with female characters (at least in the American context) showing "more verbal aggression, ingenuity, and leadership."[5] These changes include the introduction of numerous female superheroes, both in American animated cartoons and internationally.

There are differences between comics and cartoons, but many animated films and television programs are based on comic book characters. Thus, they often follow narrative formulas that are commonly identified with graphic narratives such as comics and graphic novels. Among these are the characteristics of the superhero who, in the case of Burka Avenger, is quite reminiscent of Superman in several ways. First, Jiya is located in the countryside. She is often surrounded by animals and nature, including the prominent character of the goat Golu. The emphasis on the rural here is something we also see in Superman, whose character is molded by the goodness of nature. In *Burka Avenger*, Jiya's goodness is contrasted with the city and those who are associated with it, primarily criminal characters like Munna and Tinda.

Figure 4.1   Burka Avenger with city. Photo courtesy of Unicorn Black.

Jiya, like Superman, is also an orphan; in this way, she follows the tradition of parentless superheroes, a large group that includes Captain Marvel, Batman, and Spiderman. Although Jiya's adoption by Kabaddi Jan and his wife is significant, she is still a character who is shaped by loss. Like other superheroes, she seeks to do good in a world gone bad. As Jeffery Johnson has written, "Although one of Superman's primary roles is to serve as a proper moral influence, he also often takes the proactive stance of keeping assailants at bay and thus stops Metropolis from falling into the moral abyss that has overtaken Gotham City."[6]

Burka Avenger is also significant because she is a *Muslimah*. One of the ways the central character's Muslim identity is expressed is through Jiya's life story. Orphaned as a child, she is taken in by her neighbor Kabaddi Jan and his wife. Kabaddi is also the name of a martial art popular in Pakistan and India, and *jan* is a word used in Pakistan, Afghanistan, and elsewhere as a term of endearment.[7] This martial art plays a central role in the series. It is the physical practice that helps to balance Jiya and enables her to transform into a superhero. Much like her costume, which is called a *burka* but is fashioned after a ninja, Burka Avenger's use of martial arts is reminiscent of Buddhist spiritual practice. Hollywood has often included Buddhist iconography in film, most notably by directors George Lucas and Quentin Tarantino, whose inclusion of sword-fighting and other *wuxia* elements are well known. As one scholar notes, "The importance of a long and complex training in various techniques is a common feature of the so-called *wuxia* (Chinese martial arts movies)."[8] In addition to the costume style, one of the elements of *wuxia* seen in Burka Avenger is in the character of Kabaddi Jan, who is much like a Zen master—cast as "a mild-mannered and understanding father figure."[9] He teaches Jiya the physical and spiritual practices that, when balanced, allow her to cultivate her superpowers. Much like Luke Skywalker, Jiya benefits from a motif seen in *jidaigei* movies, where a commanding Zen master tries to "guide his apprentice to wisdom and train him spiritually as well as physically."[10]

The veil is an important visual tool in *Burka Avenger*, both through its absence and presence. Jiya does not wear the veil in her daily life as a school-teacher. A symbol of the choices women in Pakistan have, the absence of the veil represents the agency exercised by the main character regarding her body. Girls and women often face pressures to wear the *hijab* in Pakistan. The use of veiling by Jiya's alter ego, Burka Avenger is an important recognition of the right of Muslim women to wear what they want, including the veil. The superhero uses veiling, her ninja-like *niqab,* to hide her body, representing a play on the idea that women need to be hidden. In this case, she uses it as a disguise, thus turning the tables on those who would compel her to wear it. As scholars have written, the veil is a practice based on the "presumption of an active female sexuality" that limits the possibility of the unleashing of the "uncontrolled sexual energy" attached to girls and women.[11]

Debate over whether the *burka* is a symbol of oppression or liberation has dominated much of the public discourse surrounding *Burka Avenger.* Writer Bina Shah has commented that the superhero's veiling makes her invisible, while journalist Mahvesh Murad stated, "When she takes back the power of the burka, she's taking back the power of every woman."[12] As for the creators of the show, which include the pop star Haroon, they firmly believe that the *burka* is a sign of her Muslim identity. As they have commented "We did not want her dressed half-naked like most Western superheroes, because she is a Muslim superhero."[13] Such a statement equates modest dress with a female Muslim's identity, which as we shall learn in the Conclusion, is also problematic. Veiling can also be used to take control of an unjust situation. This is the case for Burka Avenger, who uses the veil as tool against her oppressors.

The following section discusses Pakistani gender politics, examining its history of women's activism as well as its current issues regarding gender. These include the fight for education, which serves as a central concern in the *Burka Avenger* series. I follow this with a discussion of several episodes of the animated show, where I focus in particular on the title character—her story, personality, and activism. The final part of the chapter is dedicated to the use of veiling and unveiling by Burka Avenger, acts that represent the character's independence and exercise of agency.

FEMINISM, ACTIVISM, AND THE ARTS IN PAKISTAN

The storylines in *Burka Avenger* are focused on Pakistan's history and cur-rent political situation, including issues affecting girls and women. Pakistan is a modern nation-state with competing notions of its identity. Media reports paint a picture of a country with endless suicide attacks and kidnappings, civil unrest and corruption. Religious minorities, including Shi'i, Ahmadis, and Christians, are often the target of attacks. At the same time, Pakistan is located in a region that has a strong history of political activism and cultural traditions that challenges those seeking to control and silence females.

Pakistan's issues with gender in the modern period can be traced to the rule of General Zia al-Huq, whose regime articulated a vision of modern statehood that was explicitly tied to Islam. As Saadia Toor has written, "As a nationalist ideology, the discourse of Islamization privileged the adult Muslim male as the ideal citizen of the Pakistani nation-state while disempowering women, limiting their public visibility and mobility as well as their legal rights."[14] Zia instituted the Hudood Ordinances, which included the Zina Ordinance— a law designed to regulate women's sexuality that made extra-marital sex (either before or during marriage) a crime against the state.[15] These laws were early steps in the efforts to restrict women's agency and banish them from the public sphere, something that is seen in the pressures on dress and veiling in recent decades.

Despite these efforts, it is important to remember that Pakistan is a nation of intellectuals, artists, diverse cultures, religious traditions, and languages. The society has undoubtedly been impacted by a fear of religious extremism "suturing everyday life and contaminating people."[16] At the same time, there is a strong degree of political expression and resiliency, both against religious extremism and autocratic political rule. Pakistan has a rich culture of artistic traditions, which include contemporary theater, poetry, music, painting, and literature. During Zia's rule, a type of theater known as "parallel" or "secular alternative" theater emerged in Pakistan, performed in factory courtyards and other spaces friendly to the poor and working class.[17] Among the issues addressed in performances were those pertaining to women such as domestic violence and honor killing.[18] Poetry also became a site of dissent, inspiring women like Fehmida Riaz to write lines such as, "End this spectacle now/ Cover it up/The black chaadar has become your necessity, not mine."[19] Contemporary art is another area where women confront gender issues. One British exhibition entitled "Pakistan: Another Vision" featured artists such as Salima Hashmi, Naazish Ata Ullah, Naiza Khan, and Sabina Gillani."[20]

In Pakistan, as in much of the world, women's bodies are sites of contestation, which includes physical activities like sports and of course, clothing.[21] Today, women in Pakistan are often subjected to widespread harassment over their dress. The veil, in these cases, is used as a symbol of "true" Islam, what some Islamists argue is a mandatory requirement for girls and women. This may be why some Pakistani women view the veil as a tool of protection. According to one study that surveyed university students, "It is mentioned in all interviewees' answers that one function of Burqa is to prevent the women who wear them from the male gaze. When asked about their experience in Burqa, the women unanimously stated they feel safer and more comfortable."[22] Burka Avenger also veils as a strategy of protection, to hide her identity and protect herself from the gaze of the "Other," which is intended to represent the Taliban and more generally the Afghan. At the same time, the show offers a space for Pakistani women to be at the visual center. This is significant because of the "anxieties surrounding the textual construction of gender," which is nevertheless countered by "the poetic habitation of women's bodies in everyday rituals and objects."[23]

Television is another medium where Pakistan's gender politics are played out. As Shahid Siddiqui has argued, soap operas like *Kyonki Saas Bhi Kabbi Bau Thi* "perpetuate the stereotype of women as tricksters playing family politics."[24] This cultural stereotyping casts women in a negative light as troublemakers and meddlers, dangerous agents to the family unit and threats to patriarchal control. This stereotyping is challenged by shows like *Burka Avenger*.

Burka Avenger may be influenced by American comics and animation, in particular, the idea of the superhero. However, it is important to note that India (and by extension, Pakistan) has a long history of graphic texts, much of it situated in political rhetoric, which has influenced the production of comics and animated cartoons. While there are serious differences between Indian comics, which typically focus on religious and national figures identified with Hinduism, the region has a rich visual heritage.[25] The identification of the city with criminality, terrorism, and evil are themes found in both Indian comics and Pakistani narratives, including *Burka Avenger*. In Indian comics, the villainous Other is often Pakistani, and at other times a member of a low caste. In *Burka Avenger,* it is the Afghan.[26] The return of the oppressed is another theme found in numerous narratives, including the Indian comic, the Pakistani comic, and graphic novels like *Bloody Nasreen*, examined in the following chapter[27] While no academic studies have yet examined the question of cross-pollination of these different narrative forms on Indian and Pakistani artists, it is likely to exist at some level.

Burka Avenger reflects the Muslim-majority flavor of Pakistan. The debate over what constitutes "true Islam" is an issue at the center of *Burka Avenger*. Jiya is a positive symbol of Pakistani womanhood—intelligent, educated, and independent. The plotlines in the series also communicate a specific vision of Islam, one focused on liberation from oppression and on the fight for justice. In the first episode, a villain, Baba Bandook, has been hired by a corrupt businessman to shut down the girls' school in the village so that donations for the school can be pocketed. This plotline reflects the political realities in Pakistan, which include collusion between business interests, the government, and the Taliban that often result in violence that impacts the population.

Feminist activism in Pakistan has a long history, with projects directed at education, political rights, health care, and access to human services. Efforts to raise awareness of such achievements include many educational projects targeting children. *Burka Avenger* is one of many efforts to influence children through the mediation of friendly images; in this case, of a spirited school-teacher/superhero who uses books as weapons. The presence of a *Muslimah* superhero on Pakistani television represents an important cultural moment that signals the agency of girls and women in the society. "While the Pakistani public sphere is characterized by the constraint toward and vulnerability of women, it is also haunted by the silent and unacknowledged presence/absence of women."[28]

AN ANIMATED *MUSLIMAH* SUPERHERO

Burka Avenger's primary target is children and youth in Pakistan, where it is broadcast; however, several episodes are available on the show's website, enabling an audience far beyond South Asia. It is produced by Unicorn Black, a Pakistani entity, and funded in part by United States Agency for International Development (USAID).[29] It won a Peabody Award in 2014 as well as the award for Best TV Show at the Asian Media Awards.[30] In addition, the show won the Rising Star Award at Canada's International Film Festival and the International Emmy Kid's Award.[31] While *Burka Avenger* is revolutionary—it is the first animated television show in Pakistan to feature a *Muslimah* superhero—it has an antecedent and likely influence. Since 1971, the cartoon character Gogi, created by Nigar Nazar, has functioned as an icon of female empowerment, "the symbol of womanhood in Pakistan with all her adventures and escapades in daily life."[32]

Burka Avenger is part of a growing animation industry in Pakistan. *Team Bahadur* is Pakistan's first animated film; it is focused on a group of super-heroes—what scholars call a *supergroup*—much like the X-Men, who fight crime and evil forces.[33] Many of these projects are inspired by Pakistani comics, which have featured supergroups like the one seen in *Team Bahadur*. In *Team Muhafiz*, the supergroup of seven teenage heroes includes an Indian girl, Aarya, who teaches yoga and dance at the youth center. The heroes focus their energies on helping youth and working on social projects.[34] The comic presents seven teenagers doing good deeds that address issues including environmental preservation, drug use, gangs, criminality, pollution, and child marriage.[35]

Pakistan has a wealth of animation talent, including Oscar winner Mir Zafar Ali whose work includes *Life of Pi*, *Golden Compass*, and *Frozen*; and Novaira Masood, the visual artist known for her work on the Hollywood films *Thor*, *Jack the Giant Slayer*, and *Maleficent*.[36] Domestically, animation includes productions such as the superhero Commander Safeguard, followed by the Germ Busters, the Dettol Warriors, and *Baankay Miyaan*, which preceded *Burka Avenger* as a popular mainstream phenomenon.[37]

Burka Avenger features characters who are inspired by real people. Jiya's role as a schoolteacher and her emphasis on education have echoes of Malala Yousafzai, the Nobel Laureate from Pakistan. Education and the right of girls to an education are strong theme in the series. The fact that Jiya is a schoolteacher is one way this is communicated. As Shahid Siddiqui has written, "Education, which has a strong linkage to power, has been a rare commodity for women. In Pakistan, we see a long period of exclusion of women in terms of modern education."[38] Education is, in fact, a central focus of the series, so much so that the martial art Jiya practices is focused on the manipulation of books as weapons. The messaging here is quite clear—literacy is literally a weapon against oppression and religious fundamentalism. The producer of the series has been clear that he sees *Burka Avenger* as a way to reach the masses and influence perceptions surrounding women and gender in Pakistan. As one scholar notes,

> However, mass media should not limit the possibilities for children's understanding by presenting gender stereotypes and sexist viewpoints. Instead, mass media should contribute to children's development by presenting them with the broadest range of social models and diversity. For example, a Pakistani television producer Aaron Harun Rashid's cartoon, "Burqa Avenger," is important in the fact that it defends the idea that females should be afforded education just as males.[39]

Jiya's physical appearance communicates ideals about gender. She is strong, slender, and physically agile, a quality demonstrated in her daily exercises with Kabaadi Jaan. Her body, unlike the vast majority of female superheroes, is not sexualized. She is similar to Ms. Marvel—strong and athletic. Jiya's identity as a Muslim is carried over to her alter ego, whose use of the *burka* (an Urdu word for veil) rejects both Islamist and colonial prescriptions of veiling. As one scholar points out, "Implicitly, the program critiques the widespread negative portrayals of the burka and plays on the prevalent understandings of the 'white man's burden' to save others."[40]

Scholarship on superheroes, sexuality, and bodies has primarily focused on comics. It is important to point out that male superheroes are often androgynous, but female superheroes are often presented as highly sensual. As one scholar puts it, "Conversely, and unsurprisingly, artists are adamant about containing women's gender within highly sexed bodies."[41] *Burka Avenger* deviates from this—she is slender and strong, but her body is covered. While

Figure 4.2   Jiya/Burka Avenger. Photo courtesy of Unicorn Black.

female superheroes are at times assigned male features, her use of the veil marks her as a female, a contrast to her more "masculine" body.[42]

In addition to the physical appearance of the characters in animated cartoons, behavioral and linguistic cues that are tied to a character's presentation are important.[43] Attractiveness as a measure of personality can also be used to portray villains. Baba Bandook is the primary villain in the series. He is overweight, has a prominent mustache, and wears a turban with a gold cobra on the center. His laughter is menacing and when he opens his mouth, he has noticeable vampire fangs. Villains are at times marked physically—a morphological sign of a lack of morality. Even when these characters are not presented with purple skin (like the Joker) or some other obvious sign of alterity, they are shown to be physically unattractive. In one study, "physically unattractive characters were far more likely than others to be considered 'bad characters' whereas physically attractive characters were more likely than others to be 'good characters.'"[44]

The villains in *Burka Avenger* display signs of foreignness and, in particular, of Afghan/Taliban culture. Baba Bandook wears a turban. One of his henchmen, Tinda, wears a type of hat called a *pakol*, which is associated with Afghans. These are sartorial signs linked with the power of religious authorities (*turban*) and political instability (*pakol*). The role of the Afghan as "Other," noted earlier in this chapter, is displayed in the physical appearance of the villains in the series. The history behind these tensions is not fully explored here, but it is an important part of *Burka Avenger's* use of cultural symbols. Pakistan's relationship with Afghanistan is complicated, due in part to the fact that Pakistan has been deeply involved in its neighbor's internal affairs since the late 1970s.[45] Pakistan's support for the Taliban has been a policy largely situated in larger

Asian politics; in particular, concerns about India.[46] Despite this background, the large number of Afghan refugees living in cities like Peshawar and Karachi is often cited as a reason for the country's instability, and blamed for the rise of religious extremism within Pakistan.

While the causes of Pakistan's political problems are complex (the growth of Wahhabism, corruption of government officials, narco-economics, and other factors), Afghans are often blamed for many of Pakistan's problems, resulting in some of the stereotypes seen in popular culture like *Burka Avenger*. The high number of cultural, ethnic, and religious groups in Pakistan and Afghanistan make this an even more contentious issue. The tensions between the Baloch and Pashtun serve as one example. As Paul Titus has written, the "Pushtun reputation for religious zeal" combined with their economic success (replacing many of the Hindus and Sikhs who used to control trade in western Pakistan) has helped to create a certain vision of the Pashtun, a group associated with Afghanistan and in particular, with the Taliban.[47] As Titus explains, "The refugees are closely identified with the cause of Islam, for example, and the Baloch response to their increasing presence in the economy and social life of Balochistan has been a political one."[48] The stereotype of Pashtun is based on the view of the Taliban, when in fact Pashtuns have a history of not supporting political Islam until recently.[49] More generally, Pashtuns in Pakistan are discriminated against due to their pronunciation of Urdu and are portrayed as more misogynistic and religiously extreme. As Shehnaz Zindabad has explained,

> Generally, Pakistani Pashtuns ("Pathans" in Pakistan and India but not in Afghanistan) are mocked for the way they speak Urdu—it's very distinct, the idea goes; in Urdu, for instance, there's a specific construction that includes an "h" between letters, but that construction doesn't exist in Pashto.[50]

Burka Avenger, thus, functions as a political text with villains and heroes situated in the larger geopolitical concerns affecting the region. This is communicated in the series through expressions of gender and beauty. As we have seen, physical attractiveness is a way to communicate messaging to young children and adults the themes of morality and goodness. Typically, female characters follow the standards of beauty of the culture. In the case of animated cartoons, "attractiveness-related messages provided by this particular medium are likely to be influential in the initial stages of developing beliefs and attitudes about appearance."[51] Appearance is thus identified with personality—attractive characters are often, but not always, seen as good. In the case of superheroes, this makes sense because "attractive characters are more likely to perform prosocial acts—that is, to do things that were intended to specifically benefit others."[52]

Jiya's appearance is important. She is slender, wears a long tunic, pants, and a scarf around her neck, much like Kamala, the Pakistani-American, wears to her brother's wedding. Unlike many girls and women in animated cartoons, Jiya's body is not sexualized. She has no curves—her breasts and hips are not accentuated. Her body is radically different from most females in animated cartoons, who are drawn to appear sensual through exaggerated breasts, hips, and buttocks. The Bratz characters are an example of the "overly sexual appearance" often seen in female animated cartoon characters—in this case, including the "physicality of the dolls (big eyes and lips, no nose), and their clothes (trendy, skimpy) are sexualized and therefore sold as defiantly adult-oriented fashion."[53]

Burka Avenger's body is also an important symbolic site in the series. When in combat with villains, she never touches them with her body, suggesting that she is set apart—physically and spiritually—from these other

Figure 4.3   Jiya/Burka Avenger. Photo courtesy of Unicorn Black.

characters. It also suggests that her body is both her own and a symbol of God's piety, a belief ascribed to women who veil. In the context of Pakistan, the physical distance between Burka Avenger and the villains in the series—all of whom are male—also suggests her place in national politics. As Miranda Brar has argued,

> As she fights with corrupt and ignorant men, she maintains a safe physical distance from these "bad guys," whom she never physically strikes or touches. Though actively combatting men in public, the maintenance of physical distance between the Burka Avenger and the "bad guys" is a distinctive feature of the cultural context of her naissance. The use of the burka renders Rashid's protagonist anonymous, literally covering her identity. Her physical/spatial distance from her opponents also serve to demonstrate her symbolic value, indicating that women's participation in the nationalist movement is permissible and recognized only from within the cultural religious fabric of the Muslim nation.[54]

The physical distance seen in these encounters is coupled with a lack of sexual energy attached to Burka Avenger, as well as to Jiya. Jiya is portrayed as a pure and virginal individual, unmarried and committed to the spiritual practices seen in her martial arts. She is de-sexualized like other *Muslimah* superheroes, who with few exceptions (such as Kamala's ill-fated relationship with Kamran) are not shown in romantic entanglements. A disinterest in sex and romance is often found in superheroes, such as Batman, Superman, and Captain America, who even when pursued by women, reject their advances. However, with the *Muslimah* superhero we see something else, for the possibility of a sexual encounter is never even presented. The creator of the series has stated that this is intentional, for it is the actions of Burka Avenger, not her sexuality or attractiveness, that are important.[55]

The question of whether Burka Avenger is a queered character is an interesting one. While Jiya presents herself as a young, attractive, feminine woman, Burka Avenger does not. Her costume obscures her body and her actions as a superhero upset the more traditional gender roles in force in Pakistani society. Perhaps she has "queer potential" through her subversion of gender dress, her use of the veil to "shield herself from the male gaze," and her complicated identity.[56] Burka Avenger disrupts some of the gendered boundaries through these characteristics. Disruption of boundaries and identities are both attached to the activity of queering. As Megan Goodwin has argued, sexuality and gender are related concepts, albeit ones that are not interchangeable. As she remarks, there is a negotiated space (or multiple spaces) between gender performance and sexuality. In the American context, "heteronormativity makes sense of bodies in binary, reproductive terms."[57]

BURKA AVENGER: GENDER, POWER, AND POLITICS

Burka Avenger addresses a number of social issues ranging from gender equity to health care. While not all of these are examined here, it is important to note the ways in which the superhero counters dark forces through her physical prowess, spiritual training, and wisdom. Each episode focuses on a challenge that Burka Avenger overcomes and ends with a reflection on the importance of tolerance and national unity. In the final scene of each episode, the superhero speaks directly to the audience, offering encouragement in the form of a short lecture, which always ends with a farewell line, "Until then, remember, inner peace."

The first episode of *Burka Avenger* ("Girl's School Is Shut") introduces the main characters: Jiya, the schoolteacher; her alter ego, the superhero Burka Avenger; her foster parents, Kabaddi Jan (her mentor) and his wife; the children Mooli, Ashu, and Immu; their pet goat Golu; the villains Vadero Pajero, a crooked politician, Baba Bandook, who often does Pajero's dirty work, and his henchmen, Munna, Tinda, and Khamba. The series takes place in Halwapur, a fictitious village in rural Pakistan. The opening sequence of each episode tells the story of young Jiya's life. She is an orphan, a victim of a tragic fire that killed her parents. Raised by adoptive parents, she is now an expert in the spiritual martial art known as Takht Kabaddi, which uses pens, books, and acrobatics to fight evil.

The first episode begins with a training sequence between Jiya and Kabaddi Jan, who is named after the martial arts he instructs her in. This lesson includes Jiya catching raw eggs in her hands without breaking them. When she fails at this exercise, Kabaddi Jan reminds her that "command over mind and body" is more important than "physical strength," and that it is through "inner peace" that she can achieve anything. The mantra of inner peace is repeated throughout the series and is an important reflection of Islamic teachings centered on controlling one's negative impulses. Known as *the greater jihad*, or the *jihad al-nafs* (the battle against the ego), this is considered the Muslim's greatest task in life. As Seyyed Hossein Nasr has described it, *jihad* requires that the individual "must exert themselves at all moments of life to fight a battle, at once both inward and outward, against those forces that, if not combated, will destroy that necessary equilibrium."[58]

This equilibrium is maintained through religious exercises, which in *Burka Avenger* help Jiya achieve inner peace. In numerous instances in the series, before battling Baba Bandook she is shown in a meditative and spiritual state, focusing on achieving inner peace. This is the practice that makes her victorious. In Islam, this is the very definition of *jihad*—the battle against injustice. As Syed Ali Ashraf has written,

Jihād compels an individual to test himself through his sincerity and love for God and the Prophet. That love for God and the Prophet means love for the good, for selflessness, for all that God has prescribed and the Prophet has exemplified in order to lead man toward the final goal of mankind. That goal is to fulfill the function of viceregency of God (*khalīfat Allāh*) on earth and hatred of all evil forces, including oppression, injustice, falsehood, cheating, backbiting, suppression of human freedom, and denial of basic human rights guaranteed in the Qur'an.[59]

The Muslim's *jihad* is, as argued in the final chapter of this book, the focus of every *Muslimah* superhero, a representative of the ideal Muslim. In the first episode of *Burka Avenger*, it is clear who is winning the greater *jihad* and who is losing the battle against one's greatest own demons—egoism, greed, hatred, and violence—as expressed in the superhero and the villains she fights. Here, they attempt to shut down the school where she teaches so that Vadero Pajero can pocket the charity money for the school and Baba Bandook can have a cut of the funds meant for the children of Halwapur. After the school is shut down and padlocked, Burka Avenger appears, attacks the villains with books (instead of weapons that would physically harm them), and re-opens the school. The episode ends with the pop star Haroon giving a concert at the school, where he sings a song with the lines, "Keep the faith alive, do not despair. Your trouble stay afar." While Baba Bandook declares that he hates music, thus revealing his Taliban politics, Burka Avenger watches the concert from above. In the final scene, she states, "Whether you are a girl or a boy, education is your right." This proclamation reflects the dual hero that Jiya/Burka Avenger is. Jiya's education of children is a superhero activity equal to her adventures as Burka Avenger.

In another episode ("Kite Flying Festival Attacked"), the politics of the Taliban are introduced when Baba Bandook attempts to stop a kite festival (*Basant*). Kite flying is a popular pastime in both Pakistan and Afghanistan. The Taliban outlawed the flying of kites, deeming it un-Islamic and *bid'ah* (innovation; against Islamic teachings). The episode begins with Baba Bandook's latest creation, a robot named the Brute-anator, being destroyed when his henchman Tinda falls from the sky (after being sent to the clouds by Burka Avenger) and lands on the robot, destroying it. Bandook then proceeds to create a giant balloon, which he attaches himself to while he carries a flame-thrower, to destroy the school and the kite-flying festival. Burka Avenger arrives on the scene, and after a brief meditative exercise on inner peace, she destroys the balloon and defeats Baba Bandook. The pens with which she punctures the balloon, it should be noted, magically emerge from her hand like Wolverine's claws in the *X-Men* comic books and films.

The episode titled "Burka Avenger Fights Prejudice" turns to internal Pakistani politics; in particular, the violence inflicted upon religious minorities within the country. The episode begins with Jiya's students wearing dots symbolizing their identities. One child says he is only one of a few of his kind left, perhaps symbolizing a Christian or Hindu identity. Red dots likely symbolize Sunni Muslims, as later in the episode the children so marked will not play with a child wearing a blue dot, suggesting she is Shi'i Muslim. The scene switches to a talk show in which the host is planning to broadcast a wedding between a woman who wears a blue dot and a man who wears a red dot. Baba Bandook calls into the show and stops the wedding, convincing the studio audience that mixed marriages cannot take place. Bandook plans to divide the people of Halwapur by giving those with red dots "goop guns," which will be used to threaten the minority blue dot community members and push them out. At the moment this is taking place, Burka Avenger arrives on the scene. After she is temporarily stopped by a goop attack from Bandook, she emerges and with the help of the larger community, defeats the villains.

This episode, like others, teaches that through unity, the people of Pakistan can meet their challenges. In this case, the focus is on national unity and religious tolerance. The arch villain is signified by ignorance and hatred—he even lives in a cave like Usama bin Laden—but he fails to divide the community. As Jiya says in the episode, "In a civilized society, everyone lives together." The episode ends with the wedding being celebrated in Halwapur and a closing message from Burka Avenger, "Unity is strength."

THE SUBVERSIVE VEIL

More than any other character in this book, Burka Avenger uses veiling in a subversive way. As a prelude to discussing how the veil is deployed in the series, it is important to note that veiling in Pakistan is often represented through a politicized iconography. Women wear a variety of styles of veiling, including the simple headscarf. At the other end of the spectrum is the image of the *burqaman*, the bogeyman in Omar Khan's famous horror film *Zibahkhana* (2007), one of many featuring menacing "putrefying and rancid zombies" that populate the film.[60]

Jiya's wearing of bright and cheerful *salwar kameez*, which consists of a long tunic and pants, represents the variety of dress in Pakistan. Fashionable styles of clothing seen on the streets of Karachi, Islamabad, and Peshawar range from the very traditional to high fashion. After all, Pakistan is one of the Islamic fashion capitals in the world. Within the country, fashion designers compete with designers in Europe, some of whom incorporate traditional South Asian motifs in their designs.[61]

The veil is a powerful symbol in *Burka Avenger*. As it turns out, superheroes often adopt or reclaim objects (including culturally recognizable garments) that are used symbolically. Captain Canuck, the popular Canadian superhero, uses national symbols to express the national traits often associated with his countrymen and women. "Captain Canuck's red and white costume adorned with maple leaves signified his Canadianness, while his moralism, natural strength, and self-sacrificing persona reinforced conceptions of Canadians as polite, kind, moral, heroic peacekeepers."[62]

The superhero often uses symbols—including religious ones—in unexpected and even subversive ways. Daredevil is a character often identified with Catholicism. His use of devil horns symbolizes his tenuous relationship with his Catholic faith, honors his father (a boxer known as Jack "the Devil" Murdock), and identifies the landscape the Daredevil defends—Hell's Kitchen. As one scholar argues, the filmic interpretation of the comic plays up these elements. "The film also milks a form of Christ-like Martyrdom—Daredevil is a good Catholic boy, and guilt and devotion frame the narrative."[63] In the case of *Burka Avenger*, the heroine adopts veiling as a form of disguise. The use of the veil is a way to appropriate a tool of oppression imposed by the Taliban as a symbol of rebellion *against* the Taliban. Agency functions in a powerful way in *Burka Avenger*. The series' creator has remarked that her wearing of the *niqab* is a choice and at that, a subversive one.[64] Burka Avenger co-opts the veil for her own purposes—to fight for justice in the name of Islam. As we shall see in the following chapter, she is not alone in launching a *gender jihad* in the land of superheroes.

NOTES

1. Kiyomi Katsuzawa, "Disney's *Pocahontas*: Reproduction of Gender, Orientalism, and the Strategic Construction of Racial Harmony in the Disney Empire," *Asian Journal of Women's Studies* 6, no. 4 (2000): 55.

2. Darcy Orcutt, "Comics and Religion: Theoretical Connections," in *Graven Images: Religion in Comic Books and Graphic Novels*, eds. David A. Lewis and Christine Hoff Kraemer (London: Bloomsbury Academic: 2010): 94.

3. Hugh Klein and Kenneth S. Shiffman, "Underrepresentation and Symbolic Annihilation of Socially Disenfranchised Groups ('Out Groups') in Animated Cartoons," *The Howard Journal of Communications* 20 (2009): 57.

4. Hugh Klein and Kenneth S. Shiffman, "Race-Related Content of Animated Cartoons," *The Howard Journal of Communications* (2006): 166.

5. Teresa Thompson and Eugenia Zerbinos, "Gender Roles in Animated Cartoons: Has the Picture Changed in 20 Years?" *Sex Roles* 32, nos. 9/10 (1995): 663.

6. Jeffrey K. Johnson, "The Countryside Triumphant: Jefferson's Ideal of Rural Superiority in Modern Superhero Mythology," *The Journal of Popular Culture* 43, no. 4 (2010): 733.

7. *Kabaddi* has its origins in Hindu devotional practices. For a history of *kabaadi* in the context of South Asian history and politics, see Milind Wakankar, "Body,

Crowd, Identity: Genealogy of a Hindu Nationalist Aesthetics," *Social Text* 45 (1995): 45–73.

8. Christian Feichtinger, "Space Buddhism: The Adoption of Buddhist Motifs in Star Wars," *Contemporary Buddhism* 15, no. 1 (2014): 33.

9. Ibid.

10. Ibid.

11. Reina Lewis, *Muslim Fashion: Contemporary Style Cultures* (Durham: Duke University Press, 2015), 60.

12. Olga Khazan, "Big in . . . Pakistan," *The Atlantic Monthly* 312, no. 4 (2013): 10.

13. Ibid.

14. Saadia Toor, "Moral Regulation in a Postcolonial Nation-State: Gender and the Politics of Islamization in Pakistan," *Interventions* 9, no. 2 (2007): 259.

15. Saadia Toor, "The Political Economy of Moral Regulation in Pakistan: Religion, Gender and Class in a Postcolonial Context," in *Routledge Handbook of Gender in South Asia*, ed. by Leela Fernandes (New York: Routledge, 2014), 131.

16. Naveeda Khan, *Muslim Becoming: Aspiration and Skepticism in Pakistan* (Durham: Duke University Press, 2012): 166.

17. Danielle Abrams, "Performative Practices and Poetry in North America and Pakistan," *Women's Studies Quarterly* 35, nos. 3/4 (2007): 317.

18. Ibid.

19. Saadia Toor, "Moral Regulation," 260–61.

20. Virginia Whiles, "In and Out of Pakistan," *Third Text* 14, no. 52 (2008): 103.

21. Saadia Toor, "Moral Regulation," 266.

22. Zhou Yun, "Behind the Muslim Veil: A Qualitative Analysis of Pakistani Female Students' Views Towards Veiling," *Cross-Cultural Communication* 6, no. 1 (2010): 84.

23. Iftikhar Dadi, "Ghostly Sufis and Ornamental Shadows: Spectral Visualities in Karachi's Public Sphere," in *Comparing Cities: The Middle East and South Asia*, ed. Martina Rieker and Kamran Ali (New York: Oxford University Press): 180.

24. Shahid Siddiqui, *Language, Gender, and Power: The Politics of Representation and Hegemony in South Asia* (Karachi: Oxford University Press, 2014), 173–4.

25. Winona Landis, "Diasporic (Dis)Identification: The Participatory Fandom of Ms. Marvel," *South Asian Popular Culture* 14, nos. 1/2 (2016): 38.

26. Nandini Chandra, "The Prehistory of the Superhero Comics in India (1976–1986)," *Thesis Eleven* 113, no. 1 (2012): 69.

27. Ibid.

28. Iftikhar Dadi, "Ghostly Sufis and Ornamental Shadows," 180.

29. Anita Weiss, "Can Civil Society Tame Violent Extremism in Pakistan?" *Current History* (2016): 146.

30. "Burka Avenger Wins," *Slogan* (December 2014): 10.

31. Mahrukh Farooq, "Animation: The New Frontier," *Slogan* 20, no. 2 (2015): 8.

32. Siham Basir, "Interview: Nigar Nazar CEO, Gogi Studios," *Newsline*, June 2010, http://newslinemagazine.com/magazine/interview-nigar-nazar-ceo-gogi-studios/ (accessed February 21, 2017).

33. Mahrukh Farooq, "Animation," 8.

34. "Pakistan Gets New Teen-Heroes in 'Team Muhafiz," February 24, 2015, http://www.animationxpress.com/index.php/latest-news/pakistan-gets-new-teen-heroes-in-team-muhafiz-comic (accessed March 7, 2017).

35. Ibid.

36. Mahrukh Farooq, "Animation," 9.

37. Samina Wahid, "All About Animation," *Slogan* 20, no. 2 (2015): 10.

38. Shahid Siddiqui, *Language, Gender, and Power*, 120.

39. Nurdan Kalayci, "Analyses of the Cartoon Series from a Gender Equality Perspective: Pepee," *Education and Science* 40, no. 177 (2015): 262.

40. Shenila Khoja-Moolji, "Poststructuralist Approaches to Teaching about Gender, Islam, and Muslim Societies," *Feminist Teacher* 24, no. 3 (2015): 179.

41. Aaron Taylor, "'He's Gotta Be Strong, and He's Gotta Be Fast, and He's Gotta Be Larger Than Life': Investigating the Engendered Superhero Body," *The Journal of Popular Culture* 40, no. 2 (2007): 353.

42. Kaysee Baker and Arthur A. Raney, "Equally Super?: Gender-Role Stereotyping of Superheroes in Children's Animated Programs," *Mass Communication and Society* 10, no. 1 (2007): 37.

43. Julia R. Dobrow and Calvin L. Gidney, "The Good, the Bad, and the Foreign: The Use of Dialect in Children's Animated Television," *The Annals of the American Academy of Political and Social Science* 557 (1998): 106.

44. Hugh Klein and Kenneth S. Shiffman, "Messages about Physical Attractiveness in Animated Cartoons," *Body Image* 3 (2006): 361.

45. For a full history of Pakistan's involvement in Afghanistan's internal affairs, see Ahmed Rashid, *Taliban: Militant Islam, Oil and Fundamentalism in Central Asia* (New Haven: University Press, 2010).

46. Juan Cole, "Pakistan and Afghanistan: Beyond the Taliban," *Political Science Quarterly* 124, no. 2 (2009): 225.

47. Paul Titus, "Honor the Baloch, Buy the Pashtun: Stereotypes, Social Organization and History in Western Pakistan," *Central Asian Studies* 32, no. 3 (1998): 674, 676.

48. Paul Titus, "Honor the Baloch, Buy the Pushtun," 681.

49. Juan Cole, "Pakistan and Afghanistan," 233.

50. Shehnaz Zindabad, e-mail to author, March 22, 2017.

51. Klein and Shiffman, "Messages about Physical Attractiveness in Animated Cartoons," *Body Image* 3 (2006): 355.

52. Klein and Shiffman, "Messages about Physical Attractiveness," 361.

53. Matthew P. McAllister, "'Girls with a Passion for Fashion': The Bratz Brand as Integrated Spectacular Consumption," *Journal of Children and Media* 1, no. 3 (2007): 244, 251.

54. Miranda Brar, "The Nation and Its Burka Avenger, the 'Other' and Its Malala Yusafzai," *Prandium: The Journal of Historical Studies* 3, no. 1 (2014): 5.

55. Miranda Brar, "The Nation and Its Burka Avenger," 6.

56. Gina Waibel, "From Avengers to Heroines: Muslim Women Dismantling Hegemonic Discourses" (master's thesis, Lund University, 2016), 42.

57. Megan Goodwin, "Thinking Sex and American Religions," *Religion Compass* 5, no. 12 (2011): 775.

58. Seyyed Hossein Nasr, *Traditional Islam in the Modern World* (New York: Kegan Paul International, 1987): 29.

59. Syed Ali Ashraf, "The Inner Meaning of the Islamic Rites: Prayer, Pilgrimage, Fasting, Jihād," in *Islamic Spirituality: Foundations*, ed. Seyyed Hossein Nasr (New York: The Crossroad Publishing Company, 1991): 126.

60. Ali Khan and Ali Nobil Ahmad, "From *Zinda Laash* to *Zibahkhana*: Violence and Horror in Pakistani Cinema," *Third Text* 24, no. 1 (2010): 160.

61. Reina Lewis, *Muslim Fashion: Contemporary Style Cultures* (Durham: Duke University Press, 2015): 196.

62. Ryan Edwardson, "The Many Lives of Captain Canuck: Nationalism, Culture, and the Creation of a Canadian Comic Book Superhero," *The Journal of Popular Culture* 37, no. 2 (2003): 186.

63. Petra Kuppers, "Blindness and Affect: *Daredevil*'s Site/Sight," *Quarterly Review of Film and Video* 23 (2006): 91.

64. Srijana Mitra Das, "Aaron Haroon: Burka Avenger's Apparel Not About Sexuality—It's About Strength," *The Times of India*, August 2, 2013, http://timesofindia.indiatimes.com/interviews/Aaron-Haroon-Burka-Avengers-apparel-not-about-sexuality-its -about-strength/articleshow/21537720.cms (accessed February 5, 2017).

Chapter 5

Qahera, Raat, Bloody Nasreen, and the Vigilante Superhero

This chapter examines three *Muslimah* superheroes who live in Muslim-majority societies that are characterized by political challenges. *Qahera* features an Egyptian superhero inspired by the 2011 uprisings at Cairo's Tahrir Square. *Raat* is centered upon a Pakistani woman who fights villains on the streets of Pakistan, often wearing a terrifying skull mask. Also from Pakistan is *Bloody Nasreen*, which follows the adventures of a young woman who expresses her frustrations with violence, crime, and political instability through vigilantism. These fictional characters enhance our understanding of what it means to be a Muslim woman in a world marked by sexual violence, war, and terrorism. They are radically different from Ms. Marvel and Burka Avenger, whose use of violence is limited.

As discussed throughout this book, *Muslimah* superheroes are a result of the shift to more diverse characters in comics and other graphic narratives. Like the *X-Men*, they represent an opening up of possibilities for the superhero, who is no longer white, but may be African-American, queer, immigrant, or Muslim. As Neil Shyminski has written,

> As persecuted minorities themselves the X-Men appear well positioned to redeem the suffering and the helpless. Within the universe of the *X-Men* movies and comic books, mutant super-humans are able to utilize racially charged discourses of oppression and victimization because they are commonly figured as normative humanity's racial other.[1]

Muslimah superheroes utilize this discourse of difference. At times, they voice frustration at the victimization of Muslim girls and women by numerous factions—Islamists, Western feminists, imperial regimes, military dictatorships, and war. This victimization is expressed in the characters discussed in this chapter.

The texts examined here reflect a diversity of genres—web comics, traditional comics, and the graphic novel. *Qahera* is a web comic. *Raat* exists in both traditional comic books and in web form, as the first issue of the series is available online. *Bloody Nasreen* exists mostly on the Internet (a rumored graphic novel of the character is yet to be published). Since 9/11, there has been a proliferation of web comics and animations that have targeted Muslims and, in particular, Arabs. These have often been particularly violent, featuring an imagery of pain and death suffered by Muslims. "Narratives centered on shooting, bombing, torturing, and humiliating the Arab characters."[2] *Qahera, Raat,* and *Bloody Nasreen*, in particular, provide a radically different view of Muslims. In addition to their focus on female characters, these web comics also offer portrayals of Islam that are not dependent on the mutilation and death of Muslims. Where post-9/11 web animations are examples of "racist war propaganda" which "are refurbished and revitalized with an aura of high-tech glamour," the characters discussed in this chapter are anti-colonial women who counter this messaging.[3]

These texts are important in helping us reflect on the ways in which violence is attached to Muslim *bodies*. Qahera is a vigilante. Like other superheroes who operate outside the law, she uses violence, but has limits on how much damage she inflicts on her adversaries. Her vigilantism is directed at Muslims and non-Muslims; in particular, Arab sexists and members of the group Femen. As Deena Mohamed, the creator of *Qahera*, has written, this is a superhero with a complicated agenda that reflects the struggles Muslim women face, both from within their communities and externally.

> Consequently, the choice of subject matter itself was conceived in relation to an English-speaking audience—Muslim and non-Muslim, Arab and non-Arab, and male and female alike. While the very first comic depicts Qahera getting the better of clearly Muslim (and less clearly Egyptian) misogynistic men, it also includes a panel depicting Western feminists using this scene to argue that Muslim women are oppressed, an argument that Qahera also challenges.[4]

Vigilantism in comics often features villains whose bodies are corrupted or damaged. As Jack Fennell has argued, American comics often reflect themes of justice and vengeance. He provides a genealogy of these ideals in European and American thought and argues that the villains of comics are often subjected to symbolic violence through the corruption of their bodies. As Jack Fennell puts it, "in Western popular culture there is still an expectation that evil people should 'look evil,' which in many cases still equates to mutilation—we want our villains to look as though they have been punished in such a manner."[5] This is in addition to their physical punishment by the superhero, which is often achieved through hand-to-hand combat that uses the protagonist's special abilities, gifts, and powers. However, superheroes often inhabit corrupted bodies. *The X-Men* series is perhaps the best example of this. Wolverine's claws are huge appendages that lie within his hands, for example. *Muslimah* superheroes also can occupy corrupted, or non-human, bodies. Ms. Marvel is one example. "Kamala Khan is an inhuman affected by Terrigenesis—the process by which the exposure to Terrigen Mist activates one's inhuman genes."[6]

Up to this point, this book has focused on *Muslimah* superheroes like Burka Avenger and Ms. Marvel—individuals who have special powers and are, perhaps, not fully (or only) human. This chapter focuses on female Muslim characters who are not magical superheroes with special powers, but outraged citizens who transform into superheroes through their actions. Although Qahera and Raat are superheroes, placing them in the same genre as *Burka Avenger* and *Ms Marvel*, Bloody Nasreen is not. She is included in this study because of her vigilantism, a common theme of superhero narratives that characterizes all of the characters included in this study.

> Superheroes regularly interfere with the normal prerogatives of states, implying that legal processes are insufficient, and perhaps even that inner-directed morality is superior to other-directed legality. Not surprisingly, superhero stories often return to the question of the merits and limitations of vigilantism and unbridled or unregulated power, whether in the hands of individuals or public authorities.[7]

As discussed in chapter 1, historically, women in comics have been largely subjected *to* violence rather than being instruments *of* violence. As Gail Simone has pointed out, "Not every woman in comics has been killed, raped, depowered, crippled, turned evil, maimed, tortured, contracted a disease or had other life-derailing tragedies befall her, but given the following list, it's hard to think up exceptions."[8] The superheroine is the exception to this, although these characters are often killed off or maimed, such as when both Batgirl and Batman suffer back injuries and Batman recovers while Batgirl is "transformed into the wheelchair-bound Oracle."[9]

Of the female superheroes, Wonder Woman is perhaps the most violent, yet her use of force is limited in comparison to her male counterparts. This suggests that women are not allowed to exert the same level of violence as men. What happens, then, when female comic characters are portrayed as violent agents, breaking men's bones, or even killing them? Qahera and Nasreen are examples of agents of violence. Vigilantism is also a theme in *Ms. Marvel*, for example, and it is due to the inability (or reluctance) of the state to protect Muslims and others that her superheroism is necessary.

> Within Ms. Marvel, it is evident that Kamala decides that, in order to protect Jersey City, she cannot rely on "the State," but instead must take matters into her

own hands. While vigilante justice is a common plot point in superhero comics, Kamala's identity also illuminates the fact that "the state" already excludes, overlooks, and chooses not to protect certain citizens and locations. She, therefore, becomes her city's alternative to state protection—and state violence.[10]

Vigilantism represents the failure of the modern state to protect human beings from violence. Superheroes are characters that express a kind of independent ideology that in most cases rejects the modern state. "They [superheroes] are answerable to no one but themselves, for they are above and beyond the worlds they choose to save."[11]

Comics and other graphic narratives then often question the role of the state in fighting crime, redistributing justice, and creating a safe space for its citizenry. *Bloody Nasreen*, in particular, challenges the effectiveness of the government of Pakistan in protecting its people, who suffer from an almost endless series of suicide attacks and other forms of terroristic violence. Nasreen represents a radical feminist *jihad* that rejects the legitimacy of the modern state to protect her from violence. Unlike Qahera, whose punishment of villains is fairly mild, Raat and Bloody Nasreen resemble the more violent forms of vigilantism seen in the *Kill Bill* films. Politically, Qahera, Raat, and Nasreen represent what happens when the state is unable to protect a population against violence and vigilantism is introduced as solutions.

The work on Islam and violence tends to focus on political forms of violence, such as terrorism. Social vigilantism that uses violence is seldom discussed. This may be in part due to the feeling among scholars that terrorism is often, but not always, a form of vigilantism. However, others have argued that these are two separate categories. Stephanie Juliano has written, "Both terrorists and vigilantes are likely to seek anonymity to avoid arrest and retribution. Both also seek to fulfill a personal agenda, but the main similarities end here. The key distinction is the use of terror tactics, which includes violence, fear-mongering, and threats."[12] Qahera and Nasreen are vigilantes, much in the tradition of Anonymous, the group that fights for "noble causes" such as identifying sexual predators and revealing the secrets of criminal organizations (like the Church of Scientology).[13]

Social justice and, in particular, gender justice are at the center of these narratives. Qahera, Raat, and Bloody Nasreen reflect their social location as women in societies who pose direct challenges to misogyny and the violence it generates. Scholars have pointed out how culture functions at the micro and macro level in comics. At the micro level, culture also matters. A comic set in San Francisco might not make sense for people living in rural Alabama and vice versa. Of course, some comics have broad appeal—*Superman, X-Men, Spiderman*—which may be due in part to their utilization of national themes and iconography. At the macro level, comics (and other graphic narratives) often vary greatly. One study that compared Italian and American comics and focused on the theme of authority found that in the Italian case, "authority of all sorts was seen as valid and attempts to overthrow authority were shown to be futile," while the American case was "anti-authoritarian and ridiculed authority figures."[14] I suspect the violence attached to Nasreen provides some discomfort for Western audiences, which will be even more paramount when the graphic novel and film are released. Audiences expect the trope of the subjugated and oppressed Muslim woman, not someone who resembles a title character from the *Kill Bill* films. It is my hope that this chapter helps to explain why *Qahera*, *Raat*, and *Bloody Nasreen* shed light on questions of feminism, agency, and violence in popular culture.

QAHERA AND SOFT VIGILANTISM

Qahera represents an important historical moment in Egypt. It expresses the voice of Egyptian youth in the face of political and sexual oppression. The creation of a young Egyptian female artist, it offers a brave and power-ful meditation on Islamophobia, misogyny, revolution, and hope. As Deena Mohamed, the creator of *Qahera*, has written,

> In June 2013, at the age of 18, I created and posted online a webcomic titled Qahera. Originally posted in English and later in both English and Arabic, the comic features a central character named Qahera: this is the Arabic for "Cairo," but also for "conqueror" or "vanquisher." Qahera is an anti-misogyny, anti-Islamophobia, visibly Muslim superhero who engages with her environment critically and hopes to improve it.[15]

Qahera's visibility is communicated through her identity as an Egyptian superhero who veils. The veil is a symbol of her power. Like Burka Avenger, she uses veiling to her advantage. Where Burka Avenger uses it as a weapon against the Taliban and criminal elements in Pakistan, Qahera uses it as a tool against Islamic misogyny and Western feminism.

> Mohamed's character adheres to the codes of modesty that give her both agency and freedom to act. This places her in a position of power that is both physical and moral. She flips the paradigm regarding the veil as a form of oppression, and places her protagonist in a position to have a tangible impact within her world while wearing a *hijab*.[16]

Qahera is one of many artistic reactions to the 2013 uprising in Egypt against Hosni Mubarak and his regime. Scholars have written about these expressions in the context of modernity in Islam, describing them as "aesthetic strategies" of mediation.[17] As Iftikhar Dadi has argued, "In particular, the articulated relationship between modernity and visuality has resulted in a great flowering of visual representations of 'everyday life,' an aspect of modernity that was recognized as early as the mid nineteenth century by Charles Baudelaire in his celebrated essay, 'The Painter of Modern Life' (1964)."[18] These aesthetic strategies often emerge in spaces of oppression.

These aesthetic strategies include web comics such as *Qahera* as well as numerous other modes of cultural production. In Egypt and the larger region, artists responded in music and other creative outlets. Locally in Egypt, artists and musicians responded to the violence against women in Tahrir and on the Egyptian population at large in a variety of ways. During the eighteen days of protests at Tahrir poets performed on stages and artists painted artwork including murals, and a museum was set up that displayed "'souvenirs' from the protests, to commemorate their daily struggles in the square."[19] Musicians performed original works as well as songs that served as the anthems of the revolution.[20] The Egyptian rap group Egyptian Knightz released a song featuring Lauryn Hill titled "Rebel" that was also focused on the uprisings. After the revolution (*al-thawra*), artists continued to create art and music that spoke to the political and social issues at the center of Egyptian life. The efforts focused on "capturing the 'street'" and in particular, the spirit of Tahrir, include the establishment of a choral group called "The Choir Project" whose performance titled "Utopia" was about the events at Tahrir, as well as workshops, competitions for the most popular song of the revolution, and mural paintings around Cairo.[21]

After the protests, the government rezoned the area around Tahrir so that the protestors were confined, resulting in a constant back and forth of graffiti murals, whitewashing over them, and the return of graffiti art that has dominated several streets. Mohammed Mahmud Street has been a focus of these actions, hence its alternate name *share'i uyuun al-hurriyyah*, or "the Street of the Eyes of Freedom."[22] Among the murals of martyrs of the revolution, scenes of the protests and other imagery are images depicting women—historical and current figures that reflect Egypt's culture as well as its current political climate. One particularly evocative image is The Funeral (Mourning Women, *al-Naaehat*), which shows ancient Egyptian women carrying a sarcophagus that represents the "death of the football Ahli Ultras youngsters who were massacred on 2 February 2012 in the stadium of Port Said."[23] The murals are continuously altered—enacted, painted over, re-painted—and included the image titled *Haraaer*, which means "free fighters."

These responses reflect a rich tapestry of cultural influences, reflecting the cosmopolitan nature of Cairo. Muralists employed vocabularies "drawn from medieval Islamic calligraphy, Pharaonic temple paintings, and contemporary art."[24] Other artists employed graphic imagery that resembled American or

Japanese comic forms. *Qahera* is one such response. Qahera's name is also tied to the events of the uprising, functioning as a reference to Cairo. During the protests, army medical officers carried out "virginity tests" on female protestors; that is, forcible vaginal penetration—all of the officers were acquitted.[25] *Qahera* is a response to this violence in graphic form.

As a web comic, *Qahera* is a form of social protest broadcast through the use of technology. Mohamed utilizes the Internet as a way to express Cairene life and culture as women experience it. This life and culture is often called "the street." It is an example of what Asef Bayat points to in his work on the street and its role in social protest. As he has argued, "street politics is the modern theater of contention *par excellence*."[26] In inequitable societies, "the street is the chief locus of politics for ordinary people, those who are structurally absent from positions of power."[27]

Cairene life plays an important role in Egyptian art and culture. Graffiti artists in Egypt active in the group known as *Graffiti Harimi* believe that they are engaged in the "most popular form of activism in the public sphere."[28] The graffiti includes caricatures of women, inspirational quotes, and colloquial phrases. The actions taken by the group are seen as a collective movement, a "celebratory event that aims to take back, even in a small way, public space for women . . . the campaign will tackle and invert negative social ideas/stereotypes, and instead, build images that positive and powerful to honor the women of our society."[29]

Street art is often cited as a space for women to express their views in places that seek to silence them. Graffiti is a popular medium in the voicing of gender concerns. Afghan artist and activist Malina Suliman is well known for her blue *burqa*-clad skeleton, a self-portrait she has painted on walls throughout the Kandahar region in Afghanistan.[30] In Pakistan, street art is used to cover hate graffiti scrawled on Karachi's walls that targets women and religious minorities. In one case, a group of young Pakistani activists replaced anti-Shi'i and anti-Ahmadi slogans "by painting peace symbols, flowers, and murals over the hate speech."[31] This project has grown and like Burka Avenger, enjoys support from USAID, which as one scholar notes, "in no way diminishes the reality that the group began as a grassroots response to extremism and terrorism."[32] An initiative called "Reimagining the Walls of Karachi" has the support of a number of institutions and artists in the country aiming to encourage people to take back their streets through the power of art.[33] Graffiti art in Egypt, Afghanistan, and Pakistan represent distinct forms of protest, which at times intersects with gender politics.

How the street intersects with the web in Cairene protest art is very important. The web, in the case of *Qahera*, functions as a virtual space in which the audience can participate in the street life of Cairo. The web comic provides a place for the powerless to speak. We might think of the web comic as the city walls of the Internet. As Ada Price writes, "Creators flock to the Web for its immediacy, economic efficiency and global reach; it's also a secure place to experiment and grow."[34] Mohamed is one of many artists who have used the web as a platform for social protest in Egypt. Facebook pages dedicated to the revolution, the martyrs of the revolution, and ongoing political conflicts in Egypt often feature the art of Egyptians.

Qahera illustrates how web comics deviate from printed comics like *Ms. Marvel*. Mohamed created the first comic "as a joke" following her frustration with Islamist comments she had seen on the Internet.[35] As I have discussed, in the West, Islam is largely a construction of the imaginary that casts Muslim women as universally oppressed and powerless. *Qahera* challenges this discourse, offering a vision of Muslim women that is revolutionary but also situated in lived experience. One way this is expressed is through Qahera's wearing of the *hijab*. As one scholar points out,

> Qahera wears the hijab not to conceal her identity (as many superheroes do) but to project her identity. Indeed, her power seems to come from her traditional dress, as she is empowered by her choice to wear the hijab despite critiques of the possibilities of Islamic feminism.[36]

Despite the challenges that Egyptian women face, Deena Mohamed has been careful not to identify Muslim women as universally oppressed or in need of a white savior. Much like in Afghanistan, Iran, and other Muslim-majority countries, the tropes of the white Western savior and oppressed veiled Muslim woman have often served to dismiss the issues Muslim activists are focused upon, as well as silencing their voices in favor of white feminism. As Mohamed notes,

> Muslim women are very often put into an "oppressed, indoctrinated, in need of saving" trope, and superheroes are the precise opposite of that. That's one of the reasons I enjoyed creating her as a [female] superhero, because to many people it's a very contradictory concept . . . I like that you can easily adopt an art form usually commandeered by Western males and in doing so, make a statement on what is and isn't expected of Muslim (and also Egyptian) women.[37]

The act of silencing non-white women is known as *exclusionary feminism*, a position that requires the intervention of outsiders who "not only hold considerable privilege over marginalized communities, but are also often ignorant about the culture of those communities."[38] Qahera is an example of how this can be challenged.

The first *Qahera* comic (2013) offers a commentary on the political realities faced by Islamism and colonialism, forces that often compete for control of women's bodies. The comic opens with the face of the Arab *Muslimah*, rejecting the "gendered Western gaze" that dominates so many representations of Muslim women.[39] The first frame of the comic features Qahera's eyes beneath a furrowed brow, which is followed by a full view of the superhero clad in a gray *abaya* and cape. Her clothing includes black arm straps and a strap across her torso that hold in place the blade settled on her back.

The source of Qahera's activism is patriarchy, although a wide range of her targets are presented, including "sexual harassers, corrupt cops, kooky clerics, and Western feminists."[40] The inaugural strip takes on Islamic patriarchy. Four men listen to a religious cleric's teaching of the day: "A good wife is an obedient wife! It is your Islamic duty to keep your wife at home and in check"[41] Their wide-eyed expressions reveal a reluctance to think independently about religious matters. Muslims often call this blind allegiance to Islamic theology *taqlid* ("to follow"), which has its origins in early Islamic modernist debates in Egypt and elsewhere about the need for serious and analytical engagement with religious texts. As Khaled Abou El Fadl writes,

> In the late nineteenth and early twentieth centuries, motivated by a desire to break out of the shackles of outmoded traditions, a large number of scholars emphasized the importance of *ijtihad* (innovative and creative determinations), and severely criticized the practice of *taqlid*.[42]

Qahera leaps into action, her sword above over her head. The viewer might expect a bloodletting by the superhero in which the villain is struck down. Instead, Deena Mohamed offers humor. Qahera pauses for a moment and proclaims, "You're right, you know. Housework is women's work, absolutely. I especially enjoy doing the laundry." The cleric is shown hanging out to dry on a line with the rest of the laundry; Qahera looks on with a wry smile.

Another comic shows four women listening intently to a woman in a tank top with one hand on her hip. She replies to a scene that has just unfolded, "You see, that's why we need to rescue Muslim women!" This is an artistic representation of the critique of white feminism's savior complex, which has often insisted that Muslim women must be saved. Discussed further in the last chapter of this book, the notion of saving Muslim women is often preferred over active engagement with Muslim feminists and activists. As Aysha Hidayatullah has written, Muslim women are often "treated like native informants of a foreign religion rather than being stimulated and constructively challenged."[43]

Qahera's challenge to Femen, a controversial feminist group that, among other things, features nudity in their protests against sexism, reflects the tensions between Western and Muslim feminism. Femen is criticized by other feminists for its emphasis on a "fit body" and "hot boobs," which idealizes the female body in problematic ways.[44] By doing this, Femen privileges

Figure 5.1   Qahera with sword, Part 1: Brainstorm. Photo courtesy of Deena Mohamed.

certain bodies and the white standard of beauty. Critics have also pointed out that Femen's protests result in the projection of vulnerability and weakness through encounters of partially clothed women and the men who pull them off a stage or other public setting.[45] Femen's narrative strategy, that Muslim women are universally oppressed, is also problematic, as is the position Femen activists have taken that they need to "save" these women from Muslim men. Femen is grossly Islamophobic, making sweeping generalizations about Islam that vilify all Muslim men and cast Muslim women as hapless victims. As one of their members has stated, "We care a lot about violence and aggression, we care a lot when your fathers, brothers and husbands are raping and killing, when they call to stone your sisters, we care a lot when they burn embassies etc. and all that for Allah!"[46]

Mohamed knew that Western feminists often pervert the struggles of Muslim women to promote their own agendas. As she explains,

> Essentially, the webcomic served as both a space for self-expression and an opportunity to release my frustration with misogyny, both home and abroad. I was also careful to signal a warning to Western, liberal feminists who I knew would inevitably hijack Qahera to serve their own purposes. My wariness grew out of my own personal experiences as a Muslim girl "growing up online"; if there are no limitations on who is allowed to see your content, someone will inevitable hijack it to serve their own purposes.[47]

The comic includes a scene of Qahera at home with an open laptop featuring a web news article about a Femen protest at a mosque. In the background, we see her arsenal: costumes, swords, scimitars, pikes, ropes, and daggers. The following panel features Femen protestors yelling "Femen Akbar!" referencing a series of Femen protests which they termed "Femen jihad" that took place across Europe in 2013.[48]

Qahera's response to white feminists acting on behalf of Muslim women without their permission serves as a critique of Western paternalism. In a series of wordless panels, Qahera suits up and confronts the Femen protestors. She stands defiantly across the street from them. Upon noticing her they shout, "Look there! It's a **Muslim Woman**! This is why we're here! We have to **save** her!"[49] A demure Femen protestor is shown, suggesting that Femen's aggressive style of protest is a sham, followed by a close-up of Qahera's eyes in flames.[50] As the Femen protestors attempt to rescue Qahera and remove her *abaya*, which they label "oppression," Qahera quickly reacts, putting the length of her sword between herself and the protestor, who is taken aback. When she states, "I doubt there is much I can do to teach you," it is a way of saying that Femen's ears are closed to the voices of Muslim women.[51] After the call to rescue Muslim women, Qahera draws her sword and attacks the protestors, gathers them, binds them together with her sash, and then leaves the Femen activists dangling over a cliff and says, "Hey, so feel free to rescue me anytime."[52] The ideal of white saviorhood is destroyed in this statement, suggesting that Muslim women, be they superheroes or normal humans, can save themselves. As one scholar argues, "The rhetorical question posed at the end acts as a reminder to those who cause such violence: Do not assume that your moral (and inherently cultural) framework is any better than another's."[53]

Figure 5.2   Protestors shouting "Femen Akbar!," Part 2: On Femen. Photo courtesy of Deena Mohamed.

Qahera's vigilantism is soft. Like other superheroes, this is a vigilantism situated in an inequity of power. Qahera commits violence on others but it is acceptable, in part because her identity as a woman makes her sympathetic. As scholars have pointed out, the superhero often symbolizes the overturning of power structures—the weak become strong and the powerful are brought down.

Vigilante action can be a kind of rebellion by the weak against the strong, a further oppression by the strong against the weak, or one sort masked as the

Figure 5.3   Qahera and Femen protestors tied up, Part 2: On Femen. Photo courtesy of Deena Mohamed.

other. But it is the romantic images of vigilantes protecting the most vulnerable among us that accounts for the continuing appeal of vigilantism in the modern imagination.[54]

Comics communicate through a complex imagery, which at times reveals more than one would immediately surmise. The imagery in *Qahera* is stunning. Mohamed's use of black, white, and gray results in a striking graphic form. What is most interesting about the use of color (or lack of color) in this comic is that gray is reserved for the superhero—something that sets her apart from the world she occupies.

It is visual evidence that this woman is set apart from her environment. Superpowers and a strong agenda for Islamic women's rights are further affirmation of this fact. The grey also symbolizes something far more complex. Qahera exists in a world of absolutes. Whether she is battling some form of misogyny or white savior complex, her world is made up of polarized opposites ideologies that are represented within the black and white palette of the comic.[55]

One last point on Mohamed's work must be made—the importance of language. Qahera is bilingual, existing in both English and Arabic. As Mohamed has explained, what started out as a project in English eventually required an Arabic version due to the growing popularity of the webcomic in Egypt as well as its importance politically.[56] The theme of Islamophobia was directed at an English-speaking audience, while sexual harassment and political protest were directed at Egyptians; together they have resulted in a superhero that represents the complexities of Muslim women. It is this conversation that transformed Qahera. As Mohamed writes, "Somewhere along the line, she was redefined in the traffic between the two languages."[57]

VIGILANTISM AND HEROISM IN PAKISTANI GRAPHIC NARRATIVES

Raat is the brainchild of Wasiq Haris, a Pakistani artist and writer who created the web comic to honor the people of Pakistan.[58] Haris is also one of the individuals behind the cartoon *Team Muhafiz*, directed at Pakistani children. *Raat* is online and free, available to the public and not a business venture. As Wasiq Haris has said, this is a project "about inspiring change."[59]

Raat (which means "night" in Urdu) is not a superhero like Kamala or Jiya. She has no special powers and is not part of a mutant species or from another planet; however, Raat is still a *Muslimah* superhero. As Wasiq Haris explains, "Raat has a very strong set of moral principles which she has mainly acquired through her religion and upbringing and it is those teachings that drive her into fighting for justice at a time where injustice prevails."[60] She is a proud Pakistani Muslim woman and a vigilante who fights against criminals that plague her community.

Raat is a visually arresting character who, thanks to the talented artistry of Wasiq Haris, appears as a powerful symbol of Muslim womanhood. She wears a *dupatta*, the traditional cloth worn by women in Pakistan that covers their head, shoulders, and chest. As Haris notes, "Raat wears the dupatta not only because she is Muslim and a Pakistani but also to conceal her identity. Just like any woman, Raat loves to dress gracefully. In Raat's view, the dupatta/hijab or veil is a symbol of freedom not oppression."[61] Like Jiya/Burka Avenger, Raat uses the veil as a symbol of her Muslim identity *and* as a disguise. She is without the aid of superpowers like invisibility, the ability to fly, or shape-shift, and is physically challenged by her heroism, a quality that makes her even more relatable.

The first issue of *Raat* is titled "The Ones That Do . . . ," a reference to the choices people make in life regarding whether to do the right or wrong thing. Raat's opening image shows the main character with black eye makeup,

Figure 5.4   Montage of scenes from *Raat*. Photo courtesy of Wasiq Haris.

like a mask, holding her bloodied fists up in a fighting pose. Raat is a citizen of Karachi, a city affected by criminal violence and police corruption, both of which are documented in the first few panels. Raat identifies herself as a superhero, albeit one without any powers, when she says, "Unlike in storybooks, I have no powers, magical spells, gadgets, or a mansion full of money." These references to the superheroes of comic books, including Bruce Wayne, the alter ego of Batman (a millionaire who lives in a mansion with gadgets) helps the reader relate to the main character. She is an ordinary person doing extraordinary things. Her use of violence is expressed where she says, "People do unimaginable things to each other. History stands witness to such atrocities committed by humanity all throughout time. I intend to end that violence using violence."[62]

Raat is not the only *Muslimah* superhero who fights against injustice without the aid of magical powers. *Bloody Nasreen* is the creation of Pakistani artist Shahan Zaidi, who created the character in 2009 as his way of dealing with the rampant crime plaguing his country. The project began as concept art for a graphic novel and when Zaidi was able to introduce his idea to others in the comics and film industry, the character of Bloody Nasreen went viral. At this point, the focus of Zaidi's work shifted from the graphic novel (to be released soon) to a film adaptation of the character, which is set to be released in 2018.

Bloody Nasreen tells the story of a twenty-seven-year-old woman from Karachi who ruthlessly brandishes her own form of justice with a handgun and a *katana*.[63] The character's backstory reflects the realities of Pakistan, where kidnappings, political assassinations, and terrorism are common occurrences. According to Zaidi, "no one hears the stories about the families of the victims afterwards. Nasreen is from one of these families. And she takes revenge, and she takes it cold."[64]

Nasreen doesn't veil. In some cases, she wears a skull-covered *shalwar kameez*, a traditional dress worn by Muslims, Hindus, and other Pakistanis. The blood spatters, rips, and tears in her clothing are evidence of the violence

Nasreen has endured. She is also an adult—she wears makeup, a cigarette is drawn hanging loosely from her mouth, and in some images, she is shown in revealing dress and provocative poses.

Whether Nasreen is linked to the violent characters of American films or is a fully indigenous character, emerging out of Pakistan's own artistic and graphic traditions, is hard to determine. Pakistan is populated with female activists, including the Nobel Laureate Malala Yousafzai. The Pakistani feminist Afiya Shehrbano Zia believes,

> It [*Bloody Nasreen*] could be related to a larger message of bodily empowerment. Women may not want to wear exactly the same clothes or act like her, but the admiration can be attributed to the restrictive environment of a Pakistani woman that closes off spaces for them to be physically expressive. This character probably symbolizes a physical mobility equal to men's.[65]

Zaidi specifically created Nasreen as a role model of the "strong woman because there is a dearth of that in Pakistan."[66] Curiously absent from *Bloody Nasreen* is any mention of the girls and women in Pakistan who are activists, ranging from protestors to human rights lawyers. Instead, Zaidi focuses on terrorism and violent crime. It should be noted that feminists in Pakistan, including artists, have been active for decades, including artists. In 1983, the "15 Women Artists of Pakistan Mainfesto" stated that "we call all woman artists to take their place in the vanguard of the Pakistani women's struggle to retain their pristine image and their rightful place in society."[67]

Nasreen is a product of the chaos created by the corruption, mob violence, and terrorism in Pakistan. Her aggressive personality and post-modern style are designed to call attention not only to the ways in which such violence is inflicted upon a population, but what this violence does to the individual's very being. Muslims often speak of the darkness as a spot on one's heart that when ignored, grows until the entire heart is black. Nasreen represents this internal struggle (*jihad*) and through her violence suggests that when enough harm is done, an uncontrollable rage can take over.

Nasreen takes justice into her own hands because the government is unable to protect her and others. The theme of vigilantism is not restricted to Nasreen, of course—as we have seen, superheroes are often vigilantes. Vigilantism is often about complex political situations, adopting an ideology that is not necessarily "anti-state" but that expresses a lack of confidence in the state's ability to offer its people justice.[68]

Nasreen has sex appeal. She is drawn to reflect a slender, sexy body, with prominent breasts. At times her curves are prominent and her breasts are partially shown. This is very different from someone like Kamala Khan, whose boyish body is not on display. As discussed earlier, in comics, women are typically drawn to elicit sensuality. In one book that instructs artists how to draw women in comics, the author uses phrases like, "they must be beautiful and sexy," and "ready to die for."[69] Nasreen is presented as a beautiful, angry woman. Her clothes are torn to reveal the body, she often has a pouting expression. In these ways, Nasreen resembles the standard heroine of comics and other graphic narratives as available to men. These characters are "similarly idealized and objectified in the negative ways presented in the research on magazine advertising where women's bodies are on display and women are 'ready for sex.'"[70]

Nasreen's sex appeal makes her a controversial figure. However, through her body she suggests that the range of possibilities for Muslim women includes sexual beings. Nasreen's strength is clear—she is a fighter, she is strong, she carries weapons. In a twist on the objectification of women in media, she communicates the idea that Muslim women can be sexy on their own terms. Nasreen rejects the Orientalist imagery so often associated with women from "the East," and instead projects a loud feminist agenda that includes her right to uncover, use her body as a weapon (symbolized through her weaponry), and act in her own interests. Although not a superhero, her agency is expressed sartorially and on her body in other ways. In this way, she resembles other superheroes of the comic and film worlds.

> These characters are physically strong, athletic, proficient, confident, and intelligent, characteristics that are counter-stereotypical for female characters. Although their sex appeal may be seen as objectification of the female body, it may also be constructed as empowering by showing disdain for traditional feminine modesty.[71]

According to media reports, the *Bloody Nasreen* film will be released in 2018. The project has been in production for several years and its delayed release is likely due in part to the state of Pakistan's film industry, which has suffered a brain drain since before Partition in 1947. Poor technology, a lack of development, an exodus of actors and artists, and competition with Hindi cinema are all serious challenges.[72] However, Pakistan has had several decades of releasing excellent films, many of them with violent content that are often placed in the horror genre. When *Bloody Nasreen* does hit theaters, it will be the latest in a long string of films from Pakistan that focus on violence. Revolutionary feminists are part of Pakistani cinema, such as the 1969 film *Zarqa*, about a female Palestinian resistance fighter.[73] The 1990 Pashto-language rape-revenge film *Haseena Atimbum* (Atom Bomb) may give audiences an indication of what to expect with Nasreen, for Atom Bomb features "the female protagonist as an avenging angel fighting injustice."[74]

While we have no film yet, the images of Nasreen available on the Internet are telling. This is a character out for revenge. She is a victim of violence.

Nasreen is like other characters in popular culture who are classified as "violent women," and whose growing presence in advertising, television, film, and other areas of popular culture illustrates Third Wave feminism's emphasis on agency and free will. Nasreen's Internet presence is huge. Shahan Zaidi's artistic renderings show her in various poses—staring intently at the viewer, standing over her vanquished enemy, shooting her gun, holding her *katana* as she readies a fatal blow, and resting from doing battle. These repeated images reflect a common theme in the revenge genre, which "frequently depicts vengeance as a form of repetition."[75]

As noted above, *Bloody Nasreen* features a battered woman who carries a sword, gun, or other weapon. One assumes that she has been assaulted or attacked physically and that she is on a quest for revenge. This remaining section of the book contains observations regarding the ways in which Nasreen fits into the revenge genre, and how she resembles Beatrix, the revenge hero of the *Kill Bill* films.

Violent women seeking revenge has been a popular trope for decades, but it is perhaps associated most commonly with Quentin Tarantino's *Kill Bill* franchise, which features a woman out for blood. As scholars have argued, *Kill Bill* is a revenge tragedy, a genre that typically sees the character who seeks revenge die as a result of his or her vendetta. Tarantino disrupts this by allowing his character, Beatrix, to survive and be reunited with her child, whom she mistakenly thought was dead. Beatrix is a superhero with special powers. As one scholar points out, her special power is to come back from the dead.

> In Kill Bill, the murdered victim is also the triumphant revenger, who seemingly comes back to life to rewrite the past and resurrect the dead. Indeed, Beatrix returns from the dead not once but twice: not only does she awaken from a coma after being shot at close range, but she also manages to break out of a coffin after being buried alive.[76]

While the plotline of *Bloody Nasreen* is undetermined, we know the story of Beatrix. She is a victim of repeated sexual assault, a widow, and a mother who believes her child has been killed. The film follows her vengeance against the man who caused of her tragedy—her former employer Bill. As one scholar notes, the film begins with Beatrix awakening from her coma, a period which sees her repeatedly raped, moving into a period of encounters with her assassins, and ending with the murder of the primary villain.

> When she awakens, she goes on a "roaring rampage of revenge," killing first the hospital orderly and Buck, one of her other rapists, before picking off each member of the DiVAS in turn (all of whom participated in the massacre at her

wedding rehearsal, an event which comes to be known as the Massacre at Two Pines). Finally, she turns her attention to Bill, confronting him in his house in Mexico. It is here that she discovers her daughter, B. B. (played by Perla Haney-Jardine), is alive and well and living with Bill, her father. Beatrix kills Bill, and mother and daughter are reunited.[77]

Visually, *Bloody Nasreen* resembles the *Kill Bill* films in numerous ways. Nasreen is a vigilante. She uses a Japanese sword, or *katana*. Bloodied and battered, both Nasreen and Beatrix seek retribution for being victimized. Whether Nasreen has been sexually assaulted is unclear, but she is injured. In numerous images her lip is split and bloody, her clothes are torn, and she is covered with blood stains. Certainly, these images suggest sexual assault, utilizing the iconography of rape often see in popular culture. In one image of Nasreen, she lies on the ground, legs splayed apart, an optic that is drawn within the eye of her attacker.

Nasreen is usually shown carrying a gun in one hand and a sword in the other. The sword, a *katana*, is the weapon of the samurai. Nasreen is also shown with a katana hilt, called a *tsukamaki*, in another gesture to the samurai.[78] As numerous scholars have pointed out, the sword is used in visual narratives—including comics and film—to symbolize the moral code of the hero, which is based on the samurai. Tarantino often includes a sword in his films. As Mark Conrad has argued, it represents "a particular culture in which there is (or was) in place a very rigid framework."[79] In *Kill Bill Vol. 1*, not only is the sword used, its use is staged in a way that pays homage to Bruce Lee's last film *The Game of Death* (1978). As one scholar argues, by replacing Bruce Lee with Uma Thurman, this imagery results in a "monument to the woman fighter's faux masculine self, rather than as a tribute to her feminine physical appearance."[80]

The sword, which, incidentally, Qahera also wields, is an iconic object that has conflicting associations with sex and violence. In Japan, swords are identified with sadism and the male gaze. "Japanese manga culture and other forms of graphic texts, as well as the brand of violent and sadistic pornography closely associated with manga, have long featured the sword as an essential device for the brutal rape and torture of women."[81] This is an obvious contrast to the sword's symbolic value as the weapon of the samurai, and the code of honor attached to the Japanese warrior that Tarantino is fond of.

Nasreen represents an inversion of the threat of sexual violence that is popular in *manga*. She carries a sword as a symbol of her control over her own body as well as a sign that she will use it on anyone who attempts to violate her. Women wielding swords has become a popular theme in recent years. Scholars have argued that it transforms the individual female from a vigilante to a "competent martial equal."[82] Popular culture has often looked to Asia for inspiration in comics, literature, and film. Kurosawa and others idealized the "image of the samurai as a guard and warrior determined by deep ethical and spiritual values," as seen in the *jidaigeki* genre as well as in American films like Star Wars.[83] There is no reason to exclude the artists of Pakistan from these influences, for the presence of the *katana* in *Bloody Nasreen* is but one of many Japanese symbols seen in *Muslimah* superheroes. There is also Burka Avenger's costuming, which resembles a ninja, and her practice of martial arts, which is shown in slow motion—reminiscent of films like *Crouching Tiger, Hidden Dragon* (2000).

The focus on the body in these characters—Raat, Nasreen, and Beatrix—is situated in feminism's emphasis on sexual and physical liberation. This issue, which is examined in more detail in the following chapter, causes some consternation among Muslim feminists, who view "liberation" as a state that is not necessarily located in the performance of the body. Some scholars have gone so far as to say that violent female characters do little but glorify patriarchal forms, including the hyper-masculine violence to which we are accustomed men committing. As one study argues,

> Violent women and their violence in popular culture are often glamorized, trivi-alized, and sanitized; they are given a high profile and the status of aesthetic spectacle, and sometimes, indeed titillation. As a result, the violence is desensi-tized and disinhibited. Thus, in the seeming celebration of female empowerment as aspirational referents, violent women are constructed and circulated to signify a crisis of artificially masculinized, benign female predators and a superficial marker of power transformation in an intricate web of gendered tropes.[84]

Conversely, the focus on the body expressed in the female vigilante is wel-comed by many. Perhaps violent female characters serve as symbol of the human body, its vulnerability, and its suffering. As the feminist film critic B. Ruby Rich wrote in response to the *Kill Bill* films, "it's downright refresh-ing to find a film that makes us care about the battered and fatally flawed bodies subjected to its narrative."[85] The violent superhero also offers some-thing else—the possibility of freedom through the enactment of violence. In reflecting on characters like Raat and Bloody Nasreen and other *Muslimah* superheroes, we might ask if violence is necessarily feminist. As I argue in the following chapter, the superhero can be violent, but he or she does not have to be. Often the superhero is a symbol of the possibility of violence. Raat and Bloody Nasreen symbolize what may happen if the threat of vio-lence is met with real violence and the female superhero is what happens when "we allow ourselves to imagine the possibilities of fighting violence with violence."[86] This is, however, a possibility that is rarely pursued in the real world.

NOTES

1. Neil Shyminsky, "Mutant Readers, Reading Mutants: Appropriation, Assimilation, and the X-Men," *IJOCA* 8, no. 2 (2006): 389.

2. Cassandra Van Buren, "Critical Analysis of Racist Post-9/11 Web Animations," *Journal of Broadcasting & Electronic Media* 50, no. 3 (2006): 537.

3. Cassandra Van Buren, "Critical Analysis of Racist Post-9/11 Web Animations," 544.

4. Deena Mohamed, "On Translating a Superhero: Language and Webcomics," in *Translating Dissent: Voices From and With the Egyptian Revolution*, ed. Mona Baker (New York: Routledge, 2016), 139.

5. Jack Fennell, "The Aesthetics of Supervillainy," *Law Text Culture* 16, no. 1 (2012): 319.

6. Catherine Clark, "'Holy Agency, Batgirl!': Evaluating Young Adult Superheroines' Agency in Gotham Academy and Ms. Marvel," Honors thesis, Trinity University (2016): 32.

7. Matthew J. Costello and Kent Worcester, "Introduction. Symposium: The Politics of the Superhero," *Political Science* 47, no. 1 (2014): 86.

8. Gail Simone, "Women in Refrigerators," http://lby3.com/wir// (accessed March 14, 2017). Quoted in Neumann and Parks, "The Fan and the Female Superhero in Comic Books," *Journal of Fandom Studies* 3 no. 3 (2015): 293.

9. Neumann and Parks, "The Fan and the Female Superhero," 293.

10. Winona Landis, "Diasporic (Dis)Identification: The Participatory Fandom of Ms. Marvel," *South Asian Popular Culture* 14, nos. 1/2 (2016): 42.

11. Jamie Hughes, "'Who Watches the Watchmen?': Ideology and 'Real World' Superheroes," *The Journal of Popular Culture* 39, no. 4 (2006); 556.

12. Stephanie Juliano, "Superheroes, Bandits, and Cyber-nerds: Exploring the History and Contemporary Development of the Vigilante," *Journal of International Commercial Law and Technology* 7, no. 1 (2012): 49–50.

13. Stephanie Juliano, "Superheroes, Bandits, and Cyber-nerds," 63.

14. Arthur Berger, "Comics and Culture," *Journal of Popular Culture* 5, no. 1(1971): 170.

15. Deena Mohamed, "On Translating a Superhero," 138.

16. Jackie Duncan, "Beyond the Veil: Graphic Representations of Islamic Women," *The Compass* 1, no. 2 (2015): 2.

17. Iftikhar Dadi, "Ghostly Sufis and Ornamental Shadows: Spectral Visualities in Karachi's Public Sphere," in *Comparing Cities: The Middle East and South Asia*, ed. Martin Rieker and Kamran Ali (New York: Oxford University Press, 2009), 159.

18. Ibid.

19. Farida Makar, "'Let Them Have Some Fun'" Political and Artistic Forms of Expression in the Egyptian Revolution," *Mediterranean Politics* 16, no. 2 (2011): 310.

20. Ibid.

21. Ibid., 311.

22. Mona Abaza, "Walls, Segregating Downtown Cairo and the Mohammed Mahmud Street Graffiti," *Theory, Culture & Society* 30, no. 1 (2013): 128.

23. Mona Abaza, "Walls, Segregating Downtown Cairo," 132.

24. Nancy Demerdash, "Consuming Revolution: Ethics, Art, and Ambivalence in the Arab Spring," *New Middle Eastern Studies* 2 (2012): 7.

25. Mona Abaza, "Walls, Segregating Downtown Cairo," 123.

26. Asef Bayat, "The 'Street' and the Politics of Dissent in the Arab World," *Middle East Report*, no. 226 (Spring 2003): 11.

27. Asef Bayat, "The 'Street,'" 11.

28. Melody Patry, "Egyptian Artists Declare War on Sexual Harassment," *Index on Censorship,* May 15, 2013, https://www.indexoncensorship.org/2013/05/egyptian-artists-declare-war-on-sexual-harassment/ (accessed February 9, 2017).

29. "About," *Women Graffiti,* accessed December 15, 2016, https://www.facebook.com/pg/WomenGraffiti/about/ (February 9, 2017).

30. Megan Minto, "Artist as Activist: Malina Suliman, Afghan Street Art and Graffiti," *Eye Art Collective,* January 18, 2016, http://www.eyeartcollective.com/artist-as-activist-malina-suliman/ (accessed February 6, 2017).

31. Anita Weiss, "Can Civil Society Tame Violent Extremism in Pakistan?" *Current History* (2016): 146.

32. Anita Weiss, "Can Civil Society Tame Violent Extremism in Pakistan?" 146.

33. Adnan Murad, "A Makeover for Karachi: Artists Breathe Life into City's Walls, Replace Hate With Love, *The Express Tribune,* May 21, 2015, http://tribune.com.pk/story/889687/a-makeover-for-karachi-artists-breathe-life-into-citys-walls-replace-hate-with-love/ (accessed February 9, 2017).

34. Ada Price, "Web to Print and Back Again," *Publisher's Weekly* (August 31, 2009): 21.

35. Deena Mohamed, "On Translating a Superhero," 139.

36. Christina L. Ivey, "Combating Epistemic Violence with Islamic Feminism: Qahera vs. FEMEN," *Women's Studies in Communication* 38 (2015): 384.

37. Nadia Massih, "When Feminism Wears a Hijab," *Daily Star,* last modified October 15, 2013, http://www.dailystar.com.lb/Culture/Art/2013/Oct-15/234666-when-feminism-wears-a-hijab.ashx (accessed February 9, 2017).

38. Sandra Alena Lavadia Ilao, "Review and Assessment of Comics as a Medium for Disseminating Development-Oriented Strategies" (master's thesis, Up Open University, 2014), 35.

39. Ella Shohat, "Gender and Culture of Empire: Toward a Feminist Ethnography of the Cinema," in *Visions of the East: Orientalism in Film,* ed. Matthew Bernstein and Gaylyn Studlar (New Brunswick: Rutgers University Press, 1997), 20.

40. Marwan M. Kraidy, *The Naked Blogger of Cairo: Creative Insurgency in the Arab World* (Cambridge: Harvard University Press, 2016), 190.

41. Marwan M. Kraidy, *The Naked Blogger of Cairo*, 190.

42. Khaled Abou El Fadl, "The Ugly Modern and the Modern Ugly: Reclaiming the Beautiful in Islam," in *Progressive Muslims: On Justice, Gender, and Pluralism*, ed. Omid Safi (Oxford: Oneworld, 2003), 69.

43. Aysha Hidayatullah, *Feminist Edges of the Qur'an* (New York: Oxford University Press, 2014), 58.

44. Camilla M. Reestorff, "Mediatised Affective Activism: The Activist Imaginary and the Topless Body in the Femen Movement," *Convergence* 20, no. 4 (2014): 485.

45. Camilla M. Reestorff, "Mediatised Affective Activism," 487.

46. Inna Shevchenko, "Open Letter," *Huffington Post*: August 4, 2013. http://huffingtonpost.co.uk/2013/04/08/inna-shevchenko-muslim-womes-open-letter-amina-tyler-topless-jiad_n_3035439.html (accessed February 8, 2017). Quoted in Reestorff, 491.

47. Deena Mohamed, "On Translating a Superhero," 140.

48. Marwan M. Kraidy, *The Naked Blogger of Cairo*, 190.

49. Marwan M. Kraidy, *The Naked Blogger of Cairo*, 190.

50. Christina L. Ivey, "Combating Epistemic Violence with Islamic Feminism," 386.

51. Christina L. Ivey, "Combating Epistemic Violence with Islamic Feminism," 386.

52. Marwan M. Kraidy, *The Naked Blogger of Cairo*, 190.

53. Christina L. Ivey, "Combating Epistemic Violence with Islamic Feminism," 386.

54. Andrew E. Taslitz, "Daredevil and the Death Penalty," *Ohio State Journal of Criminal Law* 1, no. 2 (2004): 705.

55. Jackie Duncan, "Beyond the Veil," 3.

56. Deena Mohamed, "On Translating a Superhero," 142.

57. Deena Mohamed, "On Translating a Superhero," 147.

58. See the comic at www.raatcomic.com.

59. Ema Anis, "This Comic Book Series Hopes to Inspire Young Karachiites to Heal the City," *Images*, October 12, 2016, https://images.dawn.com/news/1176330 (accessed March 17, 2017).

60. Wasiq Haris, e-mail message to author, March 23, 2017.

61. Wasiq Haris, e-mail message to author, March 23, 2017.

62. Wasiq Haris, *Raat Issue #1: The Ones That Do* (2016), www.raatcomic.com (accessed March 17, 2017).

63. A *katana* is a Japanese sword.

64. Saba Eitizaz, "Superhero 'Burka Avenger' Divides Pakistan," *BBC,* July 30, 2013, http://www.bbc.com/news/world-middle-east-23503394.

65. Zofeen Ebrahim, "Bloody Nasreen: Pakistan's Very Own 'Tomb Raider,'" *Mint Press News,* September 15, 2014, http://www.mintpressnews.com/bloody-nasreen-pakistans-tomb-raider/196538/.

66. Amber Shamsi, "The Female Superhero Fighting Terrorists in Pakistan," *BBC,* August 12, 2014, http://www.bbc.com/news/world-asia-28754445 (accessed December 17, 2016).

67. Susan Ballard and Agnieszka Golda, "Feminism and Art: Unexpected Encounters," *Australian Feminist Studies* 30, no. 84 (2015): 208.

68. Andrew E. Taslitz, "Daredevil and the Death Penalty," 703.

69. Christopher Hart, *How to Draw Great-Looking Comic Book Women* (New York: Watson-Guptill, 2000), 7.

70. Karen McGrath, "Gender, Race, and Latina Identity: An Examination of Marvel Comics' Amazing Fantasy and Araña," *Atlantic Journal of Communication* 15, no. 4 (2007): 272.

71. Hillary Pennell and Elizabeth Behm-Morawitz, "The Empowering (Super) Heroine? The Effects of Sexualized Female Characters in Superhero Films on Women," *Sex Roles* 72 (2015): 212.

72. Ali Khan and Ali Nobil Ahmad, "From *Zinda Laash* to *Zibahkhana*," *Third Text* 24, no. 1 (2010): 149.

73. Khan and Ahmad, "From *Zinda Laash* to *Zibahkhana*," *Third Text* 24, no. 1 (2010): 151.

74. Khan and Ahmad, "From *Zinda Laash* to *Zibahkhana*," 157.

75. Lesel Dawson, "Revenge and the Family Romance in Tarantino's Kill Bill," *Mosaic* 47, no. 2 (2014): 123.

76. Lesel Dawson, "Revenge and the Family Romance," 122.

77. Lesel Dawson, "Revenge and the Family Romance," 125.

78. Patrick R. Benesh-Liu, "Anime Cosplay in America," *Ornament* 31, no. 1 (2007): 49.

79. Mark T. Conrad, "Symbolism, Meaning, and Nihilism in Quentin Tarantino's Pulp Fiction," in *The Philosophy of Film Noir*, ed. Mark T. Conrad (Lexington: University Press of Kentucky, 2006): 132–133.

80. Yuko Minowa, Pauline Maclaren, and Lorna Stevens, "Visual Representations of Violent Women," *Visual Communication Quarterly* 21, no. 4 (2014): 216.

81. Robbie B. H. Goh, "Sword Play: The Cultural Semiotics of Violent Scapegoating and Sexual and Racial Othering," *Semiotica* 160 (2006): 85.

82. Robbie B. H. Goh, "Sword Play," 86.

83. Christian Feichtinger, "Space Buddhism: The Adoption of Buddhist Motifs in *Star Wars*," *Contemporary Buddhism* 15, no. 1 (2014): 32.

84. Minowa, Maclaren, and Stevens, "Visual Representations of Violent Women." *Visual Communication Quarterly* 21, no. 4 (2014): 217.

85. B. Ruby Rich, "Day of the Woman," British Film Institute, June 2004, http://www.bfi.org.uk/sightandsound/feature/25 (accessed March 8, 2017). Quoted in Ruby C. Tapia, "Volumes of Transnational Vengeance: Fixing Race and Feminism on the Way to *Kill Bill*," *Visual Arts Research* 32, no. 2 (2006): 34.

86. Jack Halberstam, "Imagined Violence/Queer Violence: Representation, Rage, and Resistance," *Social Text* 37 (1993): 191.

Conclusion

Islamic Feminism and Muslim Chivalry

In the previous chapters, I have discussed *Muslimah* superheroes who demonstrate that freedom is possible. This study includes a wide range of characters—a group of superheroes who use magical stones invested with divine power, a Muslim American teenager whose life as a superhero complicates her struggles as a teenager, a Pakistani schoolteacher who dons a *niqab* to fight for children's educational rights, and an Egyptian hero who fights against Islamophobia, sexism, and exclusionary feminism. Each of these fictional characters tells us something important about the lives of Muslim girls and women. *Ms. Marvel* shows how post-9/11 Islamophobia impacts the lives of American Muslims. *Burka Avenger* teaches us about the struggles girls and women undergo to earn an education in Pakistan. In *Qahera*, we learn about the problems caused by sexism and Islamophobia. *Raat* and *Bloody Nasreen* present the struggles of the contemporary Pakistani woman.

Intersections of the fictional and the real world are not limited to *Muslimah* superheroes, of course. As scholars have argued, the use of visual narratives has often played a role is discourse about Muslims. This has been true in times of peace and during periods of war.

> From its initial articulation by the Bush administration in the days after September 11, 2001, to its current incarnation, rebranded the 'Overseas Contingency Operation' by the Obama administration, the war on terror has been mediated through an overwhelming array of visual forms and media, including photography, sculpture, painting, film, television, advertisements, cartoons, graphic novels, video games, and the Internet.[1]

In comic books, post-9/11 anxieties were expressed in characters like Captain America, whose refusal to succumb to state regulation resulted in his surrender to the government.[2]

Comics and other graphic narratives have often reflected historical events and social dynamics.

> This is demonstrated in Book Three of *Marvels*, which uses a famous story from *The Fantastic Four* issues #48–50, concerning the coming of a world-devouring entity named Galactus, as an allegory for the Cuban Missile Crisis, and Book Four portrays the death of Gwen Stacy in *The Amazing Spider-Man* #121–122 as an allegory for America's final loss of innocence during Vietnam.[3]

As discussed throughout this book, female bodies are often used as symbols of Islam in discourse surrounding the so-called "War on Terror." In most cases, they function as negative representations tied to violence, oppression, and Islamic patriarchy. The previous chapters have argued that this view of Muslims is overly simplified and that it reifies the Orientalist schema that has dominated much of the West's portrait of Islam. While Muslim girls and women suffer from harassment, abuse, and violence—like many around the world who are *not* Muslim—this is not the entire story of their lives. Iran is an Islamic republic but despite legal censures against women, many excel in education, government, and other areas. As Afsaneh Najmabadi wrote in 1998,

> Almost two decades after the 1979 Islamic Revolution in Iran, against the deepest fears of many of the secular feminist activities of the revolution, not only have women not disappeared from public life, but they have an unmistakably active presence in practically every field of artistic creation, professional achievement, educational and industrial institutions, and even in sports activities.[4]

Female theologians are also a feature of post-Revolution Iran as seen in Azam Taleqani, whose exegetical work on the Qur'an is well known within Iran and in Europe.[5] *Muslimah* superheroes also reflect political realities, which is one reason they are so powerful. Like Taleqani, they reject the controls placed on Muslim females by such diverse forces as Islamic patriarchy and Western neoliberalism.

The refusal to acquiesce to patriarchal religious instructions is one way Muslim girls and women challenge the efforts to control their bodies and minds, seen in the definition of Muslim-ness that includes heroic acts, physical strength, and social liberation. The rejection of Western neoliberalism is seen in the rejection of white feminism, which has so often equated sexual freedom with the liberation of the person, using the veil as its primary symbol. Jasmin Zine has written about the double bind Muslim women find themselves in, from both conservative religious forces and the secular state. As she puts it, "In either case, the fact that their bodies are made subservient to the decrees of patriarchal state authorities is an anti-feminist move."[6]

As discussed in the first chapter of this book, the influence held by white power structures is deeply embedded in conversations about Muslim women and liberation, and needs to be addressed honestly.

> Engagements between exalted (white) subjects (which situate these embodied subjects in their relatively powerful locations) and (non-white) others (in their embodied, relatively powerless, concreteness) are vital, if such Othering is to be subverted, and if feminists are to refuse complicity with an imperialist paradigm that has historically refrained from such exchanges with those it dominates.[7]

Because of such contingencies, a discussion of Islamic feminism is necessary. As the previous chapters have demonstrated, conversations about Muslim bodies, women, agency, and whiteness are complicated.

This final chapter explores these intersections through a careful discussion of Islamic feminism and the girls and women who are actively engaged in these struggles and the ways the fictional and real women discussed here reflect each other. At times this is quite obvious, such as the activism for girls' education championed by the fictional character Jiya/Burka Avenger and the very real Nobel Laureate Malala Yousafzai. There are other instances in which the fictional characters reflect the world in which we live, including struggles against poverty, oppression, colonial regimes, Islamist politics, and the violence these elements inflict upon the bodies and minds of Muslim girls and women. Too often these realities are ignored in discussions of gender and Islam set aside in favor of an overly optimistic view of female agency, feminism, and freedom in Islam. In Haideh Moghissi's reflection on Islamic feminism, she remarks,

> What was and is still disturbing, however, is the lack of balance in most of the affirmative accounts of Muslim women's activism. Many proponents of Muslim women's agency and Islamic feminist projects avoid any discussion of oppressive gender practices and seem to disapprove of a critical analysis of the Sharia-based reforms that are central to the Islamic feminist agenda.[8]

While Muslim feminist scholars like Amina Wadud and Kecia Ali are among the most vocal critics of these reforms and their embeddedness in Islamic law, it is nonetheless important to lift up the challenges inherent in feminism to radically change society. The narratives discussed over the previous several chapters represent a desire to symbolize these frustrations through the introduction of *Muslimah* superheroes.

Beyond this symbolic turn, what do comics, graphic novels, and animated television have to do with the lives of Muslim girls and women? Aren't graphic narratives simply forms of entertainment, disconnected from the lives of real people? As we have seen in this book, numerous scholars have argued that the opposite is true; that popular culture is not only a reflection of the world but is often a serious influence upon it. Superhero comics often "espouse and promote a particular type of idealized masculinity through the heroes' looks, action, and ideological stand."[9] Female superheroes also promote a particular view of femininity and strength. Malala Yousafzai is both an inspiration for and reflection of Jiya/Burka Avenger, who is "a skilled fighter of *takht kabaddi*, armed with a book, a sharp pen and *andaruni sakun* ('inner peace')."[10] The fact that she is wildly popular with both children and adults in Pakistan speaks to the social impact of such a revolutionary character.

As stated in previous chapters, this book is not simply a study of the recent emergence of *Muslimah* superheroes and an exploration of these narratives as cultural texts. It is an inquiry into the ways in which popular culture reflects constructions of Islam and Muslims and how graphic narratives present Muslim girls and women in radically different ways. I do not assume that these texts will overturn the meta-narrative about Islam; as other scholars have shown, even when positive Muslim characters are presented in popular culture, they do not disrupt the dominant mode of discourse. In Evelyn Alsultany's work, she documents the sympathetic Muslim characters that appeared on American television after 9/11 that did nothing to ameliorate anxieties about Islam within the general public. As she writes,

> Yet at the same time that sympathetic portrayals of Arab and Muslim Americans proliferated on US commercial television in the weeks, months, and years after 9/11, hate crimes, workplace discrimination, bias incidents, and airline discrimination targeting Arab and Muslim Americans increased exponentially.[11]

One of the problems with "sympathetic" presentations of Muslims is that they are often situated in narratives that contrast them with less sympathetic characters. The problem of the good Muslim/bad Muslim binary is found even in graphic narratives headlined by a *Muslimah* superhero. In *Ms. Marvel*, Kamala Khan and other females are at times juxtaposed with Muslim men who are stereotyped as either overly religious or controlling. As Shenila S. Khoja-Moolji and Alyssa D. Niccolini argue in their study of *Ms. Marvel*, "We note that even though strong female characters such as Khamala Khan are a direct response to dominant cultural expressions that portray Muslim women as oppressed, these images frequently rest upon the stubborn representation of Muslim men as backward, dangerous, and emotionally volatile."[12]

Yet, *Muslimah* superheroes are powerful. Visually they present an interruption to the image of the passive Muslim woman; socially they challenge patriarchy; and culturally they provoke important questions about the status, power, and agency of Muslim women. Throughout this book, I have focused on the first two of these topics; now it is time to turn to the third and final question. I begin this inquiry with two questions—What is Islamic feminism? How does it relate to negotiations of Islamic tradition and modernity?

ISLAMIC FEMINISM: DEFINITIONAL ISSUES

Islam has a long history and Islamic feminism is tied up with colonialism, racism, sexism, and other political programs, including Western feminism, all of which have been dominated by white voices. To understand Islamic feminism, it is important to understand the ways in which Western feminism participates in the discourse surrounding Islam and Muslims. Leila Ahmed describes this as "colonial feminism," which is characterized by a "selective concern" about the plight of women that employs the popular imagery of Islam (the veil) but fails to provide any support for the improvement of the lives of women (such as education).[13] For these reasons, the very notion of "Islamic feminism" is complex, bound up with politics, religion, bodies, and race, which is why it is often problematized and Islamo-centric discussions of human (including female) liberation are voiced instead.

As discussed in earlier chapters, the idea that Islam is categorically unfair to women is foundational to anti-Muslim rhetoric, part of the history of Orientalism, and a guiding theme of Islamophobia; all these approaches commit colonial violence upon the bodies of men and women. In both Iraq wars, Muslim women were a dominant symbol in the narrative of American heroism. Like those before and after him, Bush Senior fulfilled the role of the "metaphorical masculine hero because he led the rescue of a feminine captive victim from a toxic masculine rapist."[14] The same was true in Afghanistan where the "liberation" was cast in the media as a way to free Afghan girls and women from the bondage of Islam—represented most famously by the *burqa*, which served as the visual metaphor for male Muslim brutality toward women.[15]

Critics of Islamic feminism often argue that Islam is patriarchal and oppressive to women at its core, but in many cases they fail to talk about their own relationship with Islam, which as Ziba Mir-Hosseini argues, represents a "silence" that reveals the "ambivalence that many women, whether Muslim or non-Muslim, feel towards certain aspects of their identities."[16] Islamic feminism is a contested notion, complicated by the differences between schools of thought on female liberation, a colonial history, and an imperialist present that has often sought to tell Muslim girls and women what they should be struggling for. The characters examined in this study embody these complications, but in order to understand their importance locally and globally, it is necessary to understand the scope of Islamic feminism and the current dynamics of this tradition. My intention is twofold: one, to provide a concise and accurate summary of Islamic feminism; and two, to show how the characters examined in this study reflect some of the concerns voiced by Muslim women both past and present.

Islamic feminism is not an ideal descriptor for the battles, movements, and traditions involving the rights of girls and women to make choices for themselves in Muslim-majority communities. I am using it here as a way to talk about these struggles with the understanding that many of those involved in these struggles would not use the word "feminism" to describe their activism. The status of Muslim girls and women varies greatly, as do the goals of activists in different communities, which range from voting rights to changes in family law. In many cases, indigenous or local terms are used to describe the liberative work others would cast as "feminism." As Ziba Mir-Hosseini suggests, a serious discussion of Islamic feminism needs to begin with two questions: "We need to start by asking: Whose Islam? Whose Feminism? These questions continue to remain unaddressed in most discussions of Islamic feminism, whether in academic or activist forums."[17]

When examining the two terms that make up this field of inquiry, scholars have a lack of consensus. Islam is a contested term. In academia, there has been a tendency toward essentialism and blatant simplification. That is why, when discussing Islamic feminism, it is necessary to focus on a specific community. There are vast differences between Sunni and Shi'i women's movements, activists in Morocco and Indonesia, and the methods by which individuals have effected change. In the Iranian case, the 1979 Revolution, the Green Movement of 2009, and other political events have directly influenced the direction of feminist scholarship and activism. As one scholar notes, "Iranian feminists have strategized their writings based on their political and religious ideologies and locations due to the dramatic ideological changes their country has undergone in recent decades."[18] Indonesia is a Sunni majority democracy in which women (as well as men) often publish academic work on issues like child labor, forced marriage, and Qur'anic approaches to gender, all of which have been taken up by activists at the grassroots level.[19] The activities of Muslim feminists and other activists differ in numerous ways, influenced by religious identity, history, and economic class, among other factors.

Feminism is also a term that is open to numerous meanings. One definition calls it "a moral vision and a movement central to which are the struggles for personal and social transformation and activism on behalf of individual women and women as a group to change legal and cultural constraints and gender practices in favor of women."[20] Some Islamic feminists may want to work within their communities' legal and cultural systems, as they have done in Iran and elsewhere. The use of the term to describe the work of scholars and scholar-activists reveals some of the problems inherent in the adoption of a universal definition of feminism. Amina Wadud and Asma Barlas have rejected the label feminist for numerous reasons, including political and historical ones, and even some who utilize a feminist mode of analysis reject the identification because they contend that in Islam "divine truth is anti-patriarchal."[21] Feminism—that is, Western feminism—also has racial problems among them its support of colonial projects in the past and more recently,

> Third world feminists such as Chandra Mohanty, Marnia Lazreg and others have shown how non-Western women have been subject to the hegemonic discourses of Western feminisms with the effect of devaluing, prejudicing or simply denying other women's experiences.[22]

Islamic feminism also has been criticized for its dependence on religious systems of meaning. Among the critics are some who see progress as the answer to women's problems. As Mir-Hosseini has pointed out, some of those who identify as secular feminists have erroneously identified Muslim feminists with Islamism, a problem she contests by stating, "I challenge those who implicitly make these associations to make them explicit and to defend them."[23] She also dismisses the claim that Muslim feminists exclude other voices, citing the Musawah Framework for Action, which includes several secular women.[24] Others see Islam as being a sufficient belief system for liberation without a need for feminism. For some, "The political subtext of the rejection being the imperial relationship between Islam and Europe (or, more broadly, the West), namely, the political and economic ascendance of the West over the Islamic world from the nineteenth century onwards."[25]

Critics of Islamic feminism also include literalist Muslims, some of whom are responsible for its emergence in the past century. As one scholar notes, Islamic feminism in the modern age is "the 'unwanted child' of political Islam," which emerged in response to Islamists' enforcement of patriarchal notions of gender.[26] Of course, there are some Islamists—Muslims who want Islam as a foundational part of the modern state—who see feminism as "an extension of colonial politics, as a Western plot to undermine the Muslim way of life, that had to be rejected in the name of Islam."[27]

Islamic feminism is not only politically contested, it is also challenged for theological reasons. Amina Wadud, a prominent North American scholar of Islam, is perhaps the most important modern theologian who has conducted a re-evaluation of the Qur'an as the basis for Muslim transformation, focused both in areas of gender as well as other social inequities. As she points out,

> The centrality of the Qur'an and the consensus over that indicate why on-going Qur'anic analysis in necessary and why such an analysis is important to my consideration of women and social justice. Textual analysis cannot only help determine when Muslim societies are acting outside the parameters of a Qur'anic world-view and intent, but also can present a rationale for altering such actions.[28]

Kecia Ali, whose work on the subjugation of girls and women in classical Islamic law demonstrates outstanding scholarship, has argued that Islamic feminists are part of the larger academic discourse about Islam and as such, are influencing the field.[29] Fatima Mernissi argues that the gender norms of early Islam are patriarchal, but sees two Islams, one that is egalitarian and transformative ("*risalah* Islam") and another that is more political and restrictive for women.[30] She and others have contended that the status of women in Muslim societies has been in decline for many centuries, a symptom of the corrosion of Muslim ethical values, among other factors. Amina Wadud agrees with this view, insisting that "Oppression is human-made, and therefore must be human-alleviated."[31] As noted in the Introduction to this book, Wadud argues that the Qur'an offers an egalitarian and liberative model of justice that is ignored by many Muslims, who instead favor an interpretation of Islam that engenders an unjust social system. Wadud is not alone in finding gender liberation in Islamic tradition. Miriam Cooke argues that the foundations of Islamic feminism can be seen in the sacred texts (Qur'an and Sunnah) and in the long history of social justice movements in Muslim societies.[32]

Theological debates surrounding the status of women in Islam are unlikely to be settled because, as with other religious debates, social forces are more powerful. As Ziba Mir-Hosseini argues, "There always have been, and will be, competing interpretations of Islam's sacred texts. The power of any interpretation depends, not on its correctness, but on the social and political forces supporting its claims to authenticity."[33] This calls into question the potential impact Islamic feminism can have when it does not engage larger parts of society.

Islam is a global religion with numerous liberational political movements—including those that would be described as feminist. A survey of all the activist/feminist/liberative movements in Islam would be too large for this current project. A partial list would include individuals like Zaynab Al-Ghazali (Egypt), Nadia Yassine (Morocco), Nazira Zain al-Din (Lebanon), Shirin Ebadi (Iran), Raden Adjeng Kartini (Indonesia), Nabawiyya Nusa (Egypt), Bin al-Shati (Egypt), Shahla Sherkat (Iran), Sibel Eraslan (Turkey),

Amat al-Aleem Asowa (Yemen), and Rasuna Said (Indonesia).[34] As this list suggest, Islamic feminism is a global, diverse, and powerful phenomenon that includes active and rich debates surrounding Islam and women.

Islamic feminism often involves different sectors of the population. In many cases, the work of Islamic feminists is not restricted to religiously minded activists. In Iran, Afsaneh Najmabadi has argued that Islamic feminism and secular feminism are not mutually exclusive. As Fatima Seedat notes, "Najmabadi illustrates how the intersections of secularism, Islam and feminism allowed Iranian women to imagine new configurations for seemingly incompatible trajectories of thought."[35] In Southeast Asia, women have taken up causes like sex trafficking, domestic violence, and child slavery, at times within the context of Islamist movements. Indonesia, the largest Muslim country in the world, has a long history of Muslim activism focused on gender issues that began with the emergence of two political movements—the Muhammadiyyah and the Nahdlatul Ulama Movement—in the early twentieth century. As Pieternella van Doorn-Harder points out, these political movements generated women's branches whose work made a positive impact on education, medical care, and other social issues.[36] These examples illustrate the diversity of issues represented by the fight for justice in Muslim-majority countries, not just in Iran, Morocco, Egypt, and Indonesia but also Yemen, Syria, Malaysia, Pakistan, Saudi Arabia, India, and countless other Muslim communities around the world.

THE *MUSLIMAH* CODE OF CHIVALRY

The *Muslimah* superheroes that populate the worlds of comic books, graphic novels, and animated cartoons represent real struggles that affect Muslim women, including challenges to the right to control their own bodies, which often takes the form of legalized dress codes, access to health care, and the right to seek an abortion. In other cases, the stakes include human survival. Perhaps the most powerful fictive example of this is the forthcoming graphic novel *Madaya Mom*, which is currently (winter 2016) available in an online format through ABC and Marvel. It tells the story of a mother in Madaya, Syria, who struggles to keep her family alive through the siege. In the first issue, she stops eating so that her food share can be given to her children. Although Madaya Mom has no so-called superpowers, she represents the ultimate struggle of all people to survive difficult circumstances; in this case, warfare and starvation. *Madaya Mom* is a graphic narrative focused on individual heroism—a theme that runs through this study. In reflecting on Madaya Mom and other *Muslimah* superheroes, particular character traits emerge such as bravery, justice, and sacrifice. In addition to being typified by the comic/graphic novel superhero, they are also—singularly and collec-tively—Muslim values. As I argue in this concluding section, these are values expressed in the medieval code of Sufi chivalry, which ultimately sought to establish the ideals of the perfected human being.

Expressed in the characters examined in this study, values attached to the attainment of spiritual truth are also evident in the work that Muslim women (and feminist-minded men) do in their communities and in the larger world. These values are found in teachings that were followed in the orders, or brotherhoods, that have been an integral feature of Muslim life over the past millennia. As the foundational work of Muhammad ibn al-Husayn al-Sulami (10th century) argues, members of a *futuwwa* or brotherhood aspired to be "the ideal, noble, and perfect man," who "would give all, including his life, for the sake of his friends."[37] Historically, these "ethical organizing prin-ciples" included "the virtues not only of courage but of honor, gentleness, courtesy and, by and large, chastity."[38]

Many of these same qualities are seen in *Muslimah* superheroes—in their struggle for justice, bravery against enemies, and chastity, expressed in their status as single females, unmarried and childless. These Islamic values, which are understood as goals of the religious path, are focused on modeling one's behavior on the examples of Prophet Muhammad, his early companions, the *awliya* (saints), and other exemplary Muslim individuals. The Prophet's example includes his patience, sacrificial acts, generosity, and bravery.[39] These are characteristics that Muslims emulate both in Sufi orders and society at large. The rules of chivalry were also influential in the waging of war. As Henry Corbin argued, there were two stages of *futuwwa*—"military chivalry" and "spiritual chivalry."[40]

In al-Sulami's text, he lists pages of attributes that are identified with the chivalrous Muslim, including service to others and the attainment of hero-ism. "Be friends with the friend of your friend and enemies with the enemy of your friend."[41] The models of perfect humanity formed a lineage, called a *silsila* in Islam, that typically identified Muhammad and 'Ali as the founders of a brotherhood.[42] In graphic narratives, especially comics, the superhero is often part of a long lineage, who at times dies and is reborn in different forms. In the case of the death of Superman in 1992, the aftermath included "an extended funeral and the possibility that one of the four replacement Super-men might be the real deal."[43] In other cases, new generations of superheroes are related to older characters. Superman is one example. Like the superhero, the *fata* (the individual in a *futuwwa*) may not be simply human, but a "spirit (*ruh*) or an angel (*malak*)."[44]

In many cases, Sufi brotherhoods were restricted to men or relegated women to subservient roles. Nevertheless, women benefited from the rules of a particular order and in some cases, led a brotherhood. One example of this is Sokhna Magat Diop, who was considered both a saint (*wali*) and a leader of a brotherhood, or order, in Senegal.[45] Historically, Islam has a long history of female saints; the most famous is Rabi'ah of Basra, who often schooled male disciples in matters of proper morality and religious devotion. *Muslimah* superheroes embody the Islamic values that have historically served as the foundation of these brotherhoods; this is not compromised by the fact that the brotherhoods were typically all-male religious and military guilds. Muslim women have always found ways to negotiate patriarchal structures. The same is true for superheroines, who have often taken the cause up from their male predecessors. In 2014, Marvel introduced a female Thor, stating, "This is not She-Thor. This is not Lady Thor. This is not Thorita. This is THOR. This is the THOR of the Marvel Universe."[46] Burka Avenger, Ms. Marvel, Qahera, and other *Muslimah* superheroes express the spiritual qualities that are such an integral part of the *futuwwa* and are aligned with the qualities of the superhero.

Superheroes and heroines are transformative figures, passing through one state (human) to another (superhero). This often occurs following a violent and often startling event, such as a lightning bolt (Captain Marvel) or exposure to chemicals (Flash Gordon).[47] Scholars have written about this "promise of transformation" as something that involves both "identity" and the "malleable superhero body."[48] These transformations often involve physical and spiritual, or even mystical, changes. Spiderman is altered physically but other superheroes, like the characters in *The 99*, undergo a more profound change. The members of the *futuyyat* experience a mystical transformation, mirroring the many transformations that superheroes undergo in graphic narratives. In the case of one Turkish brotherhood, initiates have a ceremony that consists of "'receiving the candle,' (*tchirak almak*), 'putting on the belt' (*kushak kushanmak*), and 'getting permission' (*destur almak*)."[49] The change in clothing through a belt or robe is, of course, a standard device featured in the superhero narrative signifying the birth of the hero.

Heroes of Islam include the Prophet, of course, who rescued the Arabs—and potentially the world—from ignorance, greed, and low morality. Islam has many other heroes, including Prophet Muhammad's cousin 'Ali, who rescued the Prophet from certain death (as told in the Shi'i tradition). Also in the Shi'i tradition, we have the example of Husayn, 'Ali's son and the Prophet's grandson, who sacrificed himself to serve as an example of a just and true Muslim. Early Muslim women like Musayba b. Ka'b al-Ansariyya (who suffered wounds protecting Prophet Muhammad) and Khawla b. al-Azwar (who reportedly fought in the Battle of Yarmuk) are examples of early *Muslimah* heroes. Seeing *Muslimah* heroes engage in a *jihad*, or struggle, against injustice is not new. What is revolutionary is the casting of such individuals in graphic narrative form with stories that are disseminated to numerous communities around the globe.

Superheroes are socially relevant characters—a point made by numerous scholars. As Sean Carney has written, "Superheroes are thus allegorical figures for humanity's relationship to its own history; they are allegories for the human ability to create forms that are larger than humanity itself, and that humans then need to struggle with and repossess as their own agency."[50] The fact that these characters have, at times, leapt off the pages and entered the real world is also noteworthy. In 2015, after an Islamophobic group paid for advertisements that promoted bigotry against Muslims, activists in San Francisco transposed Kamala Khan onto these ads, radically altering their message. "The take-up of a cultural artifact to resist everyday forms of Islamophobia is precisely one of the ways in which the public pedagogies of *Ms. Marvel* can transform into action."[51]

The *Muslimah* Code of Chivalry is a model of behavior that is both Islamic and heroic. It provides an Islamic lens through which we can understand the role of Muslim women in the graphic narratives I have focused upon in this study, but also serves as a way to understand the lived, ethical Islam that is the reality for many Muslims today. The framing of this activist, liberational Islam in the *Muslimah* superhero shows what is possible and what is necessary. It is the *jihad al-nafs*, the greater *jihad* that guides the superhero's actions. Prophetic chivalry is the goal of this *jihad*. The *Muslimah* superhero is one way in which the possibility of this ideal is visualized, but it is a possibility that lies in each of us—from Kamala to Malala.

NOTES

1. Matt Delmont, "Introduction: Visual Culture and the War on Terror," *American Quarterly* 65, no. 1 (2013): 157.

2. Rebecca Wanzo, "The Superhero: Meditations on Surveillance, Salvation, and Desire," *Communication and Critical/Cultural Studies* 6, no 1 (2009): 93–4.

3. Sean Carney, "The Function of the Superhero at the Present Time," *Iowa Journal of Cultural Studies* 6 (2005): 106.

4. Afsaneh Najmabadi, "Feminism in the Islamic Republic: Years of Hardship, Years of Growth," in *Islam, Gender, and Social Change in the Muslim World*, eds. Yvonne Haddad and John Esposito (New York: Oxford University Press, 1998), 59.

5. Fereshteh Ahmadi, "Islamic Feminism in Iran: Feminism in a New Islamic Context," *Journal of Feminist Studies in Religion* 22, no. 2 (2006): 42.

6. Jasmin Zine, "Between Orientalism and Fundamentalism: The Politics of Muslim Women's Feminist Engagement," *Muslim World Journal of Human Rights* 3, no. 1 (2006): 11.

7. Sunera Thobani, "White Wars: Western Feminisms and the 'War on Terror,'" *Feminist Theory* 8, no. 2 (2007): 183.

8. Haideh Moghissi, "Islamic Feminism Revisited," *Comparative Studies of South Asia, Africa and the Middle East* 31, no. 1 (2011): 11.

9. Mervi Miettinen, "Men of Steel? Rorschach, Theweleit, and *Watchmen's* Deconstructed Masculinity," *Political Science and Politics* 47, no. 1 (2014): 104.

10. Kamila Junik-Luniewska, "From Malala to *Burka Avenger*: A Few Remarks on Changing Female Role Models in Contemporary Pakistan," *Politeja* 1, no. 40 (2016): 297–298.

11. Evelyn Alsultany, "Arabs and Muslims in the Media after 9/11: Representational Strategies for a 'Postrace' Era," *American Quarterly* 65, no. 1 (2013): 161.

12. Shenila S. Khoja-Moolji and Alyssa D. Niccolini, "Comics as Public Pedagogy: Reading Muslim Masculinities through Muslim Femininities in *Ms. Marvel*," *Girlhood Studies* 8, no. 3 (2015): 36.

13. Lila Abu-Lughod, *Do Muslim Women Need Saving?* (Cambridge: Harvard University Press, 2013), 33.

14. James W. Messerschmidt, *Hegemonic Masculinities and Camouflaged Politics: Unmasking the Bush Dynasty and Its War Against Iraq* (Boulder: Paradigm Publishers, 2010) 55.

15. Ann Russo, "The Feminist Majority Foundation's Campaign to Stop Gender Apartheid," *International Feminist Journal of Politics* 8, Issue 4 (2006): 570–71.

16. Ziba Mir-Hosseini, *Institute for Development Studies Bulletin* 42, no. 1 (2011): "Beyond 'Islam' vs. 'Feminism,'" 72.

17. Ziba Mir-Hosseini, "Beyond 'Islam' vs. 'Feminism,'" 68.

18. Huma Ahmed-Ghosh, "Dilemmas of Islamic and Secular Feminists and Feminisms," *Journal of International Women's Studies* 9, no. 3 (2008): 101.

19. Pieternella van Doorn-Harder, "Controlling the Body: Muslim Feminists Debating Women's Rights in Indonesia," *Religion Compass* 2, no. 6 (2008): 1022.

20. Haideh Moghissi, "Islamic Feminism Revisited," 79.

21. Fatima Seedat, "When Islam and Feminism Converge," *The Muslim World* 103, no. 3 (2013): 406.

22. Fatima Seedat, "When Islam and Feminism Converge," 416.

23. Ziba Mir-Hosseini, "Beyond 'Islam' vs. 'Feminism,'" 68.

24. Ziba Mir-Hosseini, "Beyond 'Islam' vs. 'Feminism,'" 75.

25. Fatima Seedat, "When Islam and Feminism Converge," 405.

26. Ziba Mir-Hosseini, "Beyond 'Islam' vs. 'Feminism,'" 71.

27. Ziba Mir-Hosseini, "Beyond 'Islam' vs. 'Feminism,'" 69.

28. Amina Wadud, "Towards a Qur'anic Hermeneutics of Social Justice: Race, Class and Gender," *Journal of Law and Religion* 12 (1995–6): 43.

29. Fatima Seedat, "When Islam and Feminism Converge," 418.

30. Fatima Seedat, "When Islam and Feminism Converge," 405.

31. Amina Wadud, "Towards a Qur'anic Hermeneutics of Social Justice," 46.

32. Fatima Seedat, "When Islam and Feminism Converge," 409.

33. Ziba Mir-Hosseini, "Beyond 'Islam' vs. 'Feminism,'" 75.

34. For a larger discussion of some of these figures, see Margot Badran, "Between Secular and Islamic Feminism(s): Reflections on the Middle East and Beyond," *Journal of Middle East Women's Studies* 1, no. 1 (2005): 6–28.

35. Fatima Seedat, "When Islam and Feminism Converge," 408.

36. Pieternella van Doorn-Harder, "Controlling the Body: Muslim Feminists Debating Women's Rights in Indonesia," 1026.

37. Quoted in Norzakiah Saparmin, "A Brief History of the Relationship between *Futuwwa* (Muslim Brotherhood) and the Sūfī's *Tarīqahs* in the Islamic Civilization," *Revelation and Science* 6, no. 1 (2016): 27. No page number given.

38. Mohsen Zakeri, "Muslim 'Chivalry' at the Time of the Crusaders: The Case of Usāma b. Munqidh," *Hallesche Beiträge zur Orientwissenschaft* 22 (1996): 39.

39. Norzakiah Saparmin, "A Brief History," 28.

40. Khachik Gevorgyan, "*Futuwwa* Varieties and the *Futuwwat-namā* Literature: An Attempt to Classify *Futuwwa* and Persian *Futuwwat-nāmas*," *British Journal of Middle Eastern Studies* 40, no. 1 (2013): 3.

41. Muhammad ibn al-Husayn al-Sulami, *The Book of Sufi Chivalry: Lessons to a Son of the Moment (Futuwwah)*, trans. Sheikh Tosun Bayrak al-Jerrahi al-Halveti (New York: Inner Traditions International, 1993), 110.

42. Gerard Salinger, "Was the *Futūwa* an Oriental Form of Chivalry?" *Proceedings of the American Philosophical Society* 94, no. 5 (1950): 485.

43. Randy Duncan, Matthew J. Smith, and Paul Levitz, *The Power of Comics: History, Form, and Culture* (New York: Bloomsbury Academic, 2015), 215.

44. Michael Chodkiewicz, "Introduction," in Muhammad ibn al-Husayn al-Sulami, *The Book of Sufi Chivalry: Lessons to a Son of the Moment (Futuwwah)*, trans. Sheikh Tosun Bayrak al-Jerrahi al-Halveti (New York: Inner Traditions International, 1993), 23.

45. Codou Bop, "Roles and the Position of Women in Sufi Brotherhoods in Senegal," *Journal of the American Academy of Religion* 73, no. 4 (2005): 1109.

46. Marvel, July 15, 2015, http://marvel.com/news/comics/22875/marvel_proudly_presents/_thor. Quoted in Ellen Kirkpatrick and Suzanne Scott, "Representation and Diversity in Comics Studies," *Cinema Journal* 55, no. 1(2015): 123.

47. Randy Duncan, Matthew J. Smith, and Paul Levitz, *The Power of Comics: History, Form, and Culture*, 209.

48. Kirkpatrick and Scott, "Representation and Diversity in Comics Studies," 123, 121.

49. G.G. Arnakis, "Futuwwa Traditions in the Ottoman Empire: Akhis, Bektashi Dervishes, and Craftsman," *Journal of Near Eastern Studies* 12, no. 4 (1953): 240.

50. Sean Carney, "The Function of the Superhero at the Present Time," 102.

51. Shenila S. Khoja-Moolji and Alyssa D. Niccolini, "Comics as Public Pedagogy: Reading Muslim Masculinities through Muslim Femininities in *Ms. Marvel*," 37.

Bibliography

Abad-Santos, Alexander. "Marvel Dismisses Female Superheroes." *The Atlantic*, September 18, 2013, https://www.theatlantic.com/entertainment/archive/2013/09/marvel-dimisses-female-superheroes/310923/ (accessed September 18, 2013).

Abaza, Mona. "Walls, Segregating Downtown Cairo and the Mohammed Mahmud Street Graffiti." *Theory, Culture & Society* 30, no. 1 (2013): 122–139.

Abbott, Lawrence L. "Comic Art: Characteristics and Potentialities of a Narrative Medium." *The Journal of Popular Culture* 19, no. 4 (1986): 155–176.

"About." *Women Graffiti,* accessed December 15, 2016, https://www.facebook.com/pg/WomenGraffiti/about/ (February 9, 2017).

Abrams, Danielle. "Performative Practices and Poetry in North America and Pakistan." *Women's Studies Quarterly* 35, nos. 3/4 (2007): 317–321.

Abu-Lughod, Lila. *Do Muslim Women Need Saving?* Cambridge: Harvard University Press, 2013.

Aguyao, Michelle. "Representations of Muslim Bodies in *The Kingdom*: Deconstructing Discourses in Hollywood." *Global Media Journal—Canadian Edition* 2, no. 2 (2009): 41–56.

Ahmad, Meha. "Islamic Superheroes Out to Change the World." *Islamic Horizons* 40, no. 5 (2011): 52–54.

Ahmad, Meher. "Muslim Girl Superhero." *The Progressive* 78, no. 4 (2014): 44–45.

Ahmadi, Fereshtah. "Islamic Feminism in Iran: Feminism in a New Islamic Context." *Journal of Feminist Studies in Religion* 22, no. 2 (2006): 33–53.

Ahmed, Leila. *A Quiet Revolution: The Veil's Resurgence, from the Middle East to America*. New Haven: Yale University Press, 2012.

Ahmed-Ghosh, Huma. "Dilemmas of Islamic and Secular Feminists and Feminisms." *Journal of International Women's Studies* 0, no. 3 (2008): 99–116.

Akou, Heather Marie. "Building a New 'World Fashion': Islamic Dress in the Twenty-First Century." *Fashion Theory* 11, no. 4 (2007): 403–422.

Aldama, Frederick Luis. *Multicultural Comics: From Zap to Blue Beetle*. Austin: University of Texas Press, 2010.

Ali, Dilshad D. "Interview: G. Willow Wilson on the Creation of the Newest Muslim-American Comic Superhero," *Patheos*, November 8, 2013, http://www.patheos.com/blogs/altmuslim/2013/11/interview-g-willow-wilson-on-the-creation-of-the-newest-muslim-american-comic-superhero/ (accessed February 13, 2017).

Ali, Kecia. *Sexual Ethics and Islam: Feminist Reflections on Qur'an, Hadith, and Jurisprudence.* Oxford: Oneworld, 2006.

Alsultany, Evelyn. "Arabs and Muslims in the Media after 9/11: Representational Strategies for a 'Postrace' Era." *American Quarterly* 65, no. 1 (2013): 161–169.

Al-Sulami, Muhammad ibn al-Husayn. *The Book of Sufi Chivalry: Lessons to a Son of the Moment (Futuwwah).* Translated by Sheikh Tosun Bayrak al-Jerrahi al-Halveti. New York: Inner Traditions International, 1983.

Al-Taee, Nasser. *Representations of the Orient in Western Music: Violence and Sexuality.* New York: Routledge, 2010.

Al-Zo'by, Mazhar. "Representing Islam in the Age of Neo-Orientalism: Media, Politics and Identity." *Journal of Arab & Muslim Media Research* 8, no. 3 (2015): 217–238.

Amouzadeh, Mohammad and Manoochehr Tavangar. "Decoding Pictorial Metaphor: Ideologies in Persian Commercial Advertising." *International Journal of Cultural Studies* 7, no. 2 (2004): 147–174.

Anis, Ema. "This Comic Book Series Hopes to Inspire Young Karachiites to Heal the City." *Images*, October 12, 2016, https://images.dawn.com/news/1176330 (accessed March 17, 2017).

Anthias, Floya. "Beyond Feminism and Multiculturalism: Locating Difference and the Politics of Location." *Women's Studies International Forum* 25, no. 3 (2002): 275–286.

Arjana, Sophia Rose. "Returning to the One: Postcolonial Muslim Liturgy." In *Liturgy in Postcolonial Perspectives: Only One Is Holy*, edited by Claudio Carvalhaes, 23–31. New York: Palgrave Macmillan, 2015.

———. *Muslims in the Western Imagination.* New York: Oxford, 2015.

Arnakis, G. G. "Futuwwa Traditions in the Ottoman Empire: Akhis, Bektashi Dervishes, and Craftsmen." *Journal of Near Eastern Studies* 12, no. 4 (1953): 232–247.

Asad, Talal. "Muslims and European Identity: Can Europe Represent Islam?" In *Cultural Encounters: Representing 'Otherness,'* edited by Elizabeth Hallam and Brian V. Street, 11–27. New York: Routledge, 2000.

Ashraf, Syed Ali. "The Inner Meaning of the Islamic Rites: Prayer, Pilgrimage, Fasting, Jih d." In *Islamic Spirituality: Foundations*, edited by Seyyed Hossein Nasr, 111–130. New York: The Crossroad Publishing Company, 1991.

Austin, Shannon. "Batman's Female Foes: The Gender War in Gotham City." *The Journal of Popular Culture* 48, no. 2 (2015): 285–229.

Badran, Margot. "Understanding Islam, Islamism, and Islamic Feminism." *Journal of Women's History* 13, no. 1 (2001): 47–52.

———. "Between Secular and Islamic Feminism/2: Reflections on the Middle East and Beyond." *Journal of Middle East Women's Studies* 1, no. 1 (2005): 6–28.

Baepler, Paul, editor. *White Slaves, African Masters: An Anthology of American Barbary Captivity Narratives.* Chicago: University of Chicago Press, 1999.

Baker, Kaysee and Arthur A. Raney. "Equally Super?: Gender-Role Stereotyping of Superheroes in Children's Animated Programs." *Mass Communication and Society* 10, no. 1 (2007): 25–41.

Ballard, Susan and Agniesza Golda. "Feminism and Art: Unexpected Encounters." *Australian Feminist Studies* 30, no. 84 (2015): 199–210.

Basir, Siham. "Interview: Nigar Nazar CEO, Gogi Studios." *Newsline*, June 2010, http://newslinemagazine.com/magazine/interview-nigar-nazar-ceo-gogi-studios/ (accessed February 21, 2017).

Bayat, Asef. "The 'Street' and the Politics of Dissent in the Arab World." *Middle East Report* 226 (2003): 10–17.

———. *Life as Politics: How Ordinary People Change the Middle East.* Stanford: Stanford University Press, 2013.

Beard, Michael. "Between West and World (Review of Orientalism by Edward Said)." *Diacritics* 9, no. 4 (1979): 2–12.

Behiery, Valerie. "Alternative Narratives of the Veil in Contemporary Art." *Comparative Studies of South Asia, Africa and the Middle East* 32, no. 1 (2012): 130–146.

Benesh-Liu, Patrick R. "Anime Cosplay in America." *Ornament* 31, no. 1 (2007): 44–48.

Berger, Arthur. "Comics and Culture." *The Journal of Popular Culture* 5, no. 1 (1971): 164–177.

Bergson, Henri. *Laughter: An Essay on the Meaning of the Comic*, edited by Cloudesley Brereton and translated by Fred Rothwell. London: MacMillan and Green Integer, 1999.

Best, Mark. "Domesticity, Homosociality, and Male Power in Superhero Comics of the 1950s." *Iowa Journal of Cultural Studies* 6 (2005): 80–99.

Bilge, Sirma. "Beyond Subordination vs. Resistance: AN Intersectional Approach to the Agency of Veiled Women." *Journal of Intercultural Studies* 31, no. 1 (2010): 9–28.

Bop, Codou. "Roles and the Position of Women in Sufi Brotherhoods in Senegal." *Journal of the American Academy of Religion* 73, no. 4 (2005): 1099–1119.

Brackett, Jeffrey M. "Religion and Comics." *Religion Compass* 9, no. 12 (2015): 493–500.

Brar, Miranda. "The Nation and Its Burka Avenger, the 'Other; and Its Malala Yusafzai: The Creation of a Female Muslim Archetype as the Site for Pakistani Nationalism." *Prandium: The Journal of Historical Studies* 3, no. 1 (2014): 108.

Brown, Jeffrey A. "Comic Book Masculinity and the New Black Superhero." *African American Review* 33, no. 1 (1999): 25–42.

"Burka Avenger Wins." *Slogan* (December 2014): 10.

Butler, Judith. "Variations on Sex and Gender: Beauvoir, Wittig, Foucault." In *The Judith Butler Reader*, edited by Sarah Salih, 21–38. Malden, MA: Blackwell Publishing, 2004.

Carney, Sean. "The Function of the Superhero at the Present Time." *Iowa Journal of Cultural Studies* 6 (2005): 100–117.

Chandra, Nandini. "The Prehistory of the Superhero Comics in India (1976–1986)." *Thesis Eleven* 113, no. 1 (2012): 57–77.

Chittick, William C. *The Self-Disclosure of God: Principles of Ibn al-'Arab 's Cosmology*. Albany: State University of New York Press, 1998.

Chodkiewicz, Michael. "Introduction." In Muhammad ibn al-Husayn al-Sulami, *The Book of Sufi Chivalry: Lessons to a Son of the Moment (Futuwwah)*, translated Sheikh Tosun Bayrak al-Jerrahi al-Halveti, 16–24. New York: Inner Traditions International, 1983.

Chute, Hillary L. and Marianne DeKoven. "Introduction: Graphic Narrative." *Modern Fiction Studies* 52, no. 4 (2006): 767–782.

Clark, Catherine. "'Holy Agency, Batgirl!': Evaluating Young Adult Superheroines' Agency in Gotham Academy and Ms. Marvel." Honors thesis, Trinity University, 2016.

Clements, James and Richard Gauvin. "The Marvel of Islam: Reconciling Muslim Epistemologies through a New Islamic Origin Saga in Naif al-Mutawa's *The 99*." *The Journal of Religion and Popular Culture* 26, no. 1 (2014): 36–70.

Cole, Juan. "Pakistan and Afghanistan: Beyond the Taliban." *Political Science Quarterly* 124, no 2 (2009): 221–249.

Conrad, Mark T. "Symbolism, Meaning, and Nihilism in Quentin Tarantino's Pulp Fiction." In *The Philosophy of Film Noir*, edited by Mark T. Conrad, 125–137. Lexington: University Press of Kentucky, 2006.

Costello, Matthew J. and Kent Worcester. "Introduction. Symposium: The Politics of the Superhero." *Political Science* 47, no. 1 (2014): 85–89.

Coulthard, Lisa. "Killing Bill: Rethinking Feminism and Film Violence." In *Interrogating Postfeminism: Gender and the Politics of Popular Culture*, edited by Yvonne Tasker and Diane Negra, 153–175. Durham: Duke University Press, 2007.

Dadi, Iftikhar. "Ghostly Sufis and Ornamental Shadows: Spectral Visualities in Karachi's Public Sphere." In *Comparing Cities: The Middle East and South Asia*, edited by Martina Rieker and Kamran Ali, 159–193. New York: Oxford University Press, 2009.

Dar, Jehanzeb. "Holy Islamophibia, Batman! Demonization of Muslims and Arabs in Mainstream Comic Books." *Counterparts* 346 (2010): 99–110.

Das, Srijana Mitra. "Aaron Haroon: Burka Avenger's Apparel Not About Sexuality—It's About Strength." *The Times of India*, August 2, 2013, http://timesofindia. indiatimes.com/interviews/Aaron-Haroon-Burka-Avengers-apparel-not-about-sexuality-its -about-strength/articleshow/21537720.cms (accessed February 5, 2017).

Daulatzai, Sohail. *Fifty Years of "The Battle of Algiers": Past as Prologue*. Minneapolis: University of Minnesota Press, 2016.

Davis, Julie and Robert Westerfelhaus. "Finding a Place for a Muslimah Heroine in the Post-9/11 Marvel Universe: New X-Men's Dust." *Feminist Media Studies* 13, no. 5 (2013): 800–809.

Dawson, Lesel. "Revenge and the Family Romance in Tarantino's Kill Bill." *Mosaic* 47, no. 2 (2014): 121–134.

Debroy, Dipavali. "The Graphic Novel in India: East Transforms West." *Bookbird: A Journal of International Children's Literature* 49, no. 4 (2011): 32–39.

Deeb, Mary-Jane. "*The 99*: Superhero Comic Books from the Arab World." *Comparative Studies of South Asia, Africa and the Middle East* 32, no. 2 (2012): 391–407.

De La Torre, Miguel. "Introduction." In *Introducing Liberative Theologies*, edited by Miguel De La Torre, xxv-xxvii. Maryknoll, NY: Orbis Books, 2015.

Delmont, Matt. "Introduction: Visual Culture and the War on Terror." *American Quarterly* 65, no. 1 (2013): 157–160.

Demerdash, Nancy. "Consuming Revolution: Ethics, Art, and Ambivalence in the Arab Spring." *New Middle Eastern Studies* 2 (2012): 1–13.

Dittmer, Jason. "Captain America's Empire: Reflections on Identity, Popular Culture, and Post-9/11 Geopolitics." *Annals of the Association of American Geographers* 95, no. 3 (2005): 626–643.

Dobrow, Julia R. and Calvin L. Gidney. "The Good, the Bad, and the Foreign: The Use of Dialect in Children's Animated Television." *The Annals of the American Academy of Political and Social Science* 557 (1998): 105–119.

Dockterman, Eliana. "Behind Marvel's Decision to Create These Controversial Female Superheroes." *Time,* August 28, 2015, time.com/4014894/marvel-female-superheroes-thor-ms-marvel/ (accessed February 16, 2017).

Doorn-Harder, Pieternella van. "Controlling the Body: Muslim Feminists Debating Women's Rights in Indonesia." *Religion Compass* 2, no. 6 (2008): 1021–1043.

Downes, Meghan. "Hybridities and Deep Histories in Indonesian *Wayang* Manga Comics." *Situations* 8, no. 2 (2015): 5–26.

Driscoll, Molly. "Meet the New Iron Man: A Black Female Teenager." *The Christian Science Monitor*, July 7, 2016, http://www.csmonitor.com/The-Culture/Arts/2016/0707/Meet-the-new-Iron-Man-a-black-female-teenager (accessed February 17, 2017).

Duncan, Jackie. "Beyond the Veil: Graphic Representations of Islamic Women." *The Compass* 1, no. 2 (2015): 1–9.

Duncan, Randy, Matthew J. Smith, and Paul Levitz. *The Power of Comics: History, Form, and Culture*. New York: Bloomsbury Academic, 2015.

Ebrahim, Zofeen. "Bloody Nasreen: Pakistan's Very Own 'Tomb Raider.'" *Mint Press News,* September 15, 2014, http://www.mintpressnews.com/bloody-nasreen-pakistans-tomb-raider/196538/ (accessed February 17, 2017).

Edmunds, Keith T. "Heroines Aplenty, but None My Mother Would Know: Marvel's Lack of an Iconic Superheroine." In *Heroines of Comic Books and Literature: Portrayals in Popular Culture*, edited by Maja Bajac-Carter, Norma Jones, and Bob Batchelor, 211–220. New York: Rowman and Littlefield, 2014.

Edwards, Holly. "A Million and One Nights: Orientalism in America, 1870–1920." In *Noble Dreams, Wicked Pleasures: Orientalism in America, 1870–1920*, edited by Holly Edwards, PAGES. Princeton: Princeton University Press, 2000.

Edwardson, Ryan. "The Many Lives of Captain Canuck: Nationalism, Culture, and the Creation of a Canadian Comic Book Superhero." *The Journal of Popular Culture* (2003): 184–201.

Edwin, Shirin. "Islam's Trojan Horse: Battling Perceptions of Muslim Women in *The 99*." *Journal of Graphic Novels and Comics* 3, no. 2 (2012): 171–199.

El Fadl, Khaled Abou. "The Ugly Modern and the Modern Ugly: Reclaiming the Beautiful in Islam." In *Progressive Muslims: On Justice, Gender, and Pluralism*, edited by Omid Safi, 33–77. Oxford: Oneworld, 2003.

Eitizaz, Saba. "Superhero 'Burka Avenger' Divides Pakistan." *BBC,* July 30, 2013, http://www.bbc.com/news/world-middle-east-23503394 (accessed February 13, 2017).

Emad, Mitra C. "Reading Wonder Woman's Body: Mythologies of Gender and Nation." *The Journal of Popular Culture* 39, no. 6 (2006): 954–984.

Esposito, John L. *Islam: The Straight Path.* New York: Oxford University Press, 2011.

Farooq, Mahrukh. "Animation: The New Frontier." *Slogan* 20, no. 2 (2015): 8–10.

Fasson, Eric. "National Identities and Transnational Intimacies; Sexual Democracy and the Politics of Immigration in Europe." *Public Culture* 22, no. 3 (2010: 507–529.

Fawaz, Ramzi. "'Where No X-Man Has Gone Before!': Mutant Superheroes and the Cultural Politics of Popular Fantasy in Postwar America." *American Literature* 83, no. 2 (2011): 355–388.

Feichtinger, Christian. "Space Buddhism: The Adoption of Buddhist Motifs in Star Wars." *Contemporary Buddhism* 15, no. 1 (2014): 28–43.

Fennell, Jack. "The Aesthetics of Supervillainy." *Law Text Culture* 16, no. 1 (2012): 305–328.

Fox, Kimberly E. "*Burka Avenger*: On Agency, Education, and Equality in Pakistani Popular Culture." Master's thesis, Iliff School of Theology, 2014.

Genter, Robert. "'With Great Power Comes Great Responsibility': Cold War Culture and the Birth of Marvel Comics." *The Journal of Popular Culture* 40, no. 6 (2007): 953–978.

Gevorgyan, Khachik. "*Futuwwa* Varieties and the *Futuwwat-n ma* Literature: An Attempt to Classify *Futuwwa* and Persian *Futuwwat-n mas.*" *British Journal of Middle Eastern Studies* 40, no. 1 (2013): 2–13.

Goh, Robbie B. H. "Sword Play: The Cultural Semiotics of Violent Scapegoating and Sexual and Racial Othering." *Semiotica* 160 (2006): 69–94.

Goodwin, Megan. "Thinking Sex and American Religions." *Religion Compass* 5, no. 12 (2011): 772–787.

Gottschalk, Peter and Gabriel Greenberg. *Islamophobia: Making Muslims the Enemy.* Lanham: Rowman & Littlefield Publishers, 2008.

Graham-Brown, Sarah. *Images of Women: The Portrayal of Women in Photography of the Middle East 1860–1950.* New York: Columbia University Press, 1988.

Greyson, Devon. "GLBTQ Content in Comics/Graphic Novels for Teens." *Collection Building* 26, no. 4 (2007): 130–134.

Gustines, George Gene. "She's Mighty, Muslim, and Leaping Off the Page." *New York Times*, November 6, 2013: C3.

Hains, Rebecca C. "Power Feminism, Mediated: Girl Power and the Commercial Politics of Change." *Women's Studies in Communication* 32, no. 1 (2009): 89–113.

Halberstam, Jack. "Imagined Violence/Queer Violence: Representation, Rage, and Resistance." *Social Text* 37 (1993): 187–201.

Hammer, Juliane. "Gender, Feminism, and Critique in American Muslim Thought." In *Routledge Handbook of Islam and the West*, edited by Roberto Tottoli, 395–410. London: Routledge, 2014.

Hancock, Rae. "Comic Books in the Classroom." *Prep School* 85 (2016): 60–61.

Hannon, Molly. "Kamala Khan, Marvel Superhero Fights Real-Life Racism." *The Daily Beast*, February 15, 2015, http://www.thedailybeast.com/articles/2015/02/15/kamala-khan-marvel-superhero-fights-real-life-racism.html (accessed February 18, 2017).

Haris, Wasiq. *Raat* Issue #1: *The Ones That Do . . .* www.raatcomic.com (2016): no p.n.

Hart, Christopher. *How to Draw Great-Looking Comic Book Women.* New York: Watson-Guptill, 2000.

Hidayatullah, Aysha A. *Feminist Edges of the Qur'an.* New York: Oxford University Press, 2014.

Hinds, Harold E. "Kaliman: A Mexican Superhero." *The Journal of Popular Culture* 13, no. 2 (1979): 229–238.

Hirji, Faiza. "Through the Looking Glass: Muslim Women on Television—An Analysis of *24, Lost,* and *Little Mosque on the Prairie.*" *Global Media Journal (Canadian Edition)* 4, no. 2 (2011): 33–47.

Holland, Tom. "Mirage in the Movie House." *Arion* 15, no. 1 (2007): 173–182.

Howell, Julia Day. "Indonesia's Salafist Sufis." *Modern Asian Studies* 44, no. 5 (2010): 1029–1051.

Huda, Qamar-ul. "The Light beyond the Shore in the Theology of Proper Sufi Moral Conduct (*Adab*)." *Journal of the American Academy of Religion* 72, no. 2 (2004): 461–484.

Hughes, Jamie A. "'Who Watches the Watchmen?': Ideology and 'Real World' Superheroes." *The Journal of Popular Culture* 39, no. 4 (2006): 546–557.

Hussain, Amir. "(Re)presenting: Muslims on North American Television." *Contemporary Islam* 4 (2010): 55–75.

Ilao, Sandra Alena Lavadia. "Review and Assessment of Comics as a Medium for Disseminating Development-Oriented Strategies." Masters thesis, UP Open University, 2014.

Ivey, Christina L. "Combating Epistemic Violence with Islamic Feminism: Qahera vs. FEMEN." *Women's Studies in Communication* 38 (2015): 384–387.

Jelodar, Esmaeil Zeiny, Noraini Md. Yusof, and Ruzy Suliza Hashim. "Muslim Women's Memoirs: Disclosing Violence or Reproducing Islamophobia?" *Asian Social Science* 10, no. 14 (2014): 215–223.

Johnson, Jeffrey K. "The Countryside Triumphant: Jefferson's Ideal of Rural Superiority in Modern Superhero Mythology." *The Journal of Popular Culture* 43, no. 4 (2010): 720–737.

Juliano, Stephanie. "Superheroes, Bandits, and Cyber-Nerds: Exploring the History and Contemporary Development of the Vigilante." *Journal of International Commercial Law and Technology* 7, no. 1 (2012): 44–64.

Junik-Luniewska, Kamila. "From Malala to *Burka Avenger*: A Few Remarks on Changing Female Role Models in Contemporary Pakistan." *Politeja* 1, no. 40 (2016): 273–300.

Jusová, Iveta. "Hisri Ali and van Gogh's Submission: Reinforcing the Islam v. Women Binary." *Women's Studies International Forum* 31 (2008): 148–155.

Kalayci, Nurdan. "Analyses of the Cartoon Series from a Gender Equality Perspective: Pepee." *Education and Science* 40, no. 177 (2015): 243–270.

Katsuzawa, Kiyomi. "Disney's *Pocahontas*: Reproduction of Gender, Orientalism, and the Strategic Construction of Racial Harmony in the Disney Empire." *Asian Journal of Women's Studies* 6, no. 4 (2000): 39–65.

Kaur, Raminder. "Atomic Comics: Parabolic Mimesis and the Graphic Fictions of Science." *International Journal of Cultural Studies* 15, no. 4 (2011): 329–374.

Kelly, Casey Ryan. "Feminine Purity and Masculine Revenge-Seeking in Taken (2008)." *Feminist Media Studies* 14, no. 3 (2014): 1–16.

Kent, Miriam. "Unveiling Marvels: *Ms. Marvel* and the Reception of the New Muslim Superheroine." *Feminist Media Studies* 15, no. 3 (2015): 522–526.

Kern, Sara Marie. "Females and Feminism Reclaim the Mainstream: New Superheroines in Marvel Comics." MA thesis, Middle Tennessee State University, 2015.

Khan, Abdul Halim Jaffer. "Hazrat Amir Khusro." *Journal of the Indian Musicological Society* 4, no. 2 (1973): 1–20.

Khan, Ali and Ali Nobil Ahmad. "From *Zinda Laash* to *Zibahkhana*." *Third Text* 24, no. 1 (2010): 149–161.

Khan, Naveeda. *Muslim Becoming: Aspiration and Skepticism in Pakistan*. Durham: Duke University Press, 2012.

Khazan, Olga. "Big in . . . Pakistan." *The Atlantic Monthly* 312, no. 4 (2013): 20.

Khoja- Moojli, Shenila. "Poststructuralist Approaches to Teaching about Gender, Islam, and Muslim Societies." *Feminist Teacher* 24, no. 1 (2014): 169–183.

Khoja-Moolji, Shenila S. and Alyssa D. Nicolini. "Comics as Public Pedagogy: Reading Muslim Masculinities through Muslim Femininities in *Ms. Marvel*." *Girlhood Studies* 8, no. 3 (2015): 23–39.

Kirkpatrick, Ellen and Suzanne Scott. "Representation and Diversity in Comics Studies." *Cinema-Journal* 55, no. 1 (2015): 120–168.

Klein, Hugh and Kenneth S. Shiffman. "Race-Related Content of Animated Cartoons." *The Howard Journal of Communications* 17 (2006): 163–182.

———. "Messages about Physical Attractiveness in Animated Cartoons." *Body Image* 3 (2006): 353–363.

———. "Underrepresentation and Symbolic Annihilation of Socially Disenfranchised Groups ('Out Groups') in Animated Cartoons." *The Howard Journal of Communications* 20 (2009): 55–72.

Klein, Sheri. "Breaking the Mold with Humor: Images of Women in the Visual Media." *Art Education* 46, no. 5 (1993): 60–65.

Kraidy, Marwan M. *The Naked Blogger of Cairo: Creative Insurgency in the Arab World*. Cambridge: Harvard University Press, 2016.

Kuppers, Petra. "Blindness and Affect: *Daredevil's* Site/Sight." *Quarterly Review of Film and Video* 23 (2006): 89–96.

Landis, Winona. "Diasporic (Dis)Identification: The Participatory Fandom of Ms. Marvel." *South Asian Popular Culture* 14, nos. 1/2 (2016): 33–47.

Lant, Antonia. "The Curse of the Pharaoh, or How Cinema Contracted Egyptomania." In *Visions of the East: Orientalism in Film*, edited by Matthew Bernstein and Gaylyn Studlar, 69–98. New Brunswick: Rutgers University Press, 1997.

Lewis, Reina. *Gendered Orientalism: Race, Femininity and Representation*. New York: Routledge, 2013.

———. *Muslim Fashion: Contemporary Style Cultures*. Durham: Duke University Press, 2015.

Link, Alex. "The Secret of Supergirl's Success." *The Journal of Popular Culture* 46, no. 6 (2013): 1177–1197.

Macdonald, Myra. "Muslim Women and the Veil: Problems of Image and Voice in Media Representations." *Feminist Media Studies* 6, no. 1 (2006): 7–23.

Macfie, Alexander Lyon. "My Orientalism." *Journal of Postcolonial Writing* 45, no. 1 (2009): 83–90.

Mahan, Jeffrey. *Media, Religion and Culture: An Introduction*. New York: Routledge, 2014.

Mahmood, Saba. *Politics of Piety: The Islamic Revival and the Feminist Subject*. Princeton: Princeton University Press, 2004.

Makar, Farida. "'Let Them Have Some Fun': Political and Artistic Forms of Expression in the Egyptian Revolution." *Mediterranean Politics* 16, no. 2 (2011): 307–312.

Martin, Douglas. "The X-Men Vanquish America," *The New York Times* August 21, 1994.

Massih, Nadia. "When Feminism Wears a Hijab." *Daily Star,* last modified October 15, 2013, http://www.dailystar.com.lb/Culture/Art/2013/Oct-15/234666-when-feminism-wears-a-hijab.ashx (accessed February 9, 2017).

Mamdani, Mahmood. *Good Muslim, Bad Muslim: America, The Cold War, and the Roots of Terror*. New York: Pantheon Books, 2004.

McAllister, Matthew P. "'Girls with a Passion for Fashion': The Bratz Brand as Integrated Spectacular Consumption" *Journal of Children and Media* 1, no. 3 (2007): 244–258.

McAllister, Matthew P., Edward H. Sewell, and Ian Gordon, "Introducing Comics and Ideology," *Comics and Ideology*, edited by Matthew P. McAllister, Edward H. Sewell, and Ian Gordon, 1–13. New York: Peter Lang, 2001.

McClain, Karline. *India's Immortal Comic Books: Gods, Kings, and Other Heroes*. Bloomington: Indiana University Press, 2009.

McClintock, Anne. *Imperial Leather: Race, Gender and Sexuality in the Colonial Contest*. New York: Routledge, 1995.

McGrath, Karen. "Gender, Race, and Latina Identity: An Examination of Marvel Comics' Amazing Fantasy and Araña." *Atlantic Journal of Communication* 15, no. 4 (2007): 268–283.

McRobbie, Angela. "Post-Feminism and Popular Culture." *Feminist Media Studies* 4, no. 3 (2004): 255–264.

Mernissi, Fatima. *The Forgotten Queens of Islam*. Translated by Mary Jo Lakeland. Minneapolis: University of Minnesota Press, 1993.

Mernissi, Fatima. *Dreams of Trespass: Tales of a Harem Childhood*. Boulder: Perseus Books, 1995.

Merskin, Debra. "Sending Up Signals: A Survey of Native American Media Use and Representation in the Mass Media." *Howard Journal of Communications* 9 (1998): 333–345.

Meskin, Aaron. "Defining Comics?" *The Journal of Aesthetics and Art Criticism* 65, no. 4 (2007): 369–379.

Messerschmidt, James W. *Hegemonic Masculinities and Camouflaged Politics: Unmasking the Bush Dynasty and Its War Against Iraq.* Boulder: Paradigm Publishers, 2010.

Michalak, Laurence. "Cruel and Unusual: Negative Images of Arabs in American Popular Culture." *American Arab Anti-Discrimination Committee Issue Paper* 15. Washington: ADC Research Institute, 1988.

Michelmore, Christina. "Old Pictures in New Frames: Images of Islam and Muslims in Post World War II American Political Cartoons.*" Journal of American and Comparative Cultures* 23, no. 4 (2000): 37–50.

Miettinen, Mervi. "Men of Steel? Rorschach, Theweleit, and *Watchmen's* Deconstructed Masculinity." *Political Science and Politics* 47, no. 1 (2014): 104–107.

Miller, Frank. *Holy Terror.* Burbank: Legendary, 2011.

Miller, P. Andrew. "Mutants, Metaphor, and Marginalism: What X-actly Do the X-Men Stand For?" *Journal of the Fantastic in the Arts* 13, no. 3 (2003): 282–290.

Minowa, Yuko, Pauline Maclaran, and Lorna Stevens. "Visual Representations of Violent Women." *Visual Communication Quarterly* 21, no. 4 (2014): 210–222.

Mir-Hosseini, Ziba. "Beyond 'Islam' vs. 'Feminism.'" *Institute of Development Studies Bulletin* 42, no. 1 (2011): 67–77.

Mitchell, Adrielle Anna. "Distributed Identity: Networking Image Fragments in Graphic Memoirs." *Studies in Comics* 1, no. 2 (2010): 257–79.

Moghissi, Haideh. "Islamic Feminism Revisited." *Comparative Studies of South Asia, Africa and the Middle East* 31, no. 1 (2011): 76–84.

Mohamed, Deena. "On Translating a Superhero" Language and Webcomics." In *Translating Dissent: Voices From and With the Egyptian Revolution*, edited by Mona Baker, 137–147. New York: Routledge, 2016.

Mohibullah, Huma and Kristi Kramer. "'Being True to Ourselves . . . Within the Context of Islam': Practical Considerations of *Hijab* Practice Among Muslim Women." *Practical Matters Journal* 9 (2016): 1–17.

Moors, Annelies. "NiqaBitch and Princess Hijab: Niqab Activism, Satire and Street Art." *Feminist Review* 98 (2011): 128–135.

———. "Fashion and Its Discontents: The Aesthetics of Covering in the Netherlands," *Islamic Fashion and Anti-Fashion: New Perspectives from Europe and North America*, edited by Emma Tarlo and Annelies Moors, 241–259. New York: Bloomsbury, 2013.

Morrison, Grant, Ethan Van Sciver, and Norm Rapmund. *New X-Men #133.* New York: Marvel, 2002.

Najmabadi, Afsaneh. "Feminism in the Islamic Republic: Years of Hardship, Years of Growth." In *Islam, Gender, and Social Change in the Muslim World*, edited by Yvonne Haddad and John Esposito, 59–84. New York: Oxford University Press, 1998.

Nasr, Seyyed Hossein. *Islamic Art and Spirituality*. Albany: State University of New York Press, 1987.

———. *Traditional Islam in the Modern World*. New York: Kegan Paul International, 1987.

Neumann, Caryn E. and Lori L. Parks. "The Fan and the Female Superhero in Comic Books." *Journal of Fandom Studies* 3 no. 3 (2015): 291–302.

Oh, David C. and Doreen V. Kutufam. "The Orientalized 'Other' and Corrosive Femininity: Threats to White Masculinity in 300." *Journal of Communication Inquiry* 38, no. 2 (2014): 149–165.

Olcese, Abigail. "Real Life, with Superpowers." *Sojourners* (2015): 39.

Orcutt, Darby. "Comics and Religion: Theoretical Connections." In *Graven Images: Religion in Comic Books and Graphic Novels*, edited by David A. Lewis and Christine Hoff Kraemer, 93–106. London: Bloomsbury Academic, 2010.

Parameswaran, Radhika E. and Kavitha Cardoza. "Immortal Comics, Epidermal Politics: Representations of Gender and Colorism in India." *Journal of Children and Media* 3, no. 1 (2009): 19–34.

Pennell, Hillary and Elizabeth Behm-Morawitz. "The Empowering (Super) Heroine? The Effects of Sexualized Characters in Superhero Films on Women." *Sex Roles* 72 (2015): 211–220.

Petersen, Robert S. *Comics, Manga, and Graphic Novels: A History of Graphic Narratives*. Santa Barbara: Praeger, 2010.

Peterson, Kristin. "More Than a Mask, Burkini and Tights: Fighting Misrepresentations through Ms. Marvel's Costume." Unpublished paper, University of Colorado, December 17, 2015.

Price, Ada. "Web to Print and Back Again." *Publisher's Weekly* (August 31, 2009): 21–22.

Priego, Ernesto. "Ms. Marvel: Metamorphosis and Transfiguration of the 'Minority' Superhero." *The Winnower* (May 11, 2016): 1–6.

Pumphrey, Nicholaus. "Avenger, Mutant, or Allah: A Short Evolution of the Depiction of Muslims in Marvel Comics." *The Muslim World* 106, no. 4 (2016): 781–794.

Ramirez, Angeles. "Control Over Female 'Muslim' Bodies: Culture, Politics and Dress Code Laws in Some Muslim and Non-Muslim Countries." *Identities: Global Studies in Culture and Power* 22, no. 6 (2015): 671–686.

Rashid, Ahmed. *Taliban: Militant Islam, Oil and Fundamentalism in Central Asia*. New Haven: Yale University Press, 2010.

Rashid, Fahmida. "99ers Power." *Islamic Horizons* 35, no. 4 (2006): 42–43.

Reestorff, Camilla M. "Mediatised Affective Activism: The Activist Imaginary and the Topless Body in the Femen Movement." *Convergence: The International Journal into New Media Technologies* 20, no. 4 (2014): 478–495.

Renard, John. *Friends of God: Islamic Images of Piety, Commitment, and Servanthood*. Berkeley: University of California Press, 2008.

Rich, B, Ruby. "Day of the Woman." *British Film Institute*, June 2004, http://www.bfi.org.uk/sightandsound/feature/25 (accessed March 8 2017).

Riesman, Abraham. "Meet G. Willow Wilson, the Muslim Woman Revolutionizing Superhero Comics." *Vulture*, March 20, 2014, http://www.vulture.

com/2014/03/g-willow-wilson-ms-marvel-kamala-khan-interview.html (accessed March 9, 2017).

Robbins, Margaret. "Female Representation in Comics and Graphic Novels: Exploring Classroom Study with Critical Visual Literacy." *SIGNAL Journal* (Fall 2014/ Winter 2015): 11–15.

Russo, Ann. "The Feminist Majority Foundation's Campaign to Stop Gender Apartheid." *International Feminist Journal of Politics* 8, no. 4 (2006): 557–580.

Sadeghi, Fatemeh. "Negotiating with Modernity: Young Women and Sexuality in Iran." *Comparative Studies of South Asia, Africa and the Middle East* 28, no. 2 (2008): 250–259.

Safi, Omid. *Memories of Muhammad: Why the Prophet Matters.* New York: HarperOne, 2010.

Said, Edward. *Orientalism.* New York: Vintage Books, 1979.

———. *Culture and Imperialism.* New York: Vintage Books, 1993.

———. *Covering Islam: How the Media and the Experts Determine How We See the Rest of the World.* New York: Vintage Books, 1997.

Salinger, Gerard. "Was the *Fut wa* an Oriental Form of Chivalry?" *Proceedings of the American Philosophical Society* 94, no. 5 (1950): 481–493.

Saner, Emine. "Ms. Marvel: Send for the Muslim Supergirl!" *The Guardian,* January 1, 2014, https://www.theguardian.com/culture/2014/jan/01/ms-marvel-muslim-superhero-graphic-novel (accessed February 9, 2017).

Santo, Avi. "'Is It a Camel? Is it a Turban? No, It's the 99': Branding Islamic Superheroes as Authentic Global Cultural Commodities." *Television & New Media* 15, no. 7 (2014): 679–695.

Saparmin, Norzakiah. "A Brief History of the Relationship between Futuwwa (Muslim Brotherhood) and the S fi's Tar qahs in the Islamic Civilization." *Revelation and Science* 6, no. 1 (2016): 27–34.

Schmitt, Ronald. "Deconstructive Comics." *The Journal of Popular Culture* 25, no. 4 (1992): 153–161.

Scott, Catharine V. "Bound for Glory: The Hostage Crisis as Captivity Narrative in Iran." *International Studies Quarterly* 44, no. 1 (2000): 177–88.

Scott, Cord. "Written in Red, White, and Blue: A Comparison of Comic Book Propaganda from World War II and September 11." *The Journal of Popular Culture* 40, no. 2 (2007): 325–343.

Seedat, Fatima. "When Islam and Feminism Converge." *The Muslim World* 103, no. 3 (2013): 404–420.

Shaheen, Jack. "Arab Images in American Comic Books." *The Journal of Culture* 28, no. 1 (1994): 123–133.

———. *Reel Bad Arabs: How Hollywood Vilifies a People.* New York: Olive Branch Press, 2001.

Shamsi, Amber. "The Female Superhero Fighting Terrorists in Pakistan." *BBC,* August 12, 2014, http://www.bbc.com/news/world-asia-28754445 (accessed December 17, 2016).

Sheety, Nour. "10 Muslim Superheroes That Totally Beat Batman." *Stepfeed*, March 17, 2017, http://stepfeed.com/10-muslim-superheroes-that-totally-own-superman-7496 (accessed March 17 2017).

Shevchenko, Inna. "Open Letter." *Huffington Post*: August 4, 2013. http://huffingtonpost.co.uk/2013/04/08/inna-shevchenko-muslim-womes-open-letter-amina -tyler-topless-jiad_n_3035439.html (accessed February 8, 2017).

Shohat, Ella. "Gender and Culture of Empire: Toward a Feminist Ethnography of the Cinema." *Visions of the East: Orientalism in Film*, edited by Matthew Bernstein and Gaylyn Studlar, 19–66. New Brunswick: Rutgers University Press, 1997.

———. "Area Studies, Gender Studies, and Cartographies of Knowledge." *Social Text 72*, 20, no. 3 (2002): 67–78.

Shohat, Ella and Robert Stam. *Unthinking Eurocentrism: Multiculturalism and the Media*. New York: Routledge, 1994.

Shyminski, Neil. "Mutant Readers, Reading Mutants: Appropriation, Assimilation, and the X-Men." *IJOCA* 8, no. 2 (2008): 387–405.

Siddiqui, Shahid. *Language, Gender, and Power: The Politics of Representation and Hegemony in South Asia*. Karachi: Oxford University Press, 2014.

Simone, Gail. "Women in Refrigerators." http://lby3.com/wir// (accessed March 14, 2017).

Singh, Jaideep. "A New American Apartheid: Racialized, Religious Minorities in the Post-9/11 Era." *Sikh Formations: Religion, Culture, Theory* 9, no. 2(2013): 115–144.

Skidmore, Max J. and Joey Skidmore. "More Than Mere Fantasy: Political Themes in Contemporary Comic Books." *The Journal of Popular Culture* 17, no. 1 (1983): 83–92.

Soares, Michael. "The Man of Tomorrow: Superman from American Exceptionalism to Globalization." *The Journal of American Popular Culture* 48, no. 4 (2015): 747–761.

Spivak, Gayatri Chakravorty. *A Critique of Postcolonial Reason: Toward a History of the Vanishing Present*. Cambridge: Harvard University Press, 1999.

Stam, Robert and Ella Shohat, *Race in Translation: Culture Wars Around the Post-colonial Atlantic*. New York: NYU Press, 2012.

Stein, Daniel, Christina Meyer, and Micha Edlich. "Introduction: American Comic Books and Graphic Novels." *Amerikastudien/American Studies: A Quarterly* 56, no. 4 (2011): 501–529.

Stevens, J. Richard. *Captain America, Masculinity, and Violence: The Evolution of a National Icon*. Syracuse: Syracuse University Press, 2016.

Stott, Rebecca. "The Dark Continent: Africa as Female Body in Haggard's Adventure Fiction." *Feminist Review* 32 (1989): 69–89.

Strömberg, Fredrik. "'Yo, rag-head!': Arab and Muslim Superheroes in American Comic Books after 9/11." *Amerikastudien/American Studies* 56, no. 4 (2011): 573–601.

Al-Suhrawardi, 'Abû Hafs 'Umar. *'Awârif al-Ma'ârif*. Cairo: Maktabat al-Qâhira, 1973.

Tapia, Ruby C. "Volumes of Transnational Vengeance: Fixing Race and Feminism on the Way to Kill Bill." *Visual Arts Research* 32, no. 2 (2004): 32–37.

Tasker, Yvonne. "Television Crime Drama and Homeland Security: From and Order to 'Terror TV.'" *Cinema Journal* 51, no. 4 (2012): 44–65.

Taslitz, Andrew E. "*Daredevil* and the Death Penalty." *Ohio State Journal of Criminal Law* 1, no. 2 (2004): 699–717.

Taylor, Aaron. "'He's Gotta Be Strong, and He's Gotta Be Fast, and He's Gotta Be Larger Than Life': Investigating the Engendered Superhero Body." *The Journal of Popular Culture* 40, no. 2 (2007): 344–360.

Teo, Hsu-Ming. *Desert Passions: Orientalism and Romance Novels.* Austin: University of Texas Press, 2012.

Thacker, Eugene. "Bio-X: Removing Bodily Contingency in Regenerative Medicine." *Journal of Medical Humanities* 23, nos. 3/4 (2002): 239–253.

Thobani, Sunera. "White Wars: Western Feminisms and the 'War on Terror.'" *Feminist Theory* 8, no. 2 (2007): 169–185.

Thompson, Teresa L. and Eugenia Zerbinos. "Gender Roles in Animated Cartoons: Has the Picture Changed in 20 Years?" *Sex Roles* 32, nos. 9/10 (1995): 651–673.

Titus, Paul. "Honor the Baloch, Buy the Pushtun: Stereotypes, Social Organization and History in Western Pakistan." *Modern Asian Studies* 32, no. 3 (1998): 657–687.

Tohidi, Nayereh. "Muslim Feminism and Islamic Reformation: The Case of Iran." In *Feminist Theologies: Legacy and Prospect*, edited by Rosemary Radford Ruether, 93–116. Minneapolis: Fortress Press, 2007.

Toor, Saadia. "Moral Regulation in a Postcolonial Nation-State: Gender and the Politics of Islamization in Pakistan." *Interventions* 9, no. 2 (2007): 255–275.

———. "The Political Economy of Moral Regulation in Pakistan: Religion, Gender and Class in a Postcolonial Context." In *Routledge Handbook of Gender in South Asia*, edited by Leela Fernandes, 129–142. New York: Routledge, 2014.

Trushell, John M. "American Dreams of Mutants: The X-Men—'Pulp' Fiction, Science Fiction, and Superheroes." *The Journal of Popular Culture* 38, no. 1 (2004): 149–168.

Twark, Jill E. "Approaching History as Cultural Memory Through Humour, Satire, Comics and Graphic Novels." *Contemporary European History* 26, no. 1 (2017): 175–187.

Vagianos, Alanna. "30 Shocking Domestic Violence Statistics That Remind Us It's An Epidemic." *The Huffington Post*, October 23, 2014, http://www.huffingtonpost.com/2014/10/23/domestic-violence-statistics_n_5959776.html (accessed February 24, 2017).

Valdez, Inés. "Nondomination or Practices of Freedom? French Muslim Women, Foucault, and the Full Veil Ban." *American Political Science Review* 110, no. 1 (2016): 18–30.

Van Buren, Cassandra. "Critical Analysis of Racist Post-9/11 Web Animations." *Journal of Broadcasting and Electronic Media* 50, no. 3 (2006): 537–554.

Wadud, Amina. "Towards a Qur'anic Hermeneutics of Social Justice: Race, Class and Gender." *Journal of Law and Religion* 12 (1995–6): 37–50.

———. *Qur'an and Woman: Rereading the Sacred Text from a Woman's Perspective.* New York: Oxford University Press, 1999.

————. *Inside the Gender Jihad: Women's Reform in Islam.* London: Oneworld Publications, 2006.

Wahid, Samina. "All About Animation." *Slogan* 20, no. 2 (2015): 10–11.

Waibel, Gina. "From Avengers to Heroines: Muslim Women Dismantling Hegemonic Discourses." MS thesis, Lund University, 2016.

Wakankar, Milind. "Body, Crowd, Identity: Genealogy of a Hindu Nationalist Aesthetics." *Social Text* 45 (1995): 45–73.

Wanzo, Rebecca. "The Superhero: Meditations on Surveillance, Salvation, and Desire." *Communication and Critical/Cultural Studies* 6, no. 1 (2009): 93–97.

Weiss, Anita. "Can Civil Society Tame Violent Extremism in Pakistan?" *Current History* (2016): 144–149.

Whiles, Virgina. "In and Out of Pakistan." *Third Text* 14, no. 52 (2008): 103–110.

Wilson, G. Willow and Adrian Alphona. *Ms. Marvel Vol. 1: No Normal.* New York: Marvel, 2014.

Wilson, G. Willow, Jacob Wyatt, and Adrian Alphona. *Ms. Marvel Vol. 2: Generation Why.* New York: Marvel, 2015.

Wilson, G. Willow, Elmo Bondoc, and Takeshi Miyazawa. *Ms. Marvel Vol. 3: Crushed.* New York: Marvel, 2015.

Wilson, G. Willow and Adrian Alphona. *Ms. Marvel Vol. 4: Last Days.* New York: Marvel, 2015.

Wilson, G. Willow, Takeshi Miyazawa, Adrian Alphona, and Nico Leon. *Ms. Marvel Vol. 5: Super Famous.* New York: Marvel, 2016.

Wilson, G. Willow, Adrian Alphona, Takeshi Miyazawa, and Mirka Andolfo. *Ms. Marvel Vol. 6: Civil War II.* New York: Marvel, 2016.

Wilson, G. Willow, Takeshi Miyazawa, Ian Herring. *Ms. Marvel #16: Damage Per Second.* New York: Marvel, 2017.

Wright, Bradford W. *Comic Book Nation: The Transformation of Youth Culture in America.* Baltimore: Johns Hopkins University Press, 2003.

Yaghi, Adam. "Popular Testimonial Literature by American Cultural Conservatives of Arab or Muslim Descent: Narrating the Self, Translating (an) Other." *Middle East Critique* 25, no. 1 (2016): 83–98.

Yun, Zhou. "Behind the Muslim Veil: A Qualitative Analysis of Pakistani Female Students' Views Towards Veiling." *Cross-Cultural Communication* 6, no. 1 (2010): 82–91.

Zakeri, Mohsen. "Muslim 'Chivalry' at the Time of the Crusaders: The Case of Us ma b. Munqidh." *Hallesche Beiträge zur Orientwissenschaft* 22 (1996): 29–50.

Zenari, Vivian. "Mutant Mutandis: The X-Men's Wolverine and the Construction of Canada." In *Culture and the State 3: Nationalisms*, edited by James Gifford and Gabrielle Zezulka-Mailloux, 53–67. Edmonton: CRC Humanities Studies, 2003.

Zine, Jasmin. "Muslim Women and the Politics of Representation," *The American Journal of Islamic Social Sciences* 19, no. 4 (2002): 1–23.

————. "Between Orientalism and Fundamentalism: The Politics of Muslim Women's Feminist Engagement." *Muslim World Journal of Human Rights* 3, no. 1 (2006): 1–24.

Index

13th Warrior, 3, 15
300, 35–36
9/11, 8, 47, 92, 115
The 99, 36–41, 125

Abaya, 8, 99, 101
Abu-Lughod, Lilah, xx, 27, 32–33
Adab, xxiv, 60–61
Afghanistan, xviii, 8, 11–12, 27, 79–80,
      84, 97, 119
African-Americans, 10, 48, 50, 53, 61,
      91
agency, xx–xxi, 4, 9, 15–16, 27–33, 51,
      74–77, 86, 107, 116–19
Ahmed, Leila, 31, 119
Algeria, 10, 27, 33
'Ali, 124–25
Ali, Kecia, 27, 117, 122
American exceptionalism, 9–10, 53–54
animation, 14–15, 36, 71–73, 77–78
Arabs, xvi–xvii, 1, 3, 5, 9–10, 13–17, 92
Asad, Talal, 3
Awliya (Muslim saints), 57, 123–26

Basant (kite festival), 84
Batgirl, 93
Batina (*The 99*), 39, 41
Batman, 6, 49, 60, 73, 82, 93, 105

Battle of Algiers, 33
Batwoman, 25
Behiery, Valerie, xxiii
Bloody Nasreen, xxv, 105–10
Bratz, 81
Burka Avenger, xxv, 71–89
Bush, George H.W., 119
Butler, Judith, xxii–xxiii

Cairo, xxv, 91, 95–97
Captain America, 9–10, 26, 47, 60, 73,
      82, 116
Captain Kanuck, 86
chivalry (*futuyyat*), xxiv, 124–26
cinema, xxiii, 15–16, 34, 107–10
Comic-Con, xv, 52
comics, 5–10, 71–72
comix, xxv, 7
cosplay, 12
costume, 12, 16, 26, 30–31, 52, 55,
      61–66, 71–75, 82, 86

Daredevil, 86
Disney, 14–15, 71
dupatta, 104
Dust (*X-Men*), 11–12

Egypt, 95–104

Excalibur (Marvel Comics), 12

The Fantastic Four, 7, 116
Fattah (*The 99*), 36
Femen, 99–103
feminism:
   critiques, xxii, 99, 116–17;
   Islamic, xx, xxii, 75–76, 78, 116–23;
   Western, 24, 78, 98–101, 120–21
France, 31–32

gendered Orientalism, xxiii, 1, 3, 26,
   98–99
graffiti, 49, 97–98
graphic novels, 12–14, 35–36, 105, 115

Hadya (*The 99*), 36, 39–40
Hammer, Juliane, xxii, 23
harem, 3, 28–29
Haris, Wasiq, 104–5
Harley Quinn, 25
Haroon, 71, 74, 84
Hijab, xix, 12, 28–32, 37–39, 48, 66–
   67, 74, 95, 98, 104. *See also*
   veiling/unveiling
Hijab porn, 3–4
Holy Terror, 35–36
homosociality/queerness, 6, 82
horror film, 85, 107

I Dream of Jeannie (television series),
   16
immigrants, 47–52
India, 5–6, 10, 52
Indonesia, 6, 30, 120, 122–23
Iran, 8, 27–28, 116, 120, 122
Iron Man (films), xxv
Islamism, 4, 32, 33, 75, 98, 121
Islamophobia, 3, 49, 54, 95, 100–1,
   104, 115, 119, 126

Japan, 5–6, 109–10
Jihad al-nafs (the greater jihad), xxiv,
   83, 126

Jihad (struggle), 83–84, 94, 101,
   125–26

Kaliman (Mexican comic), xxiv, 7–8
Kamala Khan/Ms. Marvel, xxv, 12,
   47–67, 93–94, 118, 126
Kill Bill, 94–95, 108–10
Kingdom of Heaven, 15

Little Mosque on the Prairie (Canadian
   television show), 16–17

Madaya Mom, 123
Mahmood, Saba, xx
Manga, 6, 109
martial arts, 73, 82–83, 109–10
Marvel Comics, 7, 10–12, 48–50
Maus, 13
McClintock, Anne, 2
Mernissi, Fatima, 24, 29, 122
Mickey Mouse, 14–15
Miller, Frank, 35–36
Mir-Hosseini, Ziba, 32, 119–22
Moghissi, Haideh, 117
Mohamed, Deena, xv, 1, 92, 95, 98
Monet St. Croix (*X-Men*), 10–11
monsters/monstrosity, 15–16, 23, 25,
   35–36
Muhammad (Prophet), 31, 37–38, 59–
   61, 124–26
Muslim vampires, 15–16, 23, 79
Al-Mutawa, Naif, 39–40

Najmabadi, Afsaneh, 32, 116, 123
Niqab, xxv, 3, 9, 30–31, 39, 74, 86
Noora (*The 99*), 37–38

Orientalism, xix, 1–7, 15, 26–31, 107,
   119

Pakistan, 63–65, 73–80, 84–85, 94–97,
   104–7
patriarchy, xviii, xxi, 27–28, 99, 110,
   116–17, 122, 124–25

Persepolis, 13–14
Pocahontas, 71
popular culture, xvi–xviii, 6–8, 24,
    34–36, 92, 108–10, 118
Princess Hijab, 32
Pushtun, 80

Qahera, 91–104
Qalb (heart), 33
queerness (in comics), xxii–xxiii, 6, 7,
    63, 82
Quran, xxi–xxii, 31–33, 84, 116,
    120–22

Raat, 104–5
rape, 16, 29–30, 58–59, 93, 107–10, 119
religion (in comics), 53, 55–60

Sadeghi, Fatemeh, 27
Safi, Omid, 33
Said, Edward, xv, xvii, 15
sexual democracy, 31–32
sex/sexuality, xvi, 2–4, 7, 16, 23–30,
    65–66, 74–75, 78, 81–82,
    99–100, 106–7
Shaheen, Jack, 9, 15
Shohat, Ella, xiii, 16, 35
Sleeper Cell, 16
Spiderman, 51, 116, 125
Spivak, Gayatri, xxi
Stam, Robert, 35
Star Wars, 57, 73–74, 110
Storm (*X-Men*), 11
Supergirl, 26, 65
Superman, 6, 25–26, 47, 52–53, 72–73
sword, 12, 15, 73–74, 99, 105, 108–10

Tahrir Square, 96–97
Taken, 16
Taliban, 9, 27, 32, 71, 76, 79–80
Tasfir (exegesis), xxi
Tawhid (unity of creation), xxii, 37
Team Bahadur, 77
Team Muhafiz (Pakistani cartoon), 104
teenage superheroes, 51, 77
Thor, 53, 125

Ummah (Muslim community), 33
Usamah bin Laden, 85

veiling/unveiling, xix, 4, 8, 28–33, 67,
    74, 86, 95
vigilantism, 49, 92–95
villains, 6, 9, 15–16, 25–26, 35–36, 57,
    76, 79–85, 92–94, 99, 108–9

Wadud, Amina, xxi–xxii, 117, 121–22
Widad (*The 99*), 39
Wilson, Willow, 50–51
Wolverine (*X-Men*), 11, 57–58, 84, 93
Wonder Woman, 26, 65, 93
Wujud (cosmos), xix

X-Men, 10, 58, 77, 91

Yousafzai, Malala, xviii, 78, 106,
    117–18

Zaidi, Shahan, 105–8
Zawjan (complementary partnership),
    xxi
Zen, 73–74
Zia, Afiya Sharbano, 106

About the Author

Sophia Rose Arjana is a scholar of religion who specializes in Islam, gender, and pilgrimage. Her scholarship includes the books *Muslims in the Western Imagination* (Oxford, 2015) and *Pilgrimage in Islam: Traditional and Modern Practices* (Oneworld, 2017). Dr. Arjana has traveled extensively in Muslim-majority countries, including Iran, Turkey, Morocco, Egypt, Syria, and Indonesia. She is Assistant professor of Religious Studies at Western Kentucky University.